Dispatches from the Providence Observatory: Astronomical Motifs and Sources in the Writings of H. P. Lovecraft

T. R. Livesey

I.

> The most poignant sensations of my existence are those of 1896, when I discovered the Hellenic world, and of 1902, when I discovered the myriad suns and worlds of infinite space. Sometimes I think the latter event the greater, for the grandeur of that growing conception of the universe still excites a thrill hardly to be duplicated.— H. P. Lovecraft, 1924 (*SL* 1.294).

The writings of H. P. Lovecraft are distinguished by his sense of cosmicism: the wonder and terror of the grand scope of the universe. His expression of cosmicism is often described in terms of the fleeting existence of humanity and its works against the backdrop of the infinity of space and time. Lovecraft handles this contrast by injecting his fiction with the latest developments in science—which, during the period of his lifetime, was doing more to undermine the centrality of humanity's existence than Copernicus could have imagined—to achieve a fantastic sense of realism. A thorough understanding of the science of Lovecraft's era—or his understanding of it—is crucial to appreciate the role scientific developments played as source and inspiration for his fiction.

Foundation

Lovecraft first became interested in astronomy in 1902 at age twelve, after discovering his grandmother's collection of astronomy books in his attic. He reports a year later that he thought of nothing other than astronomy, and four years later had resolved to become an absolute master of the subject (*SL* 1.69–70). In addition to writing a great deal of scientific juvenilia, Lovecraft also contributed regular newspaper columns on astronomy in the periods 1906–08 and 1914–18. Written from a layman's perspective—Lovecraft himself possessed only high-school level training in mathematics—these articles continued well into his amateur journalism period and terminated only after his editor complained that they were too technical (*CE* 3.10–11).

Among his grandmother's books was a copy of Elijah H. Burritt's *Geography of the Heavens*, a charming mid-nineteenth-century text on astronomy that included treatments of both classical constellation star lore and modern science. The introductory quotation by Lovecraft cited at the head of this paper presents his interests in the Hellenic world and astronomy as separate, almost in contrast, but part of the initial appeal of Burritt's book undoubtedly lay in Lovecraft's rediscovery of the classical world in the timeless heavens. When Lovecraft wrote "Her copy of Burritt's *Geography of the Heavens* is today the most prized volume in my library" (*SL* 1.7), he was almost certainly referring to the text as well as the *Atlas Designed to Illustrate Burritt's Geography of the Heavens*, its beautiful, oversized (14″ × 16.5″), hand-colored companion. A small sample of "The Visible Heavens of January, February, and March" is reproduced here as Figure 1.

Here we find the twins Castor and Pollux, Cancer the crab and the Praesepe, Orion and his dogs, and Taurus the bull. The familiar figures of Hellenic myth found in Burritt's *Atlas* are probably what initially caught Lovecraft's eye. Richard Hinckley Allen, author of the 1899 classic *Star-Names and Their Meanings*, recounted the influence Burritt's *Geography* and *Atlas* had on him as a boy:

> Nor should I forget to mention a very popular book in its day, the *Geography of the Heavens*, with its *Atlas* by Elijah H. Burritt, published in various editions from 1833 to 1856. This described fifty well-recognized constellations visible from the latitude of Hartford, Connecticut, 41° 46′; although his table of those in the entire heavens included ninety-six, most of which appeared in the accompanying maps, the figures being taken from Wollaston's drawings. Although not an original work of great scientific value, and erroneous as well as deficient in its stellar nomenclature, it had a sale of over a quarter of a million copies, and much influence in the dissemination of astro-

THE LOVECRAFT ANNUAL

Edited by S. T. Joshi   No. 2 (2008)

Contents

Abbreviations used in the text and notes:

AT   *The Ancient Track* (Night Shade Books, 2001)
CE   *Collected Essays* (Hippocampus Press, 2004–06; 5 vols.)
D   *Dagon and Other Macabre Tales* (Arkham House, 1986)
DH   *The Dunwich Horror and Others* (Arkham House, 1984)
HM   *The Horror in the Museum and Other Revisions* (Arkham House, 1989)
LL   *Lovecraft's Library: A Catalogue* (Hippocampus Press, 2002)
MM   *At the Mountains of Madness and Other Novels* (Arkham House, 1985)
MW   *Miscellaneous Writings* (Arkham House, 1995)
SL   *Selected Letters* (Arkham House, 1965–76; 5 vols.)

Published by Hippocampus Press, P.O. Box 641, New York, NY 10156
http://www.hippocampuspress.com

Cover illustration by Allen Koszowski. Hippocampus Press logo designed by Anastasia Damianakos. Cover design by Barbara Briggs Silbert.

Lovecraft Annual is published once a year, in Fall. Articles and letters should be sent to the editor, S. T. Joshi, c/o Hippocampus Press, and must be accompanied by a self-addressed stamped envelope if return is desired. All reviews are assigned. Literary rights for articles and reviews will reside with *Lovecraft Annual* for one year after publication, whereupon they will revert to their respective authors. Payment is in contributor's copies.

ISSN 1935-6102
ISBN13: 978-0-9814888-6-8

THE CONSTELLATIONS

Figure 1: Extract from Plate III of Burritt's *Atlas*

nomical knowledge in the generation now passing away. I am glad to pay here my own tribute to the memory of the author, in acknowledgment of the service rendered me in stimulating a boyhood interest in the skies. (Allen 15)

Lovecraft certainly would concur.

By Lovecraft's account, a milestone event in his life took place on February 12, 1903:

Incidentally—it was this very day of 1903—Feb'y 12th—(which fell, however, on *Thursday*) that I bought the very first *new* book on *astronomy* that I ever owned. It was Young's *Lessons in Astronomy*, & I got it at the R.I. News Co., for $1.25. Previously I had had only Grandma's copy of Burritt's *Geography of the Heavens*. As I returned in the evening darkness on the rear platform of an Elmgrove Ave. car—415, I think it was; one of the graceful J. M. Jones cars—I looked over the pictures & chapter heading with perhaps the most delightful sense of breathless anticipation I have ever known. Most literally, a strange cosmos of new worlds lay before me! (*SL* 2.39)

The vividness of this account—written twenty-three years after the event—indicates the importance Lovecraft attached to it. Nearly four years later, he would weave this theme—traveling home giddy with the excitement of obtaining a book that would open grand vistas of space and time—into the first three sonnets of his *Fungi from Yuggoth* cycle. Given a suitably weird tone, the third sonnet retains a vestigial trace of that day in 1903:

> I had the book that told the hidden way
> Across the void and through the space-hung screens
> That hold the undimensioned worlds at bay,
> And keep lost aeons to their own demesnes.
>
> At last the key was mine to those vague visions
> Of sunset spires and twilight woods that brood
> Dim in the gulfs beyond this earth's precisions,
> Lurking as memories of infinitude. (*AT* 65)

S. T. Joshi has argued that the fragment known as "The Book" was likely an attempt at creating a prose version of the *Fungi from Yuggoth* cycle (*Primal Sources* 190–94). Consequently, "The Book" offers another clue as to the nature of this book: "It was a key—a guide—to certain gateways and transitions of which mystics have dreamed and whispered since the race was young, and which lead to freedoms and discoveries beyond the three dimensions and realms of life and matter that we know" (*D* 63). Transcending the boundaries of the earth and traversing the limitless void lead to dimly remembered worlds of wonder; this reiterates the theme that Lovecraft rediscovered his beloved classical world through his discovery of astronomy, that the classical world lived on in the timeless celestial vault.

One difficulty with this interpretation, however, is the fact that "the book" is ancient, while Young's *Lessons in Astronomy* was new. Another line from "The Book" clarifies: "I remember how I read the book at last—white-faced, and locked in the attic room that I had long devoted to strange searchings. The great house was very still, for I had not gone up till after midnight. I think I had a family then—though the details are very uncertain—and I know there were many servants" (*D* 363). This scene is certainly reminiscent of Lovecraft's own "searchings" in the attic of 454 Angell Street, where he found Burritt's *Geography of the Heavens*. Perhaps "the book" is actually Burritt's *Geography*, with the anticipation of still greater wonders to be found in Young's *Lessons* superimposed.

Lovecraft's letter of February 12 raises another issue: how many astronomy books did he inherit from his grandmother? In that letter he claims he only had his grandmother's copy of Burritt's *Geography*. He expressed something similar in a letter from 1918: "My interest came through two sources—discovery of an old book of my grandmother's in the attic" (*SL* 1.69). In 1915, however, he suggested that there was more than one book: "it is to her excellent but somewhat obsolete collection of astronomical books that I owe my affection for celestial science" (*SL* 1.7). According to the catalogue of Lovecraft's library, Lovecraft possessed at least eight books from the mid-nineteenth-century that may have come from his grandmother. He also owned at least four books published in the 1890s, which he presumably obtained himself—unless we allow that his grandmother was still obtaining astronomy books up to the year of her death—which indicates Lovecraft occasionally would pick up older, out-of-date books. Perhaps the most puzzling is Young's *Lessons* itself. Lovecraft owned two editions, one from 1893 and the other from 1903; which edition did he obtain on that memorable day of February 12? Since he described it as "new," it must be the 1903 edition. But then where did the 1893 edition come from? Why would he buy an older edition of a book when he already had a newer one, especially in a fast-moving science like astronomy? Is it possible his grandmother really was still obtaining astronomy books just before her death? It is likely that Lovecraft is oversimplifying when he describes finding "a book in the attic," but it will likely never be known which ones, or even how many, he inherited and which he obtained on his own.

Lovecraft's astronomical newspaper columns provide an extensive account of his understanding of the planets, stars, and structure of the universe. These columns were carried in four newspapers: *Pawtuxet Valley Gleaner* (1906), Providence *Tribune* (1906–08), Providence *Evening News* (1914–18), and *Asheville Gazette-News* (1915). These writings can be divided into two broad categories: non-scientific discussion of mythological lore associated with the stars and constellations, and scientific writings. His scientific writings can be further divided into three sub-categories: recent astronomical developments or discoveries (such as the appearance of a new comet), forecasts of events for the coming month (such as the phases of the moon, rising and setting times of the various planets, upcoming meteor showers, eclipses and other perpetual phenomena), and general theoretical topics in modern astronomy. The Providence *Evening News* columns are the most extensive and diverse, covering non-scientific mythology, expositions of astronomical theory, special events in the skies and in the astronomical community, and forecasts for the coming month. The other columns are entirely scientific: *Pawtuxet Valley Gleaner* emphasizes theory and forecasts, Providence *Tribune* is entirely forecasts, and *Asheville Gazette-News* is entirely devoted to astronomical theory.

The various sources Lovecraft drew upon for these columns illustrates something about his tastes and scientific education. Joshi cites Bulfinch's *Age of Fable* and Ovid's *Metamorphoses* as sources of Graeco-Roman myths Lovecraft used for his non-scientific mythological portions of his Providence *Evening News* columns (CE 3.11). A close look at Burritt's *Geography of the Heavens*, however, suggests that in some cases its mythological material was Lovecraft's primary source. As an example, consider Bulfinch's, Burritt's, and Lovecraft's treatment of the story of Andromeda. Bulfinch's version closely follows Ovid, described in the course of the adventures of Perseus:

> Perseus, continuing his flight, arrived at the country of the Æthiopians, of which Cepheus was king. Cassiopeia, his queen, proud of her beauty, had dared to compare herself to the Sea-Nymphs, which roused their indignation to such a degree that they sent a prodigious sea-monster to ravage the coast. To appease the deities, Cepheus was directed by the oracle to expose his daughter Andromeda to be devoured by the monster. As Perseus looked down from his aërial height he beheld the virgin chained to a rock, and waiting the ap-

proach of the serpent. She was so pale and motionless that if it had not been for her flowing tears, and her hair that moved in the breeze, he would have taken her for a marble statue. (Bulfinch 145–47)

As in Ovid, there is a long digression where Andromeda initially hesitates to speak out of modesty, but then tells her tale and Perseus offers to kill the monster for her hand in marriage. There is a long battle scene, the monster is slain, the marriage takes place, Phineus and his cohorts are turned to stone.

Burritt's version is highly abbreviated: it opens with the background of Andromeda's plight, the arrival of Perseus, the monster is destroyed, and her other suitors are turned to stone:

She [Andromeda] was daughter of Cepheus, King of Ethiopia, by Cassiopeia. She was promised in marriage to Phineus, her uncle, when Neptune drowned the kingdom, and sent a sea monster to ravage the country, to appease the resentment which his favorite nymphs bore against Cassiopeia, because she had boasted herself fairer than Juno and the Nereides. The oracle of Jupiter Ammon was consulted, and nothing could pacify the anger of Neptune unless the beautiful Andromeda should be exposed to the sea monster. She was accordingly chained to a rock for this purpose, near Joppa (now Jaffa, in Syria), and at the moment the monster was going to devour her, Perseus, who was then returning through the air from the conquest of the Gorgons, saw her, and was captivated by her beauty.

> "Chained to a rock she stood; young Perseus stay'd
> His rapid flight, to woo the beauteous maid."

He promised to deliver her and destroy the monster if Cepheus would give her to him in marriage. Cepheus consented, and Perseus instantly changed the sea monster into a rock, showing him Medusa's head, which was reeking in his hand. The enraged Phineus opposed their nuptials, and a violent battle ensued, in which he, also, was turned into a stone, by the petrifying influence of the Gorgon's head. (Burritt 19)

The quotation is from Eusden's translation (Ovid 126).

Here is Lovecraft's telling of the story for an article in the Providence *Evening News*:

Andromeda was a princess of Aethiopia, daughter of King Cepheus and Queen Cassiopeia. Having declared herself more beautiful than the Nereides of the waves, Neptune, the ocean-god, sent Cetus, a vast sea monster, to harass the coast of Cepheus' kingdom as a rebuke to the vain presumption of the queen. When Cepheus consulted the oracle of Jupiter Ammon for means of relief, he was told that the curse would be withdrawn only on condition that the Princess Andromeda be bound to a rock on the shore and left for Cetus to devour. This having been done, the chained Andromeda in terror awaited the coming of the destroying monster. But meanwhile the Jove-born Perseus, fresh from his victory over the gorgon Medusa, and mounted on the winged horse Pegasus, was flying across the stricken domain. Observing Andromeda and her plight, he descended and slew the dire sea-creature that even then had approached to devour the royal victim. As Ovid says, in Eusden's translation:

> "Thus the wing'd hero now descends, now soars,
> And at his pleasure the vast monster gores.
> Full in his back, swift stooping from above,
> The crooked sabre to its hilt he drove."

The Princess thus rescued, Perseus led her in triumph to her parents and there wedded her, after turning all his rivals to stone by shewing to them the fatal head of Medusa. (CE 3.165–66)

There are, of course, variations among all three: in Burritt's version, the monster is turned to stone, not slain; Lovecraft—wishing to tie the constellation Pegasus into the story—has Perseus mounted on the winged horse, instead of flying using the winged shoes of Mercury. Nonetheless, there is more in common than different among the three, and Lovecraft's version is closest in outline and structure to Burritt's. In the first sentence of Lovecraft's and Burritt's, Andromeda and her parents are identified. In the second sentence, Cassiopeia's vanity provokes Neptune's wrath, who sends the monster Cetus to ravage the country. In the third sentence, the oracle of Jupiter Ammon is consulted, and the remedy of Andromeda's sacrifice is revealed. The oracle is identified as that of "Jupiter Ammon" only in Burritt's and Lovecraft's versions; in Bulfinch, it is simply described as "the oracle" (147), and in Ovid her fate is pronounced by "the Libyan God's unjust decree" (126). The next few sentences finish the entire story, Lovecraft's version omitting and keeping details exactly as Burritt. Both accent their prose with a touch of verse from the same source.

Lovecraft's version easily qualifies as a plagiarized version of Burritt's.

As for the sources of Lovecraft's scientific writings, he would leave us with the impression that they came from research in the Ladd Observatory library:

> From 1906 to 1918, I contributed monthly articles on astronomical phenomena to one of the lesser Providence dailies. One thing that helped me greatly was the free access which I had to the Ladd Observatory of Brown University—an unusual privilege for a kid, but made possible because of Prof. Upton—head of the college astronomical department and director of the observatory—was a friend of the family. I suppose I pestered the people at the observatory half to death, but they were very kind about it. I had a chance to see all the standard modern equipment of an observatory (including the 12″ telescope) in action, and read endlessly in the observatory library. (SL 4.398)

One envisions Lovecraft combing through the scientific journals in the Ladd Observatory library for the latest news in science and astronomy. Lovecraft is somewhat fast with the facts here: there were four papers, not "one" involved, and he was hardly a kid in 1918. Furthermore, Lovecraft suffered from the stigma of academic failure and probably avoided the observatory following his breakdown of 1908, as described in this letter from 1918:

> I no more visit the Ladd Observatory or various other attractions of Brown University. Once I expected to utilize them as a regularly entered student, and some day perhaps control some of them as a faculty member. But having known them with this "inside" attitude, I am today unwilling to visit them as a casual outsider and non-university barbarian and alien. (SL 1.78)

Nonetheless, most of Lovecraft's scientific writings on recent astronomical events and discoveries—such as the discovery of comets, results of spectroscopic analysis of nebulae and other findings—are too recent to have had time to find their way into books that would be found in an ordinary library. Some come from the popular press. For example, Lovecraft probably first read Professor William Henry Pickering's theories on lunar volcanism and life where they first appeared in the May 1902 issue of the Century Magazine. In Lovecraft's article "Is There Life on the Moon" (CE 3.26–27), virtually every point he makes comes directly from Pickering's article: changes in the crater

Linné (Pickering 90), lunar rays containing hoar-frost (91–95), changes in the craterlets inside Plato (90–91) (misprinted as "Pluto" in Lovecraft's version), vegetation (95–99), and changes in craters Messier and Messier-A. Lovecraft makes a puzzling statement about volcanism: "Now no volcano can operate without atmosphere, but there could easily be a thin gaseous envelope undetected from the Earth" (CE 3.26), which is most likely a misreading of a point made by Pickering: "Again, if there are any active volcanoes upon the moon, it is evident that they must expel something. In other words, there must be some gaseous pressure to make them active" (91).

Another case of Lovecraft reporting from the popular press appears in the March 1, 1916, installment of his Providence *Evening News* series. With respect to Dr. William R. Brooks's observation of the solar eclipse of the 3rd ultimo, Lovecraft writes that Dr. Brooks "made valuable observations during the course which he discerned not only the mountainous roughness of the moon's edge as it was darkly outlined against the solar surface, but two prominent spots near the center of the solar disc as well" (CE 3.177–78). Compare that account with that which appeared in the *New York Times* of February 4, 1916:

GENEVA, N.Y., Feb. 3.—Dr. William R. Brooks, Director of the Smith Observatory and Professor of Astronomy at Hobart College, said tonight he had made excellent observations of today's eclipse of the sun. The sky was clear. The sun and moon both were well defined, the rough edge of the moon showing clearly its mountains and craters.

There were two sun spots near the center of the disk, Dr. Brooks reported.

Despite these examples, Lovecraft had to be researching scientific sources as well: most of his news items are too dry to have been picked up from ordinary sources. An extensive review of Lovecraft's columns reveals, in fact, that he apparently relied heavily on the periodical *Popular Astronomy* for much of his material. *Popular Astronomy* was inaugurated in 1893 for the layperson, as self-described in this announcement:

"By the Word of the Lord were the Heavens Made." A new Astronomical Periodical, designed for Amateurs, Teachers, Students of Astronomy and popular readers. Plainly worded and untechnical in language. Amply illustrated. Issued monthly except July and September. Subscription price $2.50 in advance; for foreign subscribers 14 shillings. (Publications of the Astronomical Society of the Pacific, Vol. 5, No. 32, p. 223)

Based on the timing of news covered in *Popular Astronomy* and the corresponding appearance of similar articles of Lovecraft's, it is very likely that Lovecraft was an avid reader of the magazine, despite the fact that in all his published essays and letters, I can only find a single—rather oblique—reference to it (*CE* 3.292). Consider the following examples: V. M. Slipher published "Spectrographic Observations of Nebulae" in the January 1915 issue of *Popular Astronomy* (Vol. 23, pp. 21–24), in which he described some his latest findings, including the discovery of inclined lines in the spiral nebula N.G.C. 4595, inclined lines in the spectrum indicate part of the object is moving toward the Earth and part away; i.e., it is rotating. Shortly thereafter, in his *Asheville Gazette-News* column "Clusters and Nebulae" published in April of that year, Lovecraft reports:

> The rotation of nebulae on their axes has long been assumed on theoretical grounds, yet not until 1914 was this assumption verified by observation. In that year Dr. Slipher of the Lowell Observatory at Flagstaff, Arizona, found with the spectroscope that a nebula in Virgo performs such a motion. (*CE* 3.308)

N.G.C. 4595 is more commonly known as M104, the "Sombrero" Galaxy in Virgo.

In his March 1915 installment in *Asheville Gazette-News* entitled "The Earth and Its Moon," Lovecraft rehashes some of W. H. Pickering's old theories about volcanic activity, snow, and life on the moon: "Prof. W. H. Pickering, however, has lately concluded from his observations that slight traces of atmosphere, hoar-frost, and vegetation of a low type, as well as feeble remnants of volcanic force, are to be found upon our satellite" (*CE* 3.290). These comments were likely inspired by Pickering's own March 1915[1] article "Meteorology of the Moon" (*Popular Astronomy*, vol. 23, pp. 129–40), in which he reasserts

---

1. *Popular Astronomy* contained astronomical information for the coming month, so each issue was published one month in advance. Thus the March issue would arrive in February, giving HPL time to incorporate its material into his March article.

his latest observations of snow patches, snow storms, steam vents, and patches of greenishness on the surface of the moon.

In the "Comet and Asteroid Notes" section of that March 1915 issue of *Popular Astronomy*, the discovery of a new comet is announced:

> The discovery of a new comet by Mr. John E. Mellish, of Cottage Grove, Wisconsin, was announced by telegram from Harvard College Observatory, February 10. The comet was then in the constellation Ophiuchus about five degrees west and a degree south of the star σ. (*Popular Astronomy*, vol. 23, pp. 177–78)

Lovecraft's column in Providence *Evening News* published for March reports the same news: "On Feb. 10 a new comet was discovered in the constellation Ophiuchus, by J. E. Mellish of Cottage Grove, Wisconsin" (*CE* 3.141).

In the June 1915 issue of *Popular Astronomy* contains the following notice with regards to Mellish's comet: "

> The following telegram from Professor Percival Lowell, director of the Lowell Observatory, Flagstaff, Arizona, was received on the morning of May 24.

> "Comet has disrupted. Observations and photographs of Mellish comet at the Lowell Observatory by Mr. Lampland and Mr. E. C. Slipher, prove that the smaller nuclei, four in all, accompanying the comet, are slowly receding from it at the rate of about four seconds of arc a day, which indicates that the comet has broken up." (*Popular Astronomy*, vol. 23, p. 382)

That same month, Lovecraft writes:

> Mellish's comet has not fulfilled the highest expectations which it aroused in the early spring. Its brilliancy has not been at all considerable, and Profs. Lampland and Slipher of the Lowell Observatory at Flagstaff, Arizona, now report that the original mass has undergone a disruption like that which destroyed the famous comet of Biela in 1852. (*CE* 3.149–50)

In November 1915, *Popular Astronomy* carried a new book announcement:

Ten Years Work of a Mountain Observatory.—This is a 100 page pamphlet, gotten out by the Carnegie Institution of Washington as Publication No. 235. In it, Professor George E. Hale gives a brief account of the development and work of the Mount Wilson Solar Observatory. ... Professor Hale uses as popular language as is possible under the circumstances and gives the general reader a very comprehensive view of the various lines of investigation, the difficulties encountered in pursuing them and the marvelous results already obtained in several instances. (*Popular Astronomy*, vol. 23, p. 628)

Also in November 1915, Lovecraft comments on the progress of the Mount Wilson Observatory:

The eagerly awaited 100-inch reflecting telescope of the Mount Wilson Observatory in California is now approaching completion, and will probably be in active use within a year. The instrument, as before mentioned in these columns, will be the largest telescope in the world, surpassing by far even the famous old leviathan of Lord Rosse. Dr. George Ellery Hale of the observatory entertains high hopes concerning the gigantic instrument, and believes that its advent will usher in a new era of astronomical progress. According to recent estimates, a full hundred million hitherto unknown stars will reveal themselves to its expansive mirror and powerful eye-pieces or photographic plates. (*CE* 3.166)

Indeed, Hale's book contains the prediction as described: "If the indications afforded by Chapman's figures can be applied to fainter objects, there is reason to hope that a 100-inch telescope would add nearly 100,000,000 still fainter stars, many of them lying beyond the boundary of the universe as at present known" (Hale 83).

The January 1916 issue of *Popular Astronomy* carried an article by French astronomer Camille Flammarion entitled "The Giant Sun Canopus," translated by Charles Nevers Holmes, in which the enormousness of Canopus is compared to that of the sun. In the very last paragraph, Flammarion refers to some recent research on Canopus: "An English astronomer, M. O. R. Walkey, has just calculated, according to a mass of very curious probabilities, that this truly formidable star can be the center of our sidereal universe" (*Popular Astronomy*, vol. 24, p. 17). Oliver Rowland Walkey was actually involved in research that concluded that the local stellar group in which the sun belongs is centered in the direction of the constellation Carina, to which Canopus belongs (see Shapley's article "Studies of Magnitudes in Star Clusters, X. Spectral Type B and the Local Stellar System," *Proceedings of the National Academy of Science*, October 15, 1919, p. 438). Several months later, Lovecraft presents Walkey's (mangled either by Lovecraft or one of his editors as "Walkley") theory with some skepticism: "Now, however, Mr. O. R. Walkley has put forward an hypothesis which exalts the gorgeous southern star Canopus, in Argo Navis, to the position of central sun" (*CE* 3.193–94).

As an example of one of Lovecraft's anachronisms, the ancient constellation of Argo Navis had by this time been broken into several smaller ones, including Pyxis, Vela, Puppis, and Carina; Canopus in located in Carina. The misspelling of Walkey's name is presumably why he is "unidentified" in the *CE* 3 notes (p. 194).

The October 1916 issue of *Popular Astronomy* carries a short blurb on site selection for the new 72-inch reflector for the Dominion Observatory, Ottawa: "Mr. W. E. Harper gives a very interesting account of the tests which were made by him of various locations in Canada, in order to determine the most favorable location for the new 72-inch reflecting telescope which is being built for the Dominion Observatory" (*Popular Astronomy*, vol. 24, p. 546). Lovecraft carries the same story in his October 1916 article: "The Dominion Observatory near Victoria, B.C., has now put into operation, or will soon do so, a gigantic reflecting telescope which will, until the completion of the Mt. Wilson telescope, be the largest in the world" (*CE* 3.200).

As yet another example, in the November 1916 issue of *Popular Astronomy*, David H. Wilson reported his preliminary results of determining the rotational period of Venus by observing a faint streak he perceived on its surface, as well as identifying the same streak on sketches of previous observers from 1898.[2] He calculated the Cytherean rotational period as 223.9 days (*Popular Astronomy*, vol. 24, pp. 571–74). He followed up this article with a short addendum in the May 1917 issue (*Popular Astronomy*, vol. 25, p. 336) which apparently

---

2. HPL remarks on the possibility of the existence of these markings in an earlier column (*CE* 3.45). For a full account of the history of dubious research regarding markings on Venus, see Richard Baum's *The Haunted Observatory*, chapter 5, "The Himalayas of Venus."

caught Lovecraft's eye, as he summarizes Wilson's findings in his own May 1917 article:

> An interesting addition to the mass of conflicting data regarding the rotation of Venus is afforded by the recent conclusions of Mr. D. H. Wilson, who has not only made observations of his own, but given careful study to the charts and sketches of previous observers. Whilst roughly endorsing the theory of a long rotation, Mr. Wilson believes that the period does not quite equal the planet's sidereal revolution of 225 days, but that it comprises an interval of somewhat less than 224 days. (CE 3.220)

Mr. Wilson's credentials are unclear. From the context of the article, he was apparently affiliated with the University of Pennsylvania. He may have been a graduate student; I could find no other papers by him. His extreme obscurity accounts for his being unidentified in the CE 3 notes (223).

Despite this evidence that Lovecraft was an avid reader of *Popular Astronomy*, there are some discrepancies. In June 1915, Lovecraft made the following announcement:

> It was recently announced that Prof. Paul T. Delavan, the discoverer of last year's conspicuous comet, had succeeded in finding another, but the latest advices from Prof. Stroemgren [sic] of Copenhagen indicate that this body is Temple's [sic] well-known periodic comet, now drawing near its perihelion. However, it will be remembered that Delavan's comet of 1913–14 was for some time held to be West-phal's comet, so that we must not yet positively reject this astronomer's second announcement.

Lovecraft is confused on several points here. A similar announcement in found in the corresponding June 1915 issue of *Popular Astronomy*:

> **Rediscovery of the Periodic Comet Tempel (1915c Delavan).**—A cablegram from Dr. Felix Aguilar, of LaPlata, Argentina, to Harvard College Observatory announces the discovery of a comet by Delavan in the following position:
>
> May 16.8696 Gr.M.T. R.A. 0^h 33^m 01^s Dec. $-2°$ $05'$ $31''$.
>
> This is very close to the position predicted for Tempel's periodic comet (See P.A. for April, p. 310). A later position cabled from Cor-

doba, Argentina make it certain that the object is Tempel's comet. (*Popular Astronomy*, vol. 23, p. 384)

It is a mystery as to why Lovecraft would ignore the clarification and report the open possibility that an actual new comet was discovered, and how the name Stroemgren got involved. The mystery deepens by examining a little further down on the same page in *Popular Astronomy*, where the following announcement is made:

> **Approximate Ephemeris of Comet 1915a (Mellish.)**—The following ephemeris of Mellish's comet, given by E. Stromgren in A.N. 4792 shows that the comet, after going down near the south pole of the sky, will slowly return northward and may be visible again to northern observers next winter. (*Popular Astronomy*, vol. 23, p. 384)

Could Lovecraft have picked up the name Stromgren from a different announcement on the same page? In his next installment, Lovecraft prints the following clarification: "The comet lately found by Delavan has now been conclusively identified with Temple's [*sic*] periodic comet, hence is after all no new discovery" (CE 3.152). Since the matter was already settled in the scientific community, there is no corresponding announcement in *Popular Astronomy* of that month. It is possible that Lovecraft was consulting other contradictory sources which led to these discrepancies, but given the misspellings of "Tempel" and "Strömgren," it is more likely that Lovecraft was simply careless or took sloppy notes and confused the facts; discovering his error, he quietly provided a retraction on the next month and let the matter drop.

The mystery, however, does not end there. Lovecraft's confusion between Delavan's and Westphal's comets requires explanation. Delavan actually discovered *two* comets in 1913. The first, 1913d,[3] was first announced in *Popular Astronomy* as having been discovered on September 26, and described as "possibly Westphal's comet" (*Popular Astronomy*, vol. 21, p. 524). By November, the new comet is identified "certainly" with Westphal's comet of 1852[4] (*Popular Astronomy*, vol. 21,

---

3. Comets are designated by the year of discovery, and a letter indicating the order of discovery.

4. This second appearance of Westphal's comet established it as a periodic comet of period 61.2 years. It failed to return in 1976.

p. 574). On December 17, Delavan discovered another comet, designated 1913ƒ (*Popular Astronomy*, vol. 22, p. 50), and this second comet was a new find, which ultimately became known as Delavan's comet. Lovecraft first announces the comet in January 1914 (*CE* 3.101), but has the essential details confused two months later:

> The new comet which was mentioned in *The Evening News* astronomical article for January is still approaching the Earth, and my possibly be seen without a telescope in the autumn. This object was discovered last December by Prof. Paul T. Delavan of the National Observatory at La Plata, Argentine Republic. It was for some time confused with Westphar's [*sic*] comet, but its separate identity now seems fairly well established. (*CE* 3.112)

The fact that Lovecraft notes this comet was discovered in December makes it clear that he is talking about the real Delavan's comet (1913ƒ), but this comet was never confused with Westphal's. Lovecraft is probably working from faulty memory: since these events took place prior to the beginning of Lovecraft's columns in Providence *Evening News*, perhaps he was not closely following astronomical events at that point in time.

Perhaps the most startling revelation from the pages of *Popular Astronomy* is that Lovecraft quite likely appeared in it—almost! The "General Notes" of the February 1906 issue contains the following item:

> **Is there Life on the Moon?** Some one has written an account of Professor Pickering's work in relation to the Moon, under the title, *Is there Life on the Moon?* The evidences which seem to point to the possibility that there still may be some life on the cold and desolate surface of the Moon are variable spots that are not shadows. In these spots it is claimed that there are evidences of vegetation.
>
> The writer closes with this rather too strong statement: "The advances which have recently been made in selenography by Professor Pickering show that although the Moon is not a riotously luxuriant abode, it is anything but the lifeless orb commonly supposed. It may be desolate and cold, but it is not altogether dead." (*Popular Astronomy*, vol. 14, p. 122)

Unfortunately, neither name nor city of this letter writer are given, and the quoted portion does not correspond to any of Lovecraft's subsequently collected works. Nonetheless, Lovecraft is almost certainly the author: the topic is one that Lovecraft was passionate about in this period, he published an essay of identical title in the *Pawtuxet Valley Gleaner* only nine months later (CE 3.26–27), and it reads like something Lovecraft could have written. It probably was a letter to the editor, or it may have been a submission of an earlier draft of what became "Is There Life on the Moon?" Perhaps the quoted portion does not appear in the *Pawtuxet Valley Gleaner* version because he took to heart the editorial comment that it was "too strong" and excised it. If it were determined to be Lovecraft's, it would constitute his *first two sentences* to appear in print, antedating his "No Transit of Mars" letter to the *Providence Sunday Journal* by several months (CE 3.16).

Turning to Lovecraft's coverage of astronomical forecasts—timing of lunar phases, planet rising and setting times, etc.—less can be said with regard to his sources. The non-mathematically inclined Lovecraft obviously could not perform his own astronomical calculations, so he must have copied them from somewhere. Although *Popular Astronomy* carried this kind of information, it is clear Lovecraft is not using that source. Some astronomical phenomena occur simultaneously to all observers on the Earth, such as phases of the moon and lunar eclipses. Most phenomena—the rising of the sun, moon and planets, timing of solar eclipses, transits, and occultations—do not occur at the same time for all observers, and must be calculated for a given location. As an example, for October 1906, Lovecraft forecasts two occultations: μ Ceti on the 4th at 3:53, and A^3 (χ^3) Orionis on the 8th at 10:42, both presumably for Providence. *Popular Astronomy* predictions are given for Washington at 3:48 and 10:37, respectively (*Popular Astronomy*, vol. 14, p. 428). Spot checks for other events show similar discrepancies. It is likely Lovecraft used some almanac printed locally.

As for Lovecraft's star maps that appear in the Providence *Tribune*, these could not come from *Popular Astronomy* either. Looking at his map for November 1906 (CE 3.51), he has drawn η Ursa Major (the star at the very end of the handle of the Big Dipper) nearly due south, where it appears to be about to dip below, or skim, the horizon. The equivalent map in *Popular Astronomy* (*Popular Astronomy*, vol. 14, p. 561) has this star at a clearly higher elevation, as if it were drawn for a more northerly latitude—presumably the location where it is published, Northfield, MN (approximate latitude 44.5°

N). Lovecraft may have simply copied these maps from his planisphere, which was designed for latitude 40° N (CE 3.220). η Ursa Major is at declination 49° 34" north. From 40° N, only stars of declination 50° N or higher will never set and be circumpolar, which means η Ursa will just barely dip below the horizon. From Providence (latitude 41° 49" N), this star will never set, and clear the horizon by some 1° 23" (almost 2½ diameters of the full moon).[5] It is hard to draw firm conclusions from Lovecraft's crude map, but it appears to be more consistent for an observer at the planisphere's latitude than from Providence's.

As for Lovecraft's exposition of astronomical theory, there are undoubtedly numerous books, magazines, and other sources he used in his research. Based on his articles, a general outline of Lovecraft's positions and understanding of astronomical theory can be summarized.

On the Sun and Planets

Beyond a recital of the names of the planets, their order and distances from the sun, the length of their orbital periods, and a list of their various moons, Lovecraft provides few details. Indeed, this is the sad state of affairs of his time: by 1900, virtually everything that could be learned about the planets from traditional ground-based optical telescopes was known, and that was very little. Mercury is so small and so far away, observations of surface markings were extremely difficult and controversial. Lovecraft's information of observations of surface markings on Mercury was apparently drawn in part from Newcomb's *Astronomy for Everybody*, a book that appears in Lovecraft's Library. Newcomb writes:

> The first observer who thought he could see any features on the surface of this planet was Schröter, a German. When Mercury presented the form of a crescent he fancied that its south horn seemed blunted at intervals. He attributed this to the shadow of a lofty mountain; and by observing the intervals between the blunted appearance he concluded that the planet revolved on its axis in twenty-four hours and five minutes. But Sir William Herschel, who observed at the same

---

5. These rough calculations ignore considerations such as atmospheric refraction, which will be considerable at these elevations near the horizon, but a planisphere cannot account for them either.

time with much more powerful instruments, could not see anything of the kind. (Newcomb, *Astronomy for Everybody* 160)

Lovecraft's version follows similarly:

> The time of rotation of Mercury was first investigated in the late eighteenth and early nineteenth centuries by the celebrated German astronomer, Johann Schroeter, who believed that when the planet has a crescentic phase, the south horn becomes blunted once in 24 hours 5 minutes. Schroeter, assuming the phenomenon to be due to the shadow cast by a mountain of great altitude, inferred that the intervals between successive truncations represent rotations of Mercury on its axis. On the other hand, the greatest of all telescopic observers, Sir William Herschel, could never distinguish any feature whatsoever upon Mercury. (*CE* 3.114)

Lovecraft's schedule of transits of Mercury (*CE* 3.283) probably also came from Newcomb's book, which gives dates and regions of visibility (Newcomb, *Astronomy for Everybody* 163).

Venus is perpetually shrouded in clouds that obscure its surface. On several occasions, Lovecraft cites the ongoing controversy with respect the planet's rotation rate based on perceived markings on its surface and spectroscopic analysis (1914, *CE* 3.114; 1915, pp. 163–64 and 284; 1917, p. 220 and 238–39). Through February 1915, Lovecraft favors the older conclusion that Venus's day is Earth-like, approximately 24 hours, whereas afterwards he concedes the evidence is "indefinite." Perhaps he picked up something in 1915 that reopened the question in his mind.

The moon is Lovecraft's most authoritative subject. His descriptions of its seas, craters, mountains, and other features come from many hours of personal observations. His juvenile writings support Pickering's theories about lunar activity and life, but later he merely mentions them without endorsement (*CE* 3.290). Burritt's *Geography* has a very nice chapter on the moon (203–14) that Lovecraft likely drew from in his various descriptions of it phases, surface markings, and appearance. Lovecraft's quotation of Frauenhofer having seen "a lunar edifice, resembling a fortification, together with several lines of road" and Schroeter's observation of "a great city on the east side of the moon, an extensive canal in another place, and fields of vegetation" (*CE* 3.290) come almost word for word from Burritt (214). On several occasions Lovecraft misuses the expression "horizontal moon" to describe its enlarged appearance when near the horizon (CE 3.18, 33, 289). According to Burritt, the term refers to an apparent horizontal elongation—a distortion—due to the flattening of the poles (297) when the moon is right on the horizon, as opposed to its overall enlarged appearance when near the horizon (296).

The late nineteenth/early twentieth-century controversies of Mars need not be detailed here. Suffice it to say that Lovecraft took a moderate view supporting the notion that the canals of Mars existed, but rejected them as evidence of civilization (CE 3.292, 319–20). His claim that the existence of the Martian canals "was doubted until recently, when some of them were successfully photographed," was probably based on a series of photographs produced by an expedition to South America financed by Percival Lowell in 1907. Mars approaches the Earth every 26 months, but every 17 years or so the approach is very close and Mars is particularly well placed for observation. 1907 was such a year. Although the photographs from this expedition were published with much fanfare in the *Century* and *Cosmopolitan*, they were inconclusive: despite using an excellent telescope under optimal conditions, Mars's image appears only 3/16 of an inch across on the original plates (*Sky & Telescope*, November 2007, pp. 20–24). Even under the best circumstances, Mars appears in a telescope with about as much clarity as does the moon with the unaided eye, and the question of the existence of the canals would not be settled until the first space probe returned close-up photographs of the planet in 1965. Lovecraft's insinuation that the canal controversy was settled in his time is an exaggeration.

Of the outer planets—Jupiter, Saturn, Uranus, and Neptune—Lovecraft has little to say other than basic orbital duration, appearance, history of discovery of moons, and the circumstances of the discovery of the latter two. Beyond these basic facts, little more was known.

As with the planets, Lovecraft confines his description of the sun to the obvious facts and history of observations. His citation of Prof. Newcomb's estimate that the sun will continue to shine for 10,000,000 years due to gravitational contraction comes from Newcomb's *Popular Astronomy*, which Lovecraft possessed (516). Lovecraft ignores the highly controversial nature of the contraction theory, since geological and evolutionary evidence of the time suggested the

Earth was far older than the tens of millions of years the contraction theory restricted its age to (Brush 5–6).

Of the Universe Beyond the Solar System

What little was known about the solar system dwarfed what was known about the stars. Nonetheless, Lovecraft manages to cite enough basic facts about the stars' sizes, distances, colors, and movements to round out discussions about them. Of particular interest to Lovecraft—an interest that would hold his imagination for his entire life—is the vast distances to even the closest stars. In 1914 he writes of "the prodigious immensity of the space between our solar system and the rest of the universe" and the distance to the nearest star as "almost beyond human comprehension," as well as the fact that "the mind can form no conception of gulfs so vast" as the distance to the farthest stars at "stupendous intervals" (CE 3.110).[6] By 1915 his prose resembles the distinctive language of his cosmic fiction, describing stellar distances larger than "appalling gaps in space than can be comprehended by the human brain," and "monstrous spaces" (CE 3.304). In 1917, he declares that "the consideration of boundless time and space is indeed the most thought-provoking feature of astronomical science" (CE 3.222). The immensity of space and time will form a core theme throughout much of Lovecraft's fiction.

Among Lovecraft's more interesting articles is "Clusters and Nebulae," written for *Asheville Gazette-News* in 1915 (CE 3.307–11), in which he presents the observations, theories, and open questions with respect to these objects. He does an adequate job of describing the Milky Way, its appearance, disklike structure, orientation of its plane and poles, and the distribution of the brighter stars, new stars, and planetary nebulae near its plane, while the spiral nebulae tend toward the poles. This is probably his most difficult article for the modern reader to interpret, since the vast bulk of this subject has been wholly revised by science since 1915. His overview is mostly consistent with the science of the time. There was a great confusion

---

6. Either HPL or his editors inadvertently shortchanged the light year by several hundred billion miles, citing a diminutive value of 5,509,588,236,000 miles, apparently the result of a typographical error in two digits; a more reasonable figure of 5,869,588,236,000 miles is found elsewhere (CE 3.230, 304).

about the nature of the nebulae, and it was regarded as "remarkable" that some types of objects tend to appear near the galactic plane while others tend toward the poles; these were among the most enigmatic objects of the time.

Nonetheless, Lovecraft commits several misunderstandings. His statement that the nebulae "are actually composed of self-luminous gas was satisfactorily demonstrated with the spectroscope in 1864 by the late Sir William Huggins" (*CE* 3.308) ignores the dual spectroscopic nature of the nebulae. Newcomb's *Popular Astronomy* from Lovecraft's own library makes the distinction: "In the winter of 1864–'65, the spectrum of [the Orion nebula] was examined independently by Secchi and Huggins, who found that it consisted of three bright lines, and hence concluded that the nebula was composed, not of stars, but of glowing gas" (Newcomb, *Popular Astronomy* 455). But in describing the Andromeda nebula, Newcomb notes: "unlike most of the nebulae, its spectrum is a continuous one, similar to the ordinary spectra from heated bodies, thus indicating that the light emanates, not from glowing gas, but from matter in the solid or liquid state" (456). Only a handful of nebular spectra had been observed in Newcomb's time (1880), but by 1915 many more had been observed and by then it was clear that nebulae fell into two categories: those with emission spectra (bright lines), and the absorption (continuous) spectra. E. A. Fath published his research concerning the distribution of the nebulae in a 1910 issue of *Popular Astronomy*, a source to which Lovecraft obviously had access. In this article, Fath clearly distinguishes the emission from the absorption nebulae and demonstrates that the former are clustered toward the galactic plane, while the latter are the spiral forms clustered near the poles (*Popular Astronomy*, vol. 18, pp. 544–48). Lovecraft's inability to make this distinction suggests that he is out of touch with findings that were at the time years old and available in an accessible source such as *Popular Astronomy*; worse, he has an incomplete grasp of even his older sources.

Another misunderstanding Lovecraft perpetrates throughout his articles is his use of the term "proper motion." The proper motion of stars is the apparent shifting of a star's position on the celestial sphere as viewed from Earth, usually expressed as arc-seconds per year; this is not to be confused with actual movement through space, which might be expressed as miles per hour. Newcomb provides a suitable explanation that Lovecraft should have been well aware of, including a table of stars with the highest known proper motions, expressed in arc-seconds per year. He points out the general rule that brighter stars typically have higher proper motions, which arises from the fact that the brighter stars tend to be closer and therefore have a greater *apparent* speed relative to the Earth (Newcomb, *Popular Astronomy* 460–62), in the way a nearby automobile traveling at 55 m.p.h. appears to move faster than a distant jet airplane traveling at 500 m.p.h. When Lovecraft writes, "all nebulae have proper motions through space, most of them proceeding with a tremendous velocity" (CE 3.308), he is confusing proper motion with absolute motion: no proper motion has ever been detected for any of the spiral nebulae. Instead, the measured velocities he is referring to are spectroscopically measured absolute radial motion of these objects, not proper motion.

Of Cosmology

As late as 1917, Lovecraft advocated the Nebular Hypothesis of Laplace as an explanation as to the origins of stars and planets. Until the twentieth century, Laplace's theory was dominant, and Lovecraft probably learned about in from any number of sources, including Newcomb's book (Newcomb, *Popular Astronomy* 503–7). Although Lovecraft concedes that "some parts of the hypothesis of Laplace have lately been challenged," it retains his endorsement: "[it]is still the most probable explanation of the origin of the sun, the stars, and their encircling systems of planets and satellites" (CE 3.237 [originally appeared in 1915]; CE 3.310). In fact, Lovecraft is behind the times in his defense of Laplace's theory. Starting in 1900,[7] colleagues T. C. Chamberlin and F. R. Moulton began publishing a series of papers that challenged the basic plausibility of the nebular hypothesis, largely on the basis of the distribution of angular momentum in the solar system;[8] in 1905, Chamberlin published a complete theory backed by computations by Moulton that proposed that a close encounter between the sun and another star resulted in the ejection of material from the sun, which

---

7. The complete history of the Chamberlin-Moulton theory is documented by Stephen G. Brush, "The Rise and Fall of the Chamberlin-Moulton Cosmogony," *Journal for the History of Astronomy* (1978): 1–41, 77–104.

8. The basic quandary being, if the sun and planets formed together, how could the sun have over 99% of the mass of the system, while the planets have over 99% of the system's angular momentum?

eventually condensed into the planets. Although some professionals remained skeptical of details of the Chamberlin-Moulton theory, it was well received in the United States; if nothing else, Chamberlin's arguments at least unleashed serious criticism of Laplace's theory. Lovecraft was still advancing the defunct Laplace theory in 1915, just as the Chamberlin-Moulton theory peaked in popularity (Brush 79).

An interesting prediction of the nebular hypothesis is that, since planets form by the same means as stars, it follows that planetary systems—and civilizations to populate them—are likely to be plentiful (Brush 2). Newcomb devotes several pages to the topic, concluding:

> It seems, therefore, so far as we can reason from analogy, that the probabilities are in favor of only a very small fraction of the planets being peopled with intelligent beings. But when we reflect that the possible number of the planets is counted by hundreds of millions, this small fraction may be a very large number, and among this number many may be peopled by beings much higher than ourselves in the intellectual scale. (Newcomb, *Popular Astronomy* 527)

For Burritt, the plurality of worlds is a matter of gospel:

> We should therefore learn, says Dr. Chalmers, not to look on our Earth as the universe of God, but as a single, insignificant atom of it; that it is only one of the many mansions which the Supreme Being has created for the accommodation of his worshipers; and that he may now be at work in regions more distant than geometry ever measured, creating worlds more manifold than numbers ever reckoned, displaying his goodness, and spreading over all the intimate visitations of his care. (Burritt 148)

Lovecraft's own statement that the Laplace theory accounts for the formation of "the sun, the stars, and their encircling systems of planets and satellites" indicates that he too believes that planetary systems are commonplace. But under the Chamberlin-Moulton theory, planetary systems—and life itself—are the result of a very unlikely chance encounter between stars, and are therefore likely to be quite rare (Brush 86–87). As late as 1921, Lovecraft describes the Earth as an unremarkable place in the universe:

> So when it is shewn that life on our world will (relatively) soon be extinct through the cooling of the sun; that space is full of such

worlds which have died; that human life and the solar system itself are the merest *novelties* in an eternal cosmos; and that all indications point to a gradual breaking down of both matter and energy which will eventually nullify the results of evolution in any particular corner of space . . . (*In Defence of Dagon*, CE 5.51–52)

Lovecraft is not aware of, or has not grasped, the full implications of the new theory that suggests the Earth may be completely unique in the universe. Years later, Lovecraft will embrace the Chamberlin-Moulton theory and its variants, a shift that will have an interesting effect on his fiction, as discussed below.

Lovecraft is better informed of the cosmology of the universe itself. When he recycled his *Asheville Gazette-News* article on "Clusters and Nebulae" for the "August Skies" 1917 Providence *Evening News* article, he prefaced the discussion with a highly perceptive comment: "Clusters, nebulae, and the Milky Way are far more important objects in the science of astronomy than they seem to the casual observer; since from their appearance and phenomena are based nearly all our speculations regarding the structure and dimensions of the universe" (CE 3.230). Indeed, astronomers had been grappling with the question of the nature of the nebulae for hundreds of years, and would continue to do so well into the 1930s. The key questions were: why did some nebulae show emission spectra (like Orion's), but others show absorption (like Andromeda)? Why could some be resolved into stars with a sufficiently large telescope, while others remained diffuse? Some that were thought to be unresolvable proved to be resolvable when a newer, larger telescope was invented—could all of them be resolved into stars with a powerful enough telescope? Why were some types distributed toward the galactic plane, while others away from it? And perhaps most puzzling of all was the phenomenally high radial velocity that some of them exhibited. When long-duration photography was invented, it became clear that the oddballs distributed away from the galactic plane with high radial velocity usually had some sort of a spiral form. Two schools of thought developed: that the spiral nebulae were nearby and part of the Milky Way— possibly examples of stars in formation—or that they were far away, whole galactic systems of their own. J. D. Fernie has documented the history of the study of these objects. Immanuel Kant was the first commentator to suggest that the nebulae were external star systems, which he called "island universes"—a term that remained in usage through the 1920s (Fernie 1192). Over the course of time, new theories and discoveries pushed the spirals outside of the galaxy and then pulled them back in: William Herschel first supported their external nature, but then changed his mind and made them internal features (Fernie 1194–95). The invention of Lord Rosse's "leviathan" resolved many "unresolvable" nebulae into clusters of stars, reviving the island universe theory (Fernie 1196). By 1900, the island universe theory was again tabled, but by 1920 the nature of the spirals was up in the air. In that year, two champions of the alternate views, Harlow Shapley and Heber D. Curtis, met in Washington for what is now referred to as "The Great Debate": Shapley argued for the spirals being associated with our galaxy, while Curtis argued they were external systems (see Hoskin). Of course, the debate did not resolve the issue, but the issues and arguments raised provide a convenient marker to gauge various astronomical opinions of the time. Therefore, when Lovecraft speaks of "other universes," he is not being imaginative; he is embracing the vernacular of the time. Lovecraft himself is unclear about which camp he is in: he seems to take one position and then contradicts it:

> That most nebulae belong to our universe seems probable, though it was once believed that they, as well as clusters, are other universes, or external Galaxies, as it were. Whether or not such things as other universes do exist, is a question of the highest interest, involving conceptions of the most awful grandeur. It is very likely that these colossal universes of suns are widely scattered through boundless space, though separated by such terrifying and abysmal distances that their light, sent on its way at the time of their creation, has not yet reached form on to the other. It were useless here to speak of the ultimate confines of space itself. If the monstrous distances dealt with in the ordinary study of astronomy be stupefying in their immensity, what may be said of infinity itself? The idea of a boundary to all space is even more repellent than the terrible conception of the illimitable. (CE 3.231)

First, it is likely that they belong to our universe, but then it is likely that these colossal universes of suns are widely scattered. Whatever he meant, the issue is clear: the "stupendous intervals" between the stars which themselves are beyond human comprehension pale at the possibility of the distances represented by other universes of stars. When the island universe interpretation prevailed once and for all less than 10 years later, it would have at least as powerful an effect on Lovecraft's imagination as did the development of relativity theory.

II.

Not all readers are ignorant of the sciences, and a flagrant contravention of truth ruins a tale for anyone able to detect it.—H. P. Lovecraft, 1934 ("Some Notes on Interplanetary Fiction" [*CE* 2.180])

Astronomical Sources in Lovecraft's Fiction

Lovecraft argued in "Some Notes on Interplanetary Fiction" that the key to successfully imparting a sense of wonder and awe in the reader of a weird tale was to dress the central theme of the tale—the abnormality of a violation of natural law—with a stark sense of realism in order to create a convincing hoax in the reader's mind that the abnormality is *possible*. He used a number of techniques to achieve these hoaxes, including: realism and naturalness of characters, language, and setting. Perhaps his most distinctive technique for capturing a sense of realism was to integrate the sciences within his fiction as elements of the setting and atmosphere. For example, in *At the Mountains of Madness*, the long, unknown history of the Old Ones is described in terms of the vast geologic history of the earth. In "The Colour out of Space," Lovecraft draws on his chemistry background to detail the various qualitative tests to which the college professors subjected the meteorite: the borax bead (to test for various metals), malleability, its reaction to various solvents including water, acids, and other chemicals, and most interesting of all, its unidentifiable spectrum—all described in the cool, scientific language of a chemical lab report. Overall, Lovecraft uses a variety of branches of science to add realistic detail to his fiction, including biology, psychology, archeology, anthropology, and quantum physics. No science, however, receives the same level of treatment—in both frequency and detail—as astronomy.

The fact the Lovecraft was inclined to rely on astronomical phenomena to provide mood effect says a great deal about his aesthetic disposition. Astronomical references abound throughout his fiction in a myriad of forms: an unpredicted eclipse is cited one story, and auroras appear in four. Observations of planets in the sky, however, are virtually nonexistent, appearing only once. Stellar observations, on the other hand, are numerous, appearing in twenty stories. The moon—or moonlight, or its absence—is Lovecraft's overwhelming favorite vehicle for setting a certain scene or atmosphere, appearing in thirty-seven stories. Only five have no astronomical references.[9] Only rarely is the reader allowed to forget that the vast cosmos is staring down at them.

Lovecraft's astronomical flourishes are remarkably consistent with observed astronomical phenomena: he never describes obvious contradictions to observational reality such as a horned moon rising at midnight—crescent moons always rise and set with the sun. In "Dagon," for example, the narrator falls asleep in the evening and then awakens to find the "waning and fantastically gibbous moon" had risen (D 16). Full moons rise at sunset, and quarter moons rise at noon or midnight, so only a gibbous moon could rise after sunset and be "near the zenith" (D 17) during nighttime. Since it rose after sunset, it must also be waning: the details check out. In "The Other Gods," even an unpredicted lunar eclipse occurs during a full moon (D 129). Lovecraft even takes care to synchronize astronomical events with the calendar, when times and dates are given in the story: the manuscript of "The Transition of Juan Romero" contains a note: "Here is a lesson in scientific accuracy for fiction writers. I have just looked up the moon's phases for October, 1894, to find when a gibbous moon was visible at 2 a.m., and changed the dates to fit!!" (D 340). Indeed, a modern almanac confirms that a gibbous moon was visible from the American southwest at 2 A.M. on October 19, 1894, the given time and place of the story's climax.[10]

In "The Whisperer in Darkness," assaults on Akeley's place are coordinated with the absence of the moon. The first outbreak of gunfire occurs on August 12–13, 1928 (DH 231), on which the almanac indi-

---

9. A complete list of astronomical references is given in the Appendix

10. Any number of online almanacs are available for verifying these details. For facts concerning the phases of the moon, consult http://www.fourmilab. ch/earthview/vplanet.html. To display the sky—including stars, planets, and the moon from any point on earth at any time—consult http://www. fourmilab.ch/cgi-bin/Yoursky.

cates the moon was only 7% illuminated, new moon occurring on the 15th. By the end of the month, Akeley has "fewer terrors to report," but only because the full moon keeps them off (*DH* 233); this is consistent with the full moon on August 31. On September 4, Akeley laments that the moon is "going into wane anyhow" (*DH* 234), at which point it is about 80% illuminated, well on its way to becoming new, which will happen on the 14th. Akeley is right to be concerned, since the full moon loses half its brightness in only a few days; by the time of the quarter phase, the moon is only 10% as bright as it was at full.

The same attention to detail is found in "The Shadow over Innsmouth" and "The Shadow out of Time": at the time of Olmstead's escape at 2 A.M. (*DH* 350) on July 16, 1927 (*DH* 304), the decaying town is illuminated "by the beams of a moon not much past full" (*DH* 347). According to the almanac, the moon at that time is 97% illuminated, having been full on July 14. On the night of Peaslee's encounter—the morning of July 18, 1935—he describes the moon as "slightly past full" (*SOT* 70); by the almanac it is 94% full, full moon having occurred on July 16 (as also indicated in Lovecraft's notes of the story, *SOT* 93).

Lovecraft outdoes his devotion to realism in "The Shadow out of Time" by describing Peaslee's heavenly observations from the vantage point of 150 million years ago:

> Once in a while, though, there would be glimpses of the sun—which looked abnormally large—and of the moon, whose marking held a touch of difference from the normal that I could never quite fathom. When—very rarely—the night sky was clear to any extent, I beheld constellations which were nearly beyond recognition. Known outlines where sometimes approximated, but seldom duplicated. (*SOT* 45)

Although few readers were (or are) likely to appreciate the details of these remarks, they accurately reflect an extrapolation of present conditions into the distant past, based on Lovecraft's understanding of scientific thought. The enlarged appearance of the sun is an allusion to the theory that the sun derives its energy through the release of gravitational potential energy as a result of its slow but steady contraction (see Lovecraft's essay "The Sun," *CE* 3.281); it therefore follows that in the far distant past, the sun was perceptibly larger. The changes in the moon's appearance are the result of active volcanism on the lunar surface, which Lovecraft believed continued to the present day ("The Earth and the Moon," *CE* 3.290). The fact that the changes are subtle is consistent with the fact that the volcanoes themselves—i.e., the lunar craters—are not visible to the unaided eye,[11] and a wholesale reworking of the lunar surface would be required to change its appearance appreciably. The changes in the constellations are, of course, a result of the stars not being fixed, but having motions exceedingly small by human standards. The fact that some constellations remain more or less intact and others do not is probably inspired by Kapteyn's theory of star streams, in which proper motions of stars are not random, but can be divided into two groups, so some patterns move together and remain intact while others disperse ("The Stars, Part II," *CE* 3.305).

Even when astronomical phenomena themselves are not directly featured, astronomical concepts and vocabulary are employed that heighten the overall scientific and cosmic tone. For example, the Unnamable is described as "so gibbous and infamous a nebulosity" (*D* 205); after Cthulhu is struck by the *Alert*, it is described as "nebulously recombining" (*DH* 153). Ancient books contain bits of astronomical information, sometimes in the form of alchemy and astrology, as in the book found by Blake in the Starry Wisdom church (*DH* 100–101). In "The Shadow out of Time," when Peaslee's mind returns to his body, he is caught mid-sentence lecturing on William Stanley Jevons's theory linking economic boom and bust cycles to the regular cycle of sun spot maxima and minima.[12] In the assemblage of prominent Providence citi-

---

11. To the unaided *human* eye; there is no suggestion that the optical properties of the eyes of the Great Race differ from the human eye.

12. Jevons outlined his theory in two papers published in *Investigations in Currency and Finance*. In "The Solar Period and the Price of Corn," first delivered in 1875, he makes an entirely empirical study on the presumed periodicity of economic upturns and downturns, which he attributes to good and bad crop harvests, which in turn he supposes are the result of meteorological conditions influenced by sun spots. He later had second thoughts about his methodology, but was then encouraged when an economic downturn he "predicted" occurred in 1878 and a newer estimate of the period of the sun spot cycle was published which seemed to fit his cyclic boom and bust data better. The result was a second paper, "Commercial Cycles and Sun-Spots," which is little more than an elaboration of his earlier arguments.

zens to raid Joseph Curwen as described in *The Case of Charles Dexter Ward*, Lovecraft included astronomer Dr. Benjamin West (*MM* 135), who has recently distinguished himself by observing the 1769 transit of Venus from what is still known as *Transit Street* in Providence and publishing the results in *An Account of the Observation of Venus upon the Sun the Third Day of June 1769* (*Encyclopedia Brunoniana;* see also Beckwith 73). In the same story, Lovecraft uses the Dragon's Head and Tail symbols (☊ and ☋, for "ascending" and "descending" nodes) "used in almanacks" in the "bringing up" and "putting down" rituals (*MM* 204–5). The ascending and descending nodes refer to the points in space where the movement of the moon or planets crosses the plane of the earth's orbit as illustrated in Figure 2.

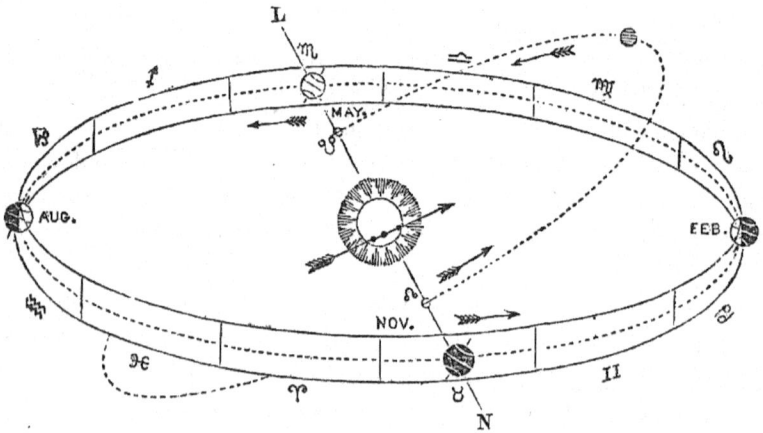

Figure 2: Nodes illustrated from Burritt's *Atlas* (p. 180)

The terminology "ascending" and "descending" nodes is very old—Johannes Kepler in 1621 notes their ancient origin in his *Epitome of Copernican Astronomy:*

> The one is "the ascending node," where the planet leaves the southern hemisphere and turns northward; the other "the descending node," which transfers the planet to the south—the words "ascending" and "descending" having been accommodated to our hemisphere, as that in which the first founders of astronomy lived. (1000)

HPL probably encountered Jevons's work as an example of yet another attempt to link sun spot activity to terrestrial events.

Weeks and Days.	Remarkable Days.	Moon south. h. m.	Moon r. & s. h. m.	Moon's pl. noon sig. o.	Aspect of Planets and other miscellaneous matter.	SUN fast. m.	SUN rises. h. m.	SUN sets. h. m.	O.style
Mond.	1 Egidius	6 16	11 3	♐ 13	☽ 1st. ♀ rises 3 22	0	5 32	6 28	20
Tuesd.	2 Eliza	7 16	morn.	♐ 27	☊ ☽ in per. ◡	0	5 33	6 27	21
Wedn.	3 Mansuetus	8 17	12 6	♑ 11	☌ ☿ ♄ ♃ sets 7 21	1	5 35	6 25	22
Thurs.	4 Moses	9 13	1 16	♑ 25	♂ rises 8 15	1	5 36	6 24	23
Friday	5 Nathaniel	10 5	2 27	♒ 9	♄ sets 7 0	1	5 37	6 23	24
Saturd.	6 Magnus	10 57	2 36	♒ 23	Dog days End.	2	5 39	6 21	25
37	*13th Sunday after Trinity.* · *Luke* 10.				*Days' length* 12 *hours* 22 *min.*				
Sunday	14 *Elev. H Cross*	4 29	9 45	♓ 6	Antares sets 9 15	4	5 49	6 11	2
Mond.	15 Nicetas	5 19	10 34	♓ 18	☾ 15th. ☋ ☽ in apo.	5	5 50	6 10	3
Tuesd.	16 Euphemia	6 8	11 27	♈ 0	7* rises 8 37 ◠	5	5 52	6 8	4
Wedn.	17 *Emberday*	6 58	morn.	♈ 12	♀ rises 4 3	6	5 53	6 7	5
Thurs.	18 Siegfried	7 46	12 24	♈ 24	☌ ♄ ☉ Altair south 8 1	6	5 54	6 6	6
Friday	19 Renatus	8 34	1 24	♉ 6	Aldebaran rises 9 45	6	5 56	6 4	7
Saturd.	20 Micleta	9 22	2 26	♉ 18	♂ rises 7 12	7	5 57	6 3	8

Figure 3: Excerpt from *Hagerstown Almanack*, September 1862

Figure 3 shows an excerpt from an 1862 almanac for Western Maryland illustrating the Dragon's Head and Tail, as Lovecraft described. The Dragon's head appears on Tuesday the 2nd, indicating that the moon crosses from below to above the plane of the earth's orbit that day. On the 15th, the Dragon's tail indicates that the moon passes back below the plane of the earth's orbit on that day. According the R. H. Allen, these points were traditionally called the Dragon's Head and Dragon's Tail by Arabian astronomers and represented by the omega-like symbol for the head and its inverse for the tail. The "Dragon" element may have been inspired by the wavy pattern of the stars of the constellation Draco (The Dragon), which suggests the undulating path of the moon. Allen also confirms "the symbols ☊ for the ascending node and ☋ for the descending, are used in text-books and almanacs" (208). Burritt additionally links the "Dragon" interpretation to the constellation Hydra:

> The introduction of two serpents into the constellations of the ancients, had its origin, it is supposed, in the circumstances that the polar one [Draco] represented the oblique course of the stars, which the Hydra, or Great Snake, in the southern hemisphere, symbolized the moon's course; hence the *Nodes* are called *the Dragon's head and tail to this day.* (72)

Indeed, well over 150 years after Burritt's time, astronomers use the angle of the ascending node along with the eccentricity, inclination, and other parameters to specify elliptical orbits, and the ascending and descending nodes are still represented by their enigmatic dragon's head and tail symbols (see, for example, Ryabov 57–58).

Care must be taken in the interpretation of astronomical phenomena, which already have cultural and mythological significance associated with them. Consider, for example, the symbol of the moon in "The Nameless City," used numerous times: "in a parched and terrible valley under the moon" (D 98), "chilly from the rays of a cold moon" (D 99), "the moon was gleaming vividly over the primeval ruins" (D 101), "when I glanced at the moon it seemed to quiver as through mirrored in unquiet waters" (D 101). It is tempting to attempt to interpret the moon here as a female symbol, as Burleson does in his study of the moon in "The Shadow out of Time" (Burleson 201–2). When Lovecraft rewrote and enlarged "The Nameless City" into *At the Mountains of Madness*, the role of the moon as a silent sentinel to the narrator's awful revelations is instead played by the sun (MM 11, 51, 102), as necessitated by the daylight exploration of the city of the Old Ones under the midnight sun. The interchangeability between sun and moon to play the same role strips the astronomical object of traditional mythological symbolism and reduces it to a mood element. Likewise, the appearance of the sun in "Dagon": "blazing down from a sky which seemed to me almost black in its cloudless cruelty" (D 15) likely appears as it does only because that is the way Lovecraft reproduced the mood from the dream that inspired it (CE 5.49).

The lack of planets in Lovecraft's sky scenes may be a deliberate attempt to avoid obvious symbolism that would be confused with astrology. More likely, however, Lovecraft felt that the planets simply didn't inspire the same sense of cosmic awe. The same cannot be said for the moon, which Lovecraft used far more than any other astronomical symbol. Again, interpretation of the moon is complicated by the many different ways Lovecraft uses it; there is also the fact that the moon's appearance—and the mood it sets—changes radically during its cycle of lunation, or, as Lovecraft puts it: "The most striking phenomena connected with the moon as seen from the earth are the phases, or different aspects caused by the progress of night and day over its surface during its monthly revolution" (CE 3.288). Of the stories in which the phase of the moon is described, in six the moon is full (or nearly full): "The White Ship," "The Outsider," "The Other Gods," "He," "The Shadow over Inns-mouth," and "The Shadow out of Time." In three, it is gibbous: "Dagon," "The Transition of Juan Romero," and "The Doom

That Came to Sarnath." Two feature a crescent moon: "Polaris" and "The Statement of Randolph Carter." "The Colour out of Space" is the only in which the moon is in the quarter phase, and is unusual in that it features a waxing moon—the other possibility being "The Doom That Came to Sarnath." The changing phase of the moon plays an important role in "The Whisperer in Darkness," in which the fungus beings are kept away by moonlight. In "The Moon-Bog," the moon is only described as "waning." In some stories the moon plays an important role, but its phase is not given, as in "The Nameless City." The sky in "The Festival" is described as "moonless." Obviously, the moon plays no unified role. Nor does the moon serve as a harbinger of good or ill fortune, since all Lovecraft's protagonists are, as a rule, luckless.

Of all Lovecraft's astronomical devices, his use of the stars distinguishes his fiction. His first attempt to mix scientific realism into his fiction occurs in "Beyond the Wall of Sleep," which features a struggle between an alien entity and its antagonist—represented by the star Algol—culminating in a battle visible from earth, known to astronomers as Nova Persei 1901 (D 35). Both Algol and GK Persei (GK Persei being the designation of the star that went nova in 1901) fall into a broad class of stars known as variable stars, which Lovecraft discusses in his *Asheville Gazette-News* article "The Stars, Part I" (*CE* 3.306). In this article, he accurately describes Algol as the eclipsing variable type that undergoes remarkable and regular variations in brightness. This star—which marks the head of the Gorgon Medusa—has been associated with great evil, mischief, and violence across many ages and cultures, its name being derived from the Arabic Rā's al Ghūl, the Demon's Head (Allen 332–33); hence Lovecraft's description of it as the "blinking beacon the name of *Algol, the Daemon-Star*" (D 34). Of the nova itself, Lovecraft says nothing beyond the short quotation from Garrett P. Serviss's *Astronomy with the Naked Eye*, p. 152.[13] Lovecraft had earlier remarked on the extreme violence of such events as nova, or "temporary" stars: "If any of these suns possessed inhabited planets, the entire race must have been exterminated by the great calamities" (*CE* 3.41). This is a notion he probably picked

---

13. Although HPL notes in his *Asheville Gazette-News* article that the new star of 1901 "is still remembered by all who beheld it," there is no evidence that HPL himself witnessed it.

up Newcomb's *Popular Astronomy*, in which the venerable astronomer considers the effect of such an event occurring on our own sun:

> Is there any possibility that our sun may be subject to such outbursts
> of light and heat as those we have described in the cases of appar-
> ently new and temporary stars? We may almost say that the contin-
> ued existence of the human race is involved in this question; for it
> the heat of the sun should, even for a few days only, be increased a
> hundred-fold, the higher order of animals and vegetable life would be
> destroyed. (Newcomb, *Popular Astronomy* 443)

Lovecraft's explanation of a temporary star—"collisions between dark
celestial objects, which suddenly liberate vast amounts of light and
heat from the concussions" (*CE* 3.306)—is easily reinterpreted as a
clash between titanic alien entities.

A temporary star may have played a role in the genesis of "Hypnos," in which the narrator's companion becomes terrified by the
open starry sky, one point in particular:

> He did not always glance at the same place in the sky—it seemed to
> be a different place at different times. On spring evenings it would be
> low in the northeast. In the summer it would be nearly overhead. In
> the autumn it would be in the northwest. In winter it would be in
> the east, but mostly if in the small hours of morning. Midwinter eve-
> nings seemed least dreadful to him. Only after two years did I con-
> nect this fear with anything in particular; but then I began to see that
> he must be looking at a special spot on the celestial vault whose posi-
> tion at different times corresponded to the direction of this glance—a
> spot roughly marked by the constellation Corona Borealis. (*D* 168)

Corona Borealis crosses the meridian at midnight about May 15, and at
mid-United States latitude it takes about eight hours to climb there
from the horizon. Therefore, it rises at 4 P.M. on that date. In general,
stars rise about two hours earlier each month, so in January (eight
months later) it rises sixteen hours earlier (midnight). Lovecraft's description of its location throughout the year is therefore accurate: high
in the sky on summer evenings, setting in autumn evenings, rising after
midnight in winter, and below the horizon midwinter evenings. The
nature of the companion's anxiety is never made clear; presumably
some vengeful threat originates from someplace in that direction. Possible clues as to what inspired Lovecraft to choose this region of the

sky come from his *Asheville-Gazette News* and *Providence Evening News:* in the former he writes: "In 1866 a star of the second magnitude appeared in Corona Borealis" (*CE* 3.306), and in the latter: "In the year 1866 one of the obscurer stars in Corona Borealis, usually invisible to the naked eye, blazed out in unexpected brilliancy, rivaling Gemma [the brightest star in the constellation] itself for a time, but soon fading back to its accustomed insignificance" (*CE* 3.187). At the climax of "Hypnos," late one January night just as Corona Borealis is rising, "there appeared from the black northeast corner a shaft of horrible red-gold light" which strikes the companion (*D* 169). Although there is no violent outburst, the red light that strikes the companion is reminiscent of the blazing light of a temporary star.

Lovecraft reuses the theme of an obsession with a particular point in the starry sky in "The Dreams in the Witch House," a tale in which the mental flights through space are also reminiscent of "Hypnos." After returning from a night of plunging through space and visiting an alien world, Gilman experiences an obsession, or attraction, toward a spot on the floor; after the course of a few hours, the direction of this attraction moves, and he eventually associates the spot with a point in the sky: "Apparently it was a point between Hydra and Argo Navis" (*MM* 275). For the given time of year (April 20), the point described by Lovecraft is below the horizon in the morning, rises at about 1 P.M., and just crosses the meridian at about 7 P.M., exactly as Lovecraft describes. A modern star atlas reveals nothing of obvious interest in this region of the sky that may have attracted Lovecraft's attention. Of course, the appropriate source to consult is Lovecraft's beloved Burritt's *Atlas*, shown in Figure 4 (Plates III & IV having been stitched together to show the relevant region of the sky). Unfortunately, yet again there appears to be nothing of any particular interest in this region of the sky. The plates in Lovecraft's edition of Burritt's *Atlas* were actually created for the 1835 edition, and were largely adapted from Alexander Jamieson's *Celestial Atlas* of 1822 (Kidwell 27; Tirion, et al., p. XXIX). The region of interest appears on plate XXVI of that atlas, shown in Figure 5:

In this atlas, the region described is occupied by the modern constellation *Felis*, "The Cat." The constellation originally appeared in J. E. Bode's 1801 *Uranographia*. Felis also appeared in the popular card set "Urania's Mirror," published around 1825, on card 32. The constellation then subsequently disappeared from charts and constel-

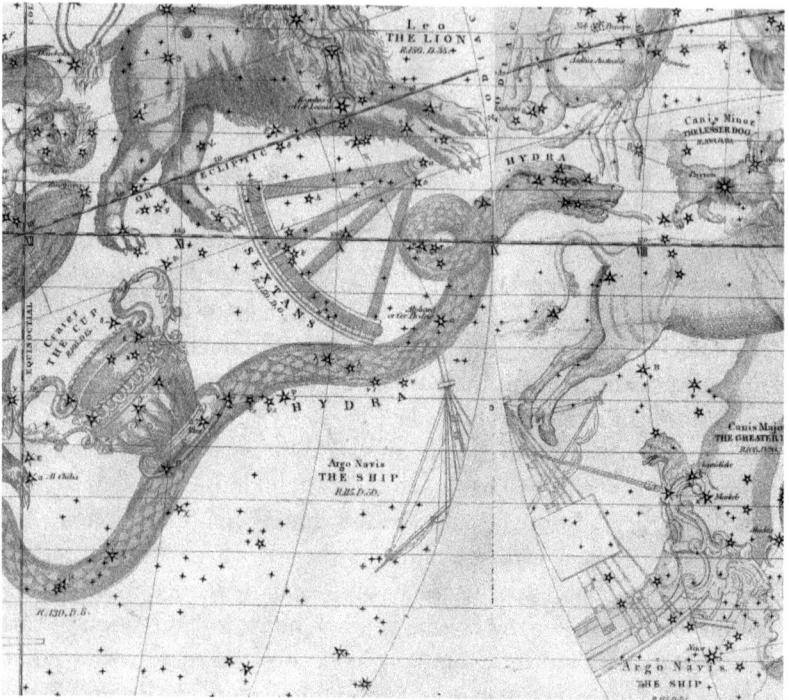

Figure 4: Excerpt of Plates III & IV of Burritt's *Atlas*. Image courtesy
David Rumsey Map Collection, www.davidrumsey.com.

lation lists. The significance, of course, is questionable: could Lovecraft be pointing to an obscure constellation representing his beloved
cats as some sort of cosmic in-joke, as suggested by blogger Chris Perridas? The region is one of the emptiest in the sky: no star brighter
than third magnitude is found anywhere near Hydra's second magnitude Alphard. Perhaps he chose this blank region of the sky deliberately as a means to avoid confusion with obvious interpretations.

On the very next night, Gilman again finds himself briefly trans-
ported to another alien world and possessed by a mysterious pull in a
different direction the next morning (*MM* 276–78). This time Lovecraft does not identify the exact spot in the sky Gilman is attracted
to—if it is even in the sky at all—but only describes it as "north—
infinitely north." On this journey, however, Lovecraft describes the
alien world, including its sky: "which glittered gorgeously in the mixed,
almost blistering glare from a polychromatic sky. Looking upward he
saw three stupendous discs of flame, each of a different hue, and at a
different height above an infinitely distant curving horizon of low

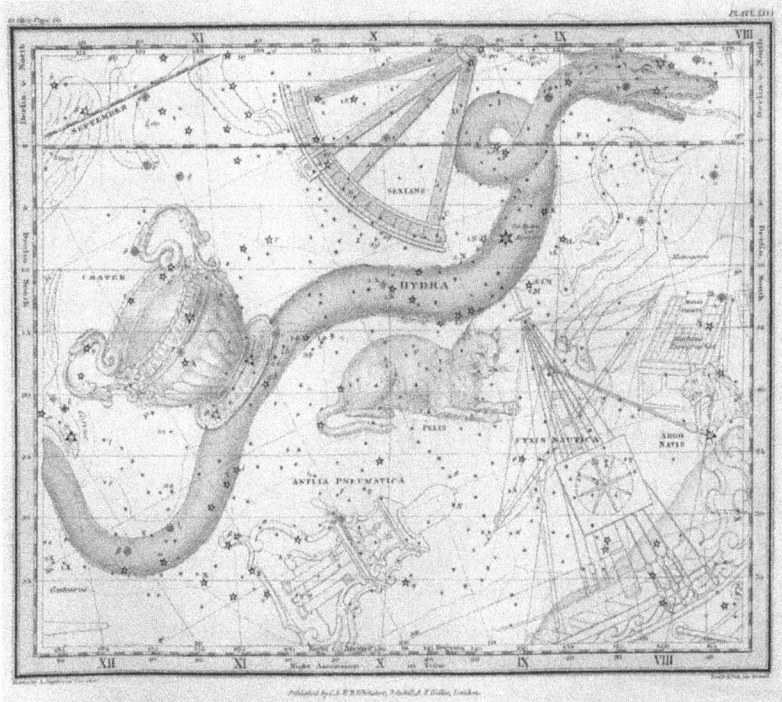

Figure 5: Plate XXVI of Jamieson's *A Celestial Atlas*

mountains" (*MM* 277). Lovecraft discusses multiple star systems in his *Asheville-Gazette News* article "The Stars II," including triples: "Systems of three actually connected stars are called 'ternary stars', of which a well-known example is Zeta Cancri. We find there one star revolving around another in a period of over 60 years, whilst a third revolved around both of these in a period of over 500 years" (*CE* 3.306; also 41–42) On April 21, Zeta Cancri is about 33° below the horizon due north at about 6:45 A.M., just the right time for Gilman to feel its pull immediately after rising from bed. Alternately, Lovecraft may have had Polaris itself in mind, which was known to be a triple star system in his time. Polaris, of course, is "infinitely north," and there is notably no suggestion that whatever Gilman is attracted to moves as the day passes. Again, we must consider these identifications speculative, but as Lovecraft crafted this world with its polychromatic sky, his imagination was probably inspired by stars like Zeta Cancri and Polaris.

To the ancients, the appearance of different stars in the night sky indicated the passage of time across the year. Even today, sky watchers recognize the arrival of new seasons with the arrival of the stars associated with them: the summer triangle in the hot months of July and August, the Great Square of Pegasus in fall, the Big Dipper in spring, and, of course, Orion in winter. Some of Lovecraft's most beautiful imagery is a product of these ancient observations: as the raiding party in *The Case of Charles Dexter Ward* sets out to confront Joseph Curwen, some of the men look back toward Providence

> lying outspread under the early spring stars. Steeples and gables rose dark and shapely, and salt breezes swept up gently from the cove north of the bridge. Vega was climbing above the great hill across the water[14] . . . Old Providence, for whose safety and sanity so monstrous and colossal a blasphemy was about to be wiped out. (*MM* 141)

The coming of spring signifies the end of the cold, dark season, and the renewal of life; for Providence the season of darkness is ending. The appearance of the stars of the spring season serve as a perfect symbol of the renewal of life the town will enjoy.

The star Fomalhaut—appearing low in the southern sky during October and November evenings—is closely associated with autumn. It is, therefore, no surprise that Lovecraft used this star to invoke the depressing mood of late fall in his *Fungi from Yuggoth* sonnet "Star Winds":

> It is a certain hour of twilight glooms,
> Mostly in autumn, when the star-wind pours
> Down hilltop streets, deserted out-of-doors,
> But shewing early lamplight from snug rooms.
> The dead leaves rush in strange, fantastic twists,
> And chimney-smoke whirls round with alien grace,
> Heeding geometries of outer space,
> While Fomalhaut peers in through southward mists.

> (*AT* 69–70)

Isolated from other bright stars, Fomalhaut[15] is often referred to as

---

14. HPL has meticulously set the time and date—about 11 P.M. on April 12— to match Vega's appearance as a prominent, but still rising object.

15. In what is probably an irrelevant coincidence, Fomalhaut is said to be associated with the fish god Dagon. See Burnham (1485) and Allen (344–45).

"the lonely star". Its loneliness accentuates its already gloomy reputation, as described by Martha E. Martin: "On early acquaintance the loneliness of the star, added to the sombre signs of approaching autumn, sometimes gives one a touch of melancholy" (80). Lovecraft refers to Fomalhaut as "that strangely fascinating orb" and quotes Garrett P. Serviss, who compares it to "a distant watch-fire gleaming in the midst of a lonely prairie" (CE 3.200; also 236–37). It is likely Lovecraft himself was affected by the melancholy nature of this harbinger of winter months ahead.

In "The Festival," Lovecraft uses winter stars and constellations to create a Yuletide setting. "The Festival" is based on Lovecraft's legendary first visit to Marblehead on December 17, 1922, so the following observations illustrated in Figure 6 are based on that place and time (SL 3.126–27). At twilight, just as the first stars are coming out, the narrator arrives just outside Kingsport and observes Aldebaran twinkling ahead among the trees. At this date, twilight passes between 5 P.M. and 6 P.M., and by this time Aldebaran has risen and gained some elevation; but since the narrator is climbing a hill, it is not unreasonable to observe Aldebaran in the trees if he is walking eastward. Later, he recalls viewing the town from the crest and seeing

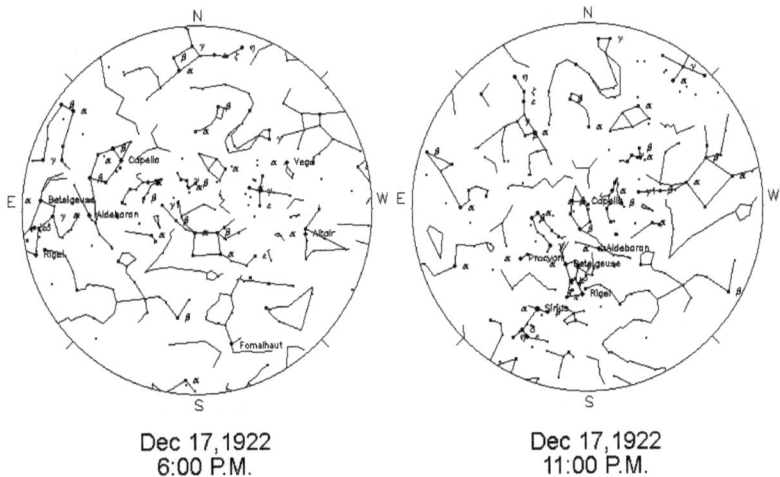

Dec 17, 1922
6:00 P.M.

Dec 17, 1922
11:00 P.M.

Figure 6: Nighttime Sky View as Described in "The Festival"

Aldebaran balance itself on the ghostly spire of the great white church on the hill; since the star is in the east and it appears over the town, he must, indeed, be facing eastward (D 212). By 6 P.M. the sky is dark, and Orion has just barely risen in time for the gleaming fanlights and small-paned windows to join it (D 209).

After having arrived at the house of his people and read a few pages from the *Necronomicon*, at 11:00 the narrator rises with his hosts and goes outdoors into a moonless night where the Dog Star leers over them (D 212). By this time, Orion is nearly due south, and the Dog Star Sirius has almost risen to its highest elevation. The moon—only a few hours away from being new—set just before the sun, and the night is, indeed, moonless. The only visible planet is Mars in Aquarius (not shown; just north of Fomalhaut); by 11 P.M., it has set. There can be no doubt that the actual events of Lovecraft's visit to Marblehead on December 17, 1922, made an enormous impression on him, and a great many of his impressions were incorporated into the tale. The final result, however, is probably highly polished. For example, in his correspondence he notes that sunset occurred between 4:05 and 4:10. This is highly accurate. In fact, it is too accurate: it seems unlikely Lovecraft would be carefully timing the event with his watch, even if we assume his watch was set to that level of accuracy. More than likely, he went back afterward to an almanac and noted the exact time of this spectacular sunset. It also seems unlikely that Lovecraft—as allergic to cold as he was—would still be out sightseeing at 11 P.M. in mid-December. The overall impressions undoubtedly guided his creativity, but the actual writing was probably aided by a careful reconstruction of the night sky using his basic astronomical background.

"Polaris" is Lovecraft's most explicitly astronomically based story. Its narrator is transfixed all night at his window watching Polaris, the pole star, as the other stars of heaven reel around it:

> Down from the heights reels the glittering Cassiopeia as the hours wear on, while Charles' Wain lumbers up from behind the vapour-soaked swamp trees that sway in the night-wind. Just before dawn Arcturus winks ruddily from above the cemetery on the low hillock, and Coma Berenices shimmers weirdly afar off in the mysterious east. (D 20)

Given that Arcturus has risen just before dawn, the story must take place sometime near the end of October. "Dawn" is taken to mean "twilight," since the faint stars of Coma Berenices (the brightest of which is only fourth magnitude) would not be visible beyond any significant brightening of the sky. Twilight was found to occur just before 4:45 on October 25, with Arcturus just above the horizon as shown in Figure 7:

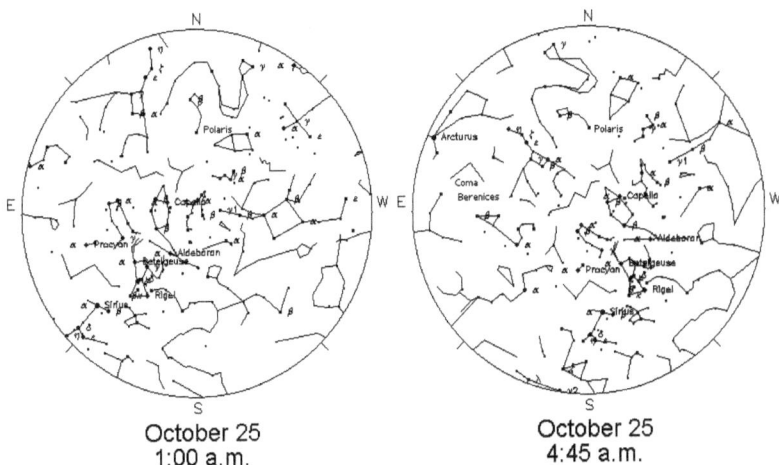

October 25
1:00 a.m.

October 25
4:45 a.m.

Figure 7: Nighttime Sky View as Described in "Polaris"

Lovecraft's description of the sky perfectly matches the orientation of the sky on that night. At the "small hours of the morning" (1 A.M.), Cassiopeia is directly overhead, and between that time and dawn, Charles' Wain (Ursa Major, or the Big Dipper) sweeps from near the horizon to greater heights along a wide arc. At dawn, Coma Berenices is directly east. The Pole Star remains fixed, of course, as it always does.

"Polaris" is known to have been inspired in part by a dream (Joshi, *H. P. Lovecraft: A Life* 162–63), but it may also have been inspired by a nonfiction article by Charles Nevers Holmes entitled "Polaris," which appeared in *Popular Astronomy* in 1916. Since Lovecraft was still writing for the Providence *Evening News* at this time, he almost certainly read Holmes's piece. This article is a summary of some interesting facts and history associated with the star Polaris, written in a poetic and whimsical tone, with some popular science thrown in.[16] It contains nothing about dream worlds or squat, hellish Inutos, but there are points about Polaris itself and the stars around it. Holmes, of course, covers the 26,000-year cycle of procession, which will bring other stars to the celestial pole (636–37), the central theme to Love-

16. If nowhere else, HPL would have learned that Polaris is a ternary system from this article (637–38), for later use in "The Dreams in the Witch House."

craft's "Polaris." He also covers how the observer's latitude affects the location of the pole star, pointing out: "were we exactly at the north geographical pole, this northern Sky-Pole would be precisely overhead" (636), which Lovecraft's narrator experiences first-hand: "And overhead, scarce ten degrees from the zenith, glowed that watching Pole Star" (*D* 21). Although Holmes chose winter in which to describe the layout of the sky around Polaris, it reads remarkably similar to Lovecraft's autumn version:

> Darkness on all sides, darkness everywhere except far, far overhead, in the firmament sparkling with jewels of fire. In the south incomparable Sirius is scintillating like a fiery diamond; above Sirius Orion glitters; above Orion ruddy Aldebaran and beautiful Capella. Northwardly the eye of our star-gazer roves, all seems dark and devoid of suns after the glorious galaxy in the south. But due north a smaller star twinkles, not particularly noticeable, about half-way from Capella to where blue Vega sparkles on the horizon. It is Polaris, and at once the star-gazer knows exactly the sky-directions around him. On his own planet-home, wars and rumors of wars may come, nations, dynasties rise and fall, generations pass away, he himself will die; but overhead framed by the ebon background of star-lighted night, Polaris will glitter unextinguishably on, the pole star of his grandfathers, the north star of his grand children. (638)

Holmes even includes a short poem to honor the star:

> Where Cepheus reigns weakly in the sky
> And Draco yawns with widely open jaws,
> Where Ursa Major circles low and high
> Propelled by power of celestial laws;
> Where Ursa Minor daily, nightly, turns
> Around a sky-set axis of man's Home,
> Polaris like supernal beacon burns,
> A pivot-gem amid our star-lit Dome. (633)

This is a very different poem from what Lovecraft wrote for his "Polaris," but in the big picture, it is not hard to imagine Lovecraft's imagination being inspired by Holmes's article and bringing all these astronomical elements together for his own fictional purposes.

Lovecraft's primary motive in fiction writing was to capture certain moods or motifs which "virtually demand formulation & expression" (*SL* 5.201). The quantity of astronomical images in his fiction is a testament to how important these images were to him. This astronomical imagery adds beauty as well as realism to his writing, but both are effective only because Lovecraft had the technical background to convey astronomical descriptions convincingly. Naturally, Lovecraft was not perfect and committed an occasional gaffe, an obvious example appearing in *The Dream-Quest of Unknown Kadath:* after having arrived at the far side of the moon (*MM* 319), Carter beholds "The great shining disc of the earth, thirteen times greater than that of the moon as we see it, had risen" (*MM* 323). Of course, the earth never rises over any part of the lunar far side, which Lovecraft has already stated "is always turned away from the earth."[17] The story is, after all, a fantasy in which boats and cats traveling between the earth and the moon should obliterate any expectation of realism in describing the earth's appearance from the lunar surface. More importantly, the story was never property revised, and as inconsequential a detail it might seem, it is highly likely Lovecraft would have found and fixed the discrepancy during revision.

Lovecraft's astronomical realism is all the more impressive when compared to the efforts of his imitators. Consider August Derleth, for example, who had no astronomical background. Derleth made passing attempts to imitate Lovecraft's use of astronomical imagery in many tales, including "The Return of Hastur," "The Gable Window," "The Shadow out of Space," and others. His most ambitious attempt to incorporate astronomical motifs appears in *The Lurker at the Threshold*, a work that demonstrates Derleth's lack of astronomical knowledge and lack of interest in getting simple details right. At first glance, he does a reasonable job in describing the basic orientation of the sky on the night Quamis returns:

> [Dewart] stood with both arms extended towards the heavens in the west, where at this hour shone the stars and constellations of the winter nights, very low on the horizon—Aldebaran in the Hyades, part of Orion, and slightly higher, Sirius, Capella Castor and Pollux, as

---

17. Actually, the earth never rises over *any* point on the lunar surface. Because one face of the moon is locked toward the earth, as seen from any point on the lunar near side the earth remains fixed in one part of the sky while the sun, planets and stars whirl around beyond it. From the margins of the near side, the earth bobs above and below the lunar horizon due to libration.

well as the planet Saturn—though these were somewhat dimmed by the proximity of the moon. (106)

This scene takes place "past midnight." Derleth does not date this scene, complicating analysis. It must take place sometime between "late March" (91) and April 7, 1924 (111). The moon provides another clue: "a gibbous moon had swung into the western sky from its earlier position east of the zenith" (105).

Taken together, these observations describe the appearance of the sky from Salem, Massachusetts, on or about 11 P.M. March 16, 1924, as shown in Figure 8. The essentials, as Derleth describes them, are all present: Aldebaran and Orion setting in the west, other winter starts somewhat higher, Saturn and the gibbous moon. In that month, the moon was first quarter on the 13th, full on the 21st, and last quarter on the 27th, so it could only be described as gibbous after the 13th but before the 21st, and after the 21st but before the 27th. Since it is past due south at midnight, it must be waxing gibbous, which suggests a date before the 21st. Dates after the 16th become harder to reconcile, because with each day the moon becomes fuller and moves farther east, and Aldebaran and Orion slip farther and farther toward the horizon.

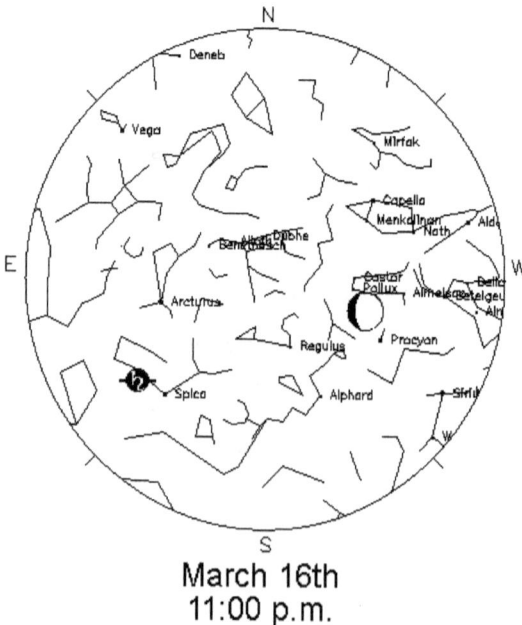

March 16th
11:00 p.m.

Figure 8: Nighttime Sky View of March as Described in
The Lurker at the Threshold

Nor can the hour be much later: by midnight on the 16th, Aldebaran will have set. The hour might line up better if Daylight Savings Time were in effect, but mid-March is rather early for that. Derleth would have only needed a planisphere to orient the stars and the date properly, and he is known to have owned Lovecraft's (*CE* 3.14). Determining that only Saturn would be visible, and getting the phase of the moon would have required consulting an almanac of some sort. All things considered, Derleth—writing in 1945—must have gone to some trouble to get this scene from 1924 as close as he did. Nonetheless, the scene could not have taken place after midnight in late March: the stars and moon just don't line up.

Other attempts at astronomical realism in *Lurker*, however, reflect even worse on Derleth's astronomical background. In several instances he associates the star Aldebaran with the star cluster the Hyades, including "Aldebaran in the Hyades" from the quote above, and later describing that Hastur "shall come again from the dark star which is near Aldebaran in the Hyades" (133). In fact, as seen from earth, Aldebaran is in the same line of sight as the Hyades, but it has a different proper motion and therefore is not part of the cluster itself, but is actually much closer. This much was known in the nineteenth century. Writing in 1917, Lovecraft himself describes them as separate entities: "Taurus, with its bright Aldebaran and its two attractive clusters, the Pleiades and the Hyades" (*CE* 3.236). Derleth commits a flagrant contravention of truth in describing the alien scene Bates glimpses through the rose window:

> The landscape before my eyes was pitted and torn, and was assuredly non-terrestrial, and the sky overhead was filled with strange, baffling constellations, of which I knew none save one, very close, which bore a resemblance to the Hyades, as if that group had come closer to earth by thousands upon thousands of light years. (86)

Apparently, the window is some sort of visual portal to an alien world overlooking the Hyades. But how could a layperson—or probably any person—recognize the Hyades distorted in size and taken out of the context of earth's skies? Also, how could he tell that this one constellation was very close? From earth, it is not possible to tell which stars are close just by looking at them. The central V-shaped core of stars of the Hyades occupy a volume of about eight light years in diameter, so an observer would have to be a comparable distance away to see them in their sky, as opposed to *being* their sky. It also seems incredible that this alien world lays in the exact line of sight of earth, so that the cluster would have the same general outline. Only an earth-gazer would mistake the V-shaped star pattern as an intrinsic, universally recognizable attribute of the cluster. Worst of all is the suggestion that the Hyades are "thousands upon thousands" of light years away, a figure so out of proportion it is ludicrous: from that distance, the Hyades would have to be composed entirely of extremely rare super-luminous stars spread out over such a fantastically huge volume of space that they could hardly be considered a cluster. The true distance to the Hyades was determined in 1908 to be about 130 light years in a landmark paper by Lewis J. Boss, using a very cleaver application of geometry. Derleth was simply way out of his depth and not doing his homework.

Convincing testimony relies on the believability of the testifier. Even the reader who lacks the ability to crosscheck facts and verify observations is likely to be impressed with testimony that is rich in detail and told with conviction. Expressing personal moods and impressions may have been Lovecraft's motive for his fiction, but it was his ability to express them that has made such an impression on readers: even readers who do not know about the dream that inspired "Dagon" or the trip to Marblehead that inspired "The Festival" can feel the experience described largely because of the wealth of technical details provided to make the description believable. While it may not be possible to experience a moment of "truth" by locating a copy of the *Necronomicon*, it is possible to experience the same sensation by discovering the moon really was just past full the night of July 17, 1935, and that there really was a celestial outburst on February 22, 1901.

III.

Anybody with simple or stereotyped ideas about the universe has a lot of disillusioning reading before him nowadays.—H. P. Lovecraft (*SL* 3.87).

Scientific Influences on Lovecraft's Fiction

All writings are products of the era in which they were created. Interpretations of writings must, therefore, account for the styles,

tastes, values, and cultural and intellectual development of their respective era. Writings in rapidly evolving fields—such as the sciences
since the nineteenth century—are particularly prone to misunderstanding if taken out of the context of their era: the value of Copernicus's circular orbits, Newton's "action at a distance," the Bohr atom,
and other ideas discarded by twenty-first-century science must be as-
sessed by their contemporary standards, given the mathematical,
computational, and observational limitations of their time. The same
is true for literature that incorporates the sciences: correct interpretation and assessment of such works are only possible if accompanied
by a suitable understanding of the scientific thought and understanding of the time in which the literature was produced. The remainder
of this essay will place Lovecraft's use of astronomical and cosmological science in his fiction in the context of his era.

Examples where modern scientific thought is inappropriately applied to the interpretation and critical assessment of Lovecraft are readily found in the literature. Consider, for example, the editorial notes for
the Hippocampus Press edition of "The Shadow out of Time," which
suggest the enlarged size of the sun 250 million years ago described by
Peaslee (SOT 45) is due to the fact that "[the sun] would have had a
greater mass, not having burned off as much of itself as it now has"
(SOT 106), an anachronistic application of the theory of stellar nucleo-
synthesis. A contemporary example of the state of scientific theory
that Lovecraft was familiar with is Sir James Jeans's The Universe
Around Us (SL 3.87). Jeans discusses several mechanisms of matter being converted into energy as possible sources for the sun's energy, all of
which leave the sun relatively unchanged over the history of the earth
(174–81). He notes, for example, that the combination of four hydro-
gen atoms into one helium atom corresponds to a weight loss of only 1
part in 130, and that "a star would retain its weight practically unal-
tered though its life" (176). Jeans, however, favors more efficient
mechanisms, which would extend the life of stars to millions of millions of years (175–76). If this were the case, the sun could not change
appreciably in a mere 250 million: "The sun is hardly like to have altered much since its planets were born, for the intervening 2000 million years or so represent but a minute fraction of the sun's total life"
(222). Lovecraft's expectation that the sun would appear larger in the
past can only be explained by his reluctance to abandon the Helmholtz
contraction theory, despite the fact that it was obsolete when he was

advocating it back in 1915 (CE 3.281). This also illustrates his extreme conservatism with respect to accepting new scientific ideas.

Likewise, the SOT editorial note to the altered appearance of the moon—"Perhaps the suggestion is that the moon had fewer or different craters at this time than it does now, as meteorites may have struck the satellite in the interim" (SOT 107)—is also inconsistent with the prevailing view of the time (and Lovecraft's view: see CE 3.90) that lunar volcanism was largely responsible for shaping the moon's surface, a view that persisted until after World War II: one researcher describes how his impact interpretation of lunar craters in 1941 was regarded as "heresy" by colleagues, and his paper rejected by numerous professional journals, and accepted only by Popular Astronomy (Baldwin 368–70). A better explanation of Peaslee's observation of the moon is that perhaps the moon had fewer or different craters at this time than it does now, as volcanic activity reshaped the moon's surface in the interim.

Perhaps the most glaring example of questionable science applied to Lovecraftian criticism is found in his use of the luminiferous ether as the means by which the fungus beings of Yuggoth in "The Whisperer in Darkness" propel themselves through space "on clumsy, powerful wings which have a way of resisting the ether" (DH 217); the Old Ones of Antarctica are said to have the same ability (MM 61). On this detail, Fritz Leiber noted: "This notion was good speculative fiction back in the 1920's when the ether was still a fringe-fashionable science concept, and today the notion of sailing or perhaps even winging through space is back in speculative style again, light pressure taking the place of ether" (144). In response to Leiber's comment, Richard L. Tierney wrote:

> Lovecraft was actually ignoring a major facet of science as it was known to most intelligent persons at the time he wrote his stories; namely, the Michaelson-Morley [sic] experiment which had disproved the 'cosmic aether' theory three decades earlier and which had necessitated thereby the theory of relativity. Fritz Leiber tries to pass off this matter as a relatively minor point, by pointing out that 'vast membranous wings' could have been used somewhat like sails to track through space, utilizing the energy of photon-impact; but Lovecraft never mentions the idea, and to defend his use of the 'cosmic aether' is only to say that deliberate ignorance of the facts as known to science seems merely an attempt to establish a misconception as being somehow more 'aesthetic' than the truth. (Quoted in Leiber 151–52)

While it is true that Lovecraft wrote "The Whisperer in Darkness" some forty-three years after the famous Michelson-Morley experiment and twenty-five years after Einstein's special theory of relativity, Tierney's comments fail to appreciate not only the way scientific discoveries often slowly disseminate through the scientific community and to the public, but also grossly mischaracterizes the intent of the experiment, its authors' conclusions, and Einstein's reaction to it. The luminiferous ether was conjectured as the medium though which electromagnetic light waves traveled; since this ether presumably permeated the entire universe, the Michelson-Morley experiment of 1887 attempted to measure the earth's motion through the ether by measuring the change in the speed of light beams directed parallel and perpendicular to this motion. As such, it was not intended to detect the ether itself, but rather the *ether wind*—the movement of the earth through the either. That the experiment failed to find any change in the speed of light is well known. At the time, however, these results were in no way interpreted as proof of the non-existence of the ether: perhaps there was something wrong with the apparatus, or perhaps the ether was somehow carried along near the earth's surface, or at least in their laboratory. Since the earth's motion around the sun was supposed to comprise some of the earth's motion through the ether, the experiment was designed to be repeated at three-month intervals to cover the different directions of the earth's motion relative to the stars. After only a single session of null results, however, they abandoned the experiment, concluding in their own paper: "It is obvious from what has gone before that it would be hopeless to attempt to solve the question of the motion of the solar system by observations of optical phenomena at the surface of the earth" (quoted in Swenson 60).

In the same year as the Michelson-Morley experiment, Heinrich Hertz's demonstration of radio waves appeared to confirm ethereal waves, relegating the Michelson-Morley result as an anomaly. Over the course of the next forty years, Michelson, Morley, and their successors repeated the same basic experiment with variations—using larger, more sensitive equipment, from mountaintops, in glass structures—all in an attempt to find an environment in which the ether was free to flow (Swenson 60–65). During the two decades following the publication of Einstein's special theory, several scientific papers giving serious treatment to the ether were published. For example, in 1910, Owen Ely published an article in *Popular Astronomy*—almost certainly read by Lovecraft—that described various presumed attributes of the ether, the null result of Michelson-Morley, and attempts to explain the null result; there is no mention of Einstein or his work. In 1922, H. Bateman acknowledged the relativitist's objections but nonetheless argued that light had to wave in *something*, and proceeded to describe that thing. Finally, in 1925, Dayton C. Miller—a former collaborator of Morley—published "The Significance of the Ether-Drift Experiments of 1925 at Mt. Wilson," in which he confirmed a small but measurable variation in the speed of light in the ether, suggesting that the earth had an absolute motion of about 200 km/s toward the constellation Draco, for which he won a $1000 prize from the American Association for the Advancement of Science (Swenson 66). Admittedly, by this time, interest in ether drift experiments was on the decline, but Miller was himself highly respected—Secretary and later President of the American Physical Society, as well as a member of the National Academy of Sciences (Swenson 65, 66)—and he had admirers, such as R. K. Young, who confidently wrote in 1926: "it would appear that some of the premises [of relativity] must be altered, since the basic experiment which suggested it is shown to have different results from those formerly held to be true" (14). Miller's results, however, could not be replicated, and by 1931, interest in ether drift theory within the professional community essentially evaporated. Miller continued to publish ether drift papers well into the 1930s and died in 1941, still convinced in the veracity of his results. After exhaustive data reduction on newly invented electronic computers in 1954, Miller's very small shifts in the speed of light were attributed to uncontrolled temperature fluctuations across his instrument (Swenson 68).

Maverick astronomer T. J. J. See also wrote extensively in support of ether theories from the 1920s well into the 1950s—over 300 pages on his "New Theory of the Aether" in *Astronomische Nachrichten* between 1920 and 1926 alone, in which he attacked the theories of Einstein and just about everyone else, and argued for his own theory that unified gravitational, electrical, and magnetic phenomena under the action of tiny particles called "etherons," which traveled 57% faster than light (Sherrill 42). Unlike Miller, See was largely regarded by the professional community as a crackpot, having by 1920 been accused of sloppy work, left several positions due to personal and professional conflicts, been banned from publishing in the *Astronomical Journal*, and effectively banished to an obscure naval observatory in California (Sherrill 28–33). See was nonetheless highly influential to the general public, creating a great deal of skepticism in relativity and quantum theories through many books, articles, and public lectures (Sherill 25). See cultivated a strong relationship with the press, which helped promote his unorthodox ideas: see Sherrill (44) for a full-page feature newspaper article from 1928 covering his ether theory. Lovecraft himself wrote favorably of See's research into the rotation of Venus, ranking him among "the latest and most authoritative astronomers" (CE 3.114). See's legacy demonstrates that even if it weren't for Miller and a few of his ether hold-outs, ether theory would have been alive and well in the public eye well into the late 1920s.

Even if the null results of the Michelson-Morley experiments had been accepted, they only address the issue of the *ether drift*, not the ether itself. Lovecraft does not describe the fungus beings as riding the ether wind, but rather as pushing against it with their wings. A. S. Eddington, one of the leading figures of relativity theory, argued in his *The Nature of the Physical World* (31), which Lovecraft read (SL 3.87), that although it is meaningless to talk of moving through the ether, "this does not mean the aether is abolished." Eddington describes the ether not as a physical medium in which light waves, but rather as the agent that holds the attributes of space which describe light and gravitation.[18] In 1934, Einstein himself wrote something similar: "physical space and the ether are only different terms for the same thing; fields are physical states of space" (281). The study of ether theory is complicated by the fact that it was never fully defined, and different writers at different times regarded it differently. Jeans rightly points out that the ether was never disproved, but merely reverted to a concept that was no longer particularly useful (318). One thing, however, is perfectly clear: in 1930, the ether was by no means known by most intelligent persons to have been disproved three decades earlier. Leiber probably summarized the situation best in describing the ether as still a fringe-fashionable science concept in the 1920s.

This discussion is not, however, meant to suggest that Lovecraft

---

18. Eddington's comment "The man who could make gravitation out of cogwheels would have been a hero in the Victorian age" (209) is probably a reference to T. J. J. See.

was thoroughly up-to-date on scientific theories, carefully reading the latest scientific journals in an effort to determine exactly what his fiction could and could not get away with. He was an educated and enthusiastic layperson, but had no particular insight into the veracity or deeper scientific implications of those theories that fascinated him. For example, it is tempting to credit Lovecraft with the foresight to recognize the importance of the theory of plate tectonics as described in *At the Mountains of Madness* (*MM* 66, 69), decades before the theory had any significant acceptability in the scientific community. In fact, all Lovecraft had available to him to suggest this theory was the similarity between the outlines of South America and Africa, something schoolchildren marveled over and geologists dismissed as coincidence. Similarly, Edmund Wilson credits Lovecraft with predicting the effects of the atomic bomb in "The Colour out of Space," but offers no support linking the wasting disease of that story with radiation sickness (49); the effects of man-made technology were probably the last thing Lovecraft had in mind. Some of Lovecraft's more outlandish ideas have, over time, found strange parallels in modern physics: in "The Whisperer in Darkness," Akeley reports that he could not photograph the fungus beings because they are "composed of a form of matter totally alien to our part of space—with electrons having a wholly different vibration-rate" (*DH* 240).[19] Dr. Lisa Randall, a modern leading expert of particle physics and cosmology at Harvard, has hypothesized something remarkably similar: that our universe is one of many "branes" that together comprise a multiverse, and that these other branes might contain different forces and types of matter (Bartusiak 20). Any attempt to credit Lovecraft with anticipating these later scientific developments is as baseless as Pope Pius XII linking the Christian version of creation with the Big Bang theory (Haught 109). Instead, Lovecraft's major contribution to speculative fiction is his recognition that the emerging sciences would transform the universe into something far more unearthly than anyone could have seriously imagined at the start of the twentieth century.

At some point during the 1920s, Lovecraft finally abandoned Laplace's theory of planetary formation—which held that the planets

---

19. The notion of electrons having a characteristic "vibration rate" is drawn from Schrödinger's version of quantum theory, which HPL probably picked up from Eddington (211–20).

were formed from the same nebular material as the sun—for the Chamberlin-Moulton theory. As previously described, the Chamberlin-Moulton theory (slightly modified by Jeans-Jeffreys in 1917[20]) conjectured that the planets condensed from material ripped from the sun by a very close passage of another star. This seemingly inconsequential shift in thought about the origin of the solar system suggested that planetary systems like ours were *extremely rare*, given the vast distances that normally separated stars:

> Up to a decade or a decade & a half ago it was commonly thought that such worlds are virtually unlimited—i.e., that a large number of stars possess planetary systems like the sun's. Recently, however, the mathematical calculations of Jeans & Eddington have very gravely challenged that concept, & have tended to indicate that a planet-system represents a kind of celestial accident of relatively rare occurrence. The number of planets existing at any one time, then, is perhaps very limited. (*SL* 5.154)[21]

This shift had an important impact on Lovecraft's fiction: in 1918, he wrote that he had always held the idea of the earth's insignificance (*SL* 1.70), but by the late 1920s the earth had become very special in the Cthulhu Mythos: a place where wave after wave of extremely powerful entities and races came from vast distances and even other dimensions, to found mighty civilizations and collect its precious resources. Man might be insignificant, but the earth itself was apparently important enough for these entities to fight great wars for supremacy over it, or at least to carve out their share of it. Lovecraft's realignment toward the tidal theory is a subtle but crucial step in the evolution of his mythos: the reduction of the number of worlds in the cosmos from

20. See Brush (82–86).

21. In this same letter, HPL claims Eddington predicted that only about six planets in the whole cosmos are likely to have highly developed life; actually, Eddington acknowledges that in the long run, developed life is unlikely restricted to the earth, but at the present time "not one of the profusion of stars in their myriad clusters looks down on scenes comparable to those which are passing beneath the rays of the sun" (178). Also, HPL mentions an alternate theory of Dinsmore Alter, under which planetary formation is common. Alter's theory is described in his paper published in *Astrophysical Journal* in 1934. I do not know where HPL encountered it. It never gained any acceptance.

an unlimited number to only a handful opens the possibility that the earth could be the concern of so many powerful entities. In "The Call of Cthulhu" (1926), the earth is merely the planet to which Cthulhu arrived from the stars. The first hints that the earth is of special importance to outside entities are made in "The Dunwich Horror" (1928), but the true history of the earth as an important crossroads of the cosmos is not fully developed until "The Whisperer in Darkness" (1930), *At the Mountains of Madness* (1931), and "The Shadow out of Time" (1934–35). Lovecraft may have been swayed toward the tidal theory by arguments made in Shapley's *Starlight* (100–103), which Lovecraft is known to have read by 1929 (*SL* 3.97), but possibly as early as 1926. Lovecraft also read of the tidal theory in Eddington (176–78), in which the solar system is described as "a freak." Lovecraft's change in heart is well documented in his writings: in a 1917 article from the Providence *Evening News*, he still endorsed the Laplace theory (*CE* 3.237), but by 1929 he fully embraced the tidal theory: "all stars are temporary in the long run, that the birth of planets from them is comparatively rare, (induced by tidal action of other stars that pass by them under rare conditions)" (*SL* 2.266). Lovecraft even engaged in a little historical revisionism, noting that the origin of the solar system due to closely passing stars has "been dominant since 1905 or 1906" (*SL* 3.438),[22] despite his rejection of the theory long after that time. The timeline of Lovecraft's acceptance of the tidal theory correlates well with the earth's growing prominence in his fiction.

Shapley's *Starlight* influenced Lovecraft's fiction in other ways. One passage describing meteors is highly suggestive as a germ idea of "The Colour out of Space":

> [Meteors] may be wandering fragments from interstellar space, not heretofore associated with the solar system. The chemistry of meteorites is carefully studied with each new discovery, but as yet no element unknown to the earth's surface has been found and no novelty appears in the materials sufficient to indicate origin in a remote part of space where the chemistry and mineralogy might be peculiar. (Shapley 78–79)

The chemistry of the meteor in "Colour" is carefully studied, but its

22. An obvious reference to the Chamberlin-Moulton theory, which was introduced in 1905.

properties were nothing but peculiar: "It presented no identifying features whatsoever; and at the end of the tests the college scientists were forced to own that they could not place it. It was nothing of this earth, but a piece of the great outside; and as such dowered with outside properties and obedient to outside laws" (*DH* 59). "Colour" is in fact a well scripted *exception* to Shapley's statement about meteorites, coming "from some place whar things ain't as they is here" (*DH* 72).

Based on the letter in which he mentions *Starlight*, Lovecraft was probably most impressed with the revelation that the spiral nebulae were not part of the Milky Way, but vast island universes in their own right—now referred to as "external galaxies"—separated by distances that made the distances between stars seem small: "But all the distances described in the two books I lent you are as nothing compared with the nearly unthinkable chasms envisaged by modern astronomy" (*SL* 3.97). Since Lovecraft had already described the distance to the nearest star as "beyond human comprehension," and that "the mind can form no conception of gulfs so vast" as the most distant stars (*CE* 3.110), describing the distances to the galaxies must have taxed even his use of adjectives. The spiral nebulae/island universe controversy had been raging since before William Herschel's time, and was still raging when Lovecraft considered both sides of the argument, leaning against island universes, in 1917 (*CE* 3.231). The question largely was settled in 1924 by Edwin Hubble, who managed to measure the distances to several nebulae at millions of light years, far outside the Milky Way. Shapley had been on the wrong side of the debate, and when Hubble's news reached him he is said to have exclaimed, "Here is the letter that destroyed my universe" (Trimble 1142). It must, therefore, have pained him to concede the likelihood that the nebulae were external, although he implies that the question was still open (Shapely 133). As a result of these observations, the boundaries of the observable universe had been dramatically pushed outward. In "Hypnos" (1922), Lovecraft's narrator explores the vast universe, but this is a universe of deeper consciousness and dream. By the time Lovecraft wrote "The Whisperer in Darkness," the scientific universe had grown sufficiently to encompass Lovecraft's imagination. When Mr. B-67 tells Wilmarth he has been to "37 different celestial bodies—planets, dark stars, and less definable objects—including eight outside our galaxy and two outside the curved cosmos of space and time" (*DH* 260), he means in actual corporeal form (his corporeal brain, anyway), not in dreams or drugs or beyond the wall of sleep. This represents a major shift for Lovecraft, whose narrators' epic adventures in previous stories had been metaphysical. The physical universe had become big enough and exotic enough to serve as Lovecraft's stage. Shapley's universe may have been destroyed, but Lovecraft's had just opened up.

As dramatic as advances in the measurement of the distances to the distant spiral nebulae, the origin of the solar system and even the nature of atomic structure, no scientific advance influenced Lovecraft's writing as did the impact of Einstein's theories of relativity: concepts such as distortions of time, extra-dimensional space, and non-Euclidean geometry comprise the hallmarks of Lovecraft's fiction. Although Einstein published his first major works in 1905, he was virtually unknown outside the field of a small number of specialists until 1919. Lovecraft may have first read about Einstein's theories in an article, "Relativity in Astronomy," written by W. Rufus published in *Popular Astronomy* in 1918, which provides a general overview of the basic tenets of relativity, including inconsistent observations of time and length as reported by observers moving relative to each other and the predictions of gravity bending starlight. For the most part, however, Einstein's work remained obscure until the announcement in November 1919 that two expeditions observed the total solar eclipse of May 29 and confirmed the bending of starlight passing near the sun, as predicted by Einstein's theory of general relativity (see Figure 9). The public reaction to the news was practically unprecedented in the history of science and propelled Einstein himself to household name status (Coles 37–39). Numerous articles appeared in the popular press in the months after the announcement attempting to explain Einstein's theory and its implications to the non-scientific public—a difficult task given the mathematically abstract nature of the subject. The coverage naturally attracted Lovecraft's attention, and he documented his preliminary understanding and opinions on the subject in a letter to the Gallomo in April 1920 (*Letters to Alfred Galpin* 75–79). Lovecraft deserves some latitude in the correctness of his assessments, given his own admittance of his lack of authority and his having only "unsatisfactory and fragmentary articles" available to him. Indeed, a survey of articles covering relativity appearing in the *New York Times* between November 9, 1919 (the announcement of the eclipse results), and April 1, 1920, reveals little substantive hard information on the theory as well as some misinformation.

It is nonetheless instructive to examine how Lovecraft digests and reacts to the information at hand. He divides Einstein's work into two parts: one dealing with light, gravity, and ether, and the other with time and space, by which he means more or less the theories of general and special relativity, respectively. Based on the content of Lovecraft's comments and expressions such as "Einstein believes," "Einstein is cautious," and "Einstein denies," it is likely Lovecraft read the interview with Einstein, "Einstein Expounds His New Theory," published in the *New York Times*. Lovecraft's argument that the passage of time directly correlates with "the growth and development of an organic being or race of organic beings" suggests that he also read an article published in the *Times*, written by R. D. Carmichael, author of one of the few books on relativity available at the time: in describing the relativity of time, Carmichael describes how if an organism were hurled through space,

> it would be possible for the organism, after a flight of whatever distance, to return to its starting point practically unchanged, while an exactly similar organism which remained motionless at the starting point might have given place to new generations. (Carmichael, "Given the Speed, Time Is Naught")

—a circumstance Lovecraft used in an argument to prove the impossibility of the relativity of time:

> When the birth of two children reaches our perception simultaneously, we know that no matter what the subsequent conditions attending each, the future steps of their development will exhibit a correspondence. We know that there are no conditions whereby one will present himself to our perceptions as a child side by side with the presentation of the other as an adult.

Virtually everything substantial Lovecraft has to say on relativity is found in these two articles.[23] His statement, "This point,[24] however,

---

23. HPL may have also read the article "Dutch Colleague Explains Einstein" by physicist H. A. Lorentz. Lorentz's explanations, however, were somewhat more technical and unaccompanied by any diagrams or illustrations, making it unlikely HPL or anyone else learned much from it.

24. That is, the failure to detect any displacement of lines in the solar spec-

would positively disprove the larger and more complex relativity theory, but would not disprove the possibility of a material light affected by gravitation," suggests that Lovecraft did not read Einstein's article "Time, Space, and Gravitation" in the January 1920 issue of *Science*, in which Einstein asserts the whole theory must stand or fall together: "The great attraction of the theory is its logical consistency. If any deduction from it should prove untenable, it must be given up. A modification of it seems impossible without destruction of the whole" (10). Instead, Lovecraft appears to be following a suggestion made in the *Times* article "Eclipse Showed Gravity Variation," which states: "If this failure [shifting of lines in the solar spectrum] were taken as final it would mean that parts of Einstein's theory would need revision, but the parts already verified would remain." Over the course of the next few years, Lovecraft—as well as the whole scientific community—would have to reconcile positive tests results for relativity with its overall deeper implications for time and space.

Lovecraft's arguments raise several interesting points. His fear that Einstein's dismissal of the ether invalidates the entire wave theory of light is apparently his own interpretation: not only is it not true (relativity says nothing about the wave or particle nature of light), but also no similar conclusion appears in the contemporary articles surveyed. It is possible that Lovecraft is confusing relativity theory with the photoelectric effect—another of Einstein's theories—which does reestablish certain aspects of Newton's corpuscular theory of light; however, there is nothing that suggests Lovecraft was even aware of this theory, and again no mention of Einstein's other work is found in the contemporary articles surveyed. Lovecraft is apparently still of the nineteenth-century mindset that the ether was an actual physical medium for light and there could be no waves if there were no medium to wave in, an idea that had died out even before the advent of relativity (Eddington 31).

Also of interest is Lovecraft's claim that Einstein's theory may be "running ahead of experimental and practical science with speculations *for which observed phenomena and accepted hypotheses make no demand.*" Lovecraft is ignoring Einstein's successful explanation of the long-standing mystery of the perihelion advance of the planet Mercury's orbit, a perturbation from the planet's predicted orbit that could

---

trum, today referred to as gravitational redshift.

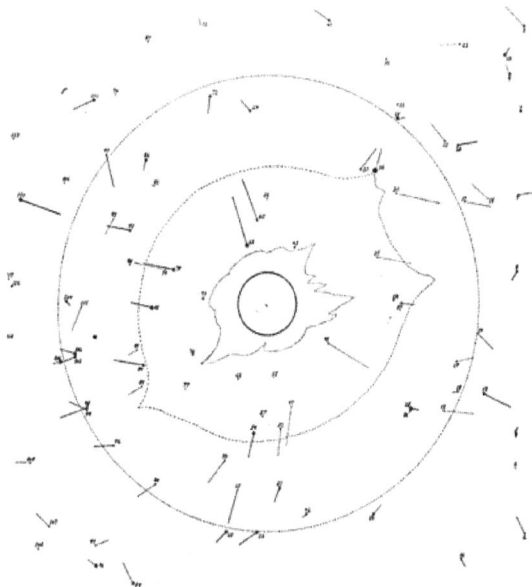

Figure 9: Displacement of locations of stars near the sun during
eclipse of September 21, 1922
(*Lick Observatory Bulletin*, Number 346, p. 48)

not be satisfactorily explained by Newton's theory of gravity. This unexplained perturbation led to the theory that the discrepancy was
caused by the influence of an unknown planet, dubbed "Vulcan," orbiting inside Mercury's orbit. The problem is described in Newcomb's
Popular Astronomy (292–95), and Lovecraft himself had described the
problem as early as 1906 (*CE* 3.30, 331). Numerous newspaper articles
surveyed in the *Times* remark on this important successful application
of Einstein's theory: "Eclipse Showed Gravity Variation," "Lights All
Askew in the Heavens," "Jazz in the Scientific World," "A New Physics, Based on Einstein," "Einstein Expounds His New Theory," Lorentz
("Dutch Colleague Explains Einstein"), "Lodge Pays Tribute to Einstein
Theory," Carmichael ("Einstein's Third Victory"). Despite the publicity
of this success, Lovecraft does not even mention it in his remarks on
Einstein's theory. It seems unlikely that he deliberately tried to down-
play it, yet his failure to grasp its significance in light of his astronomical background represents a serious lapse on his part.

Another curious omission in Lovecraft's remarks is the absence of
any mention of the effect of relativity theory on traditional notions of

Euclidean geometry. The fact that relativity theory somehow required modifications to the understanding of the geometry of space was one of the few means available for writers to convey the revolutionary aspect of Einstein's work to the man on the street, and was cited in many articles surveyed: "Eclipse Showed Gravity Variation," "Lights All Askew in the Heavens," "Light and Logic," "Jazz in the Scientific World," "A New Physics, Based on Einstein," Carmichael ("Einstein's Third Victory"). Apparently, the notion of curved space—which would eventually become one of Lovecraft's signature elements in his fiction—was so alien to him that he simply dismissed it without comment.

Perhaps the most remarkable observation to be drawn from Lovecraft's early commentary on relativity is his assertion that certain features of the theory must be incorrect, because they contradict what human perception and senses show obviously to be true. If Lovecraft's imagination had been stirred by the notion that humanity's understanding of the universe was restricted by limited powers of human sense and perception (Joshi, *H. P. Lovecraft: A Life* 204–5), he might have welcomed the relativity of time and space as an example of universal truth that the human mind cannot conceive. Instead, he places complete faith in the human conception of time, proclaiming: "If our senses are not reliable in informing us of the various time-relations; if there is no such thing as order and precedence as we know it, then our perceptive apparatus is strangely out of harmony with that regularity which seems omnipresent in the cosmos." Likewise, Lovecraft uses what are called "commonsense objections" to argue for the absoluteness of space. Eddington provides an example of a commonsense argument less detailed, but essentially identical to Lovecraft's: "Space—*his* space—is so vivid to him. This object is obviously here; that object is just there. I know it; and I am not going to be shaken by any amount of scientific obscurantism about contraction of measuring rods" (16). These objections are thought to arise more from collective human experience limited to non-relativistic settings rather than limited human perception itself (Eddington 16–19; Bohm 185–230). Nonetheless, they rely on trust in what the senses seem to convey, even if they contradict the physicist and the mathematician. Science gave Lovecraft a glimpse of something that appeared to transcend human experience, and he rejected it on the basis of his reliance on what his senses told him was possible.

Lovecraft undoubtedly followed news of the Einstein theory. He may have been influenced by a series of articles appearing in *Popular Astronomy* written by an old and respected source, William H. Pickering, who Lovecraft once called "the greatest living selenographer" (*CE* 3.26) In the first of these articles, "The Theory of Relativity" (June 1920), Pickering attempted to explain topics about relativity in plain language, including the aberration of light, the constant speed of light, Lorentz transformations, gravitation, time as the fourth dimension, and rest mass. Lovecraft may have been satisfied with some of Pickering's explanations, but Pickering's own imperfect understanding of the theory introduced some misinformation: he completely misunderstands the concept of time dilation and attributes the loss of absolute simultaneity as simply the result of the finite speed of light.[25] Pickering may have also reinforced Lovecraft's notion that discarding the ether meant discarding the entire wave theory of light. Nonetheless, Pickering's account is a more or less balanced attempt to explain relativity as it was understood at the time.

The second of Pickering's articles, "Shall We Accept Relativity" (April 1922), however, openly questions the experimental results of the three tests supposedly validating Einstein's theory: the perihelion shift of Mercury, the bending of starlight, and the shifting of solar spectral lines toward the red. In the case of Mercury, Pickering offers the theory that Mercury is perturbed by diffuse matter orbiting inside the planet's orbit, a wholly unoriginal idea that had been suggested and rejected many times since the nineteenth century. As for the bending of starlight, Pickering questions the accuracy of the results, commenting on numerous sources of potential error. Here, Pickering is reiterating legitimate accuracy concerns raised by other skeptics. As for the third proof, Pickering only points out that, to date, no shifting of lines in the

---

25. *Time dilation* refers to the relativistic effect whereby two observers traveling relative to each other will observe each other's clocks running more slowly than their own. *Absolute simultaneity* refers to the condition where all observers will agree whether for two events, one follows the other, the other follows the first, or they occur simultaneously. Under special relativity, it is possible for two observers to disagree on the simultaneity of two events. Under Newtonian laws, all identical clocks run that the same rate regardless of their states of motion, and all observers always agree on the consecutively or simultaneity of two events.

solar spectrum had been demonstrated convincingly.[26] Pickering concludes by quoting Einstein's dictum that any modification of the theory
would undermine all of it, implying that failure in any test would disprove the entire theory. This article, or ones similar to it, probably
shifted Lovecraft away from his previous attitude that some parts of
relativity might be true while others false and substituted in its place
doubt that any light bending had been observed in the first place.

Pickering's third article, "Aberration and Relativity" (June 1922),
advances a new explanation of *aberration*, an astronomical phenomenon that causes the apparent position of stars to shift as the result of
the earth's motion around the sun coupled with the finite speed of
light. Pickering's theory supposes an atmosphere of ether is dragged
along with the earth, and explains the phenomenon with a series of
geometric arguments; the fact that the ether is dragged with the earth
explains the null results of the Michelson-Morley and invalidates the
basis of special relativity:

> Much beside this that runs counter to our common sense, such as the
> shortening of bodies in the direction of their motion, and Min-
> kowski's theory that time is a form of space will thus be left as mere
> philosophical speculations, without any physical basis of fact. Should
> the photographs to be taken at the coming solar eclipses of 1922 and
> 1923 confirm the rejected photographs taken by Crommelin in 1919,[27]
> which supported Newton instead of Einstein, and there is but little
> doubt that such will be the case, it is to be hoped that then astro-
> nomical science will at last escape from this mathematical mare's nest
> of Relativity, into which a considerable portion of the English speak-
> ing world, following a few leaders, seems to have been led, and again
> return to the saner views held during what the Relativitists are now
> pleased to call the Prerelativity period. (343)

---

26. Turbulence in the sun's atmosphere complicated the measurement of
gravitational redshift in its spectrum. The effect was tentatively verified in
the spectrum of the white dwarf companion of Sirius in 1925.

27. Pickering is referring to photographs taken during the 1919 eclipse that
were rejected from consideration of the final results because they were out
of focus. Skeptics were highly critical of their exclusion, since they seemed
to show a stellar deflection better explained by Newton's theory than Einstein's (Coles 34–36). For an explanation of how Newton's laws also predicted light bending, see Coles (29–31).

Pickering's theory was probably received as welcome news to Lovecraft, since it provided another theoretical basis for rejecting Einstein altogether and reestablishing the Newtonian order. It also probably raised Lovecraft's expectation that the coming solar eclipses would show either no light deflection, or a deflection consistent with Newton's laws—half that of Einstein's.

In his 1920 letter to the Gallomo, Lovecraft was willing to accept the gravitational bending of starlight as "apparently proved fairly well." By 1923, he probably seriously doubted the 1919 observations and fully expected the eclipse observations of 1922 to vindicate him. His shock that the results—released in the spring of 1923, and this time widely observed by many expeditions—positively confirmed Einstein's predictions is evident in his letter written to Morton:

> I have no opinions—I believe in nothing . . . My cynicism and skepticism are increasing, and from an entirely new cause—the Einstein theory. The latest eclipse observations seem to place this system among the facts which cannot be dismissed, and assumedly it removes the last hold which reality or the universe can have on the independent mind. All is chance, accident, and ephemeral illusion—a fly may be greater than Arcturus, and Durfee Hill my surpass Mount Everest—assuming them to be removed from the present planet and differently environed in the continuum of space-time. (*SL* 1.231)

Having been conditioned to fully expect negative results, the positive results appear to have forced Lovecraft to confront the reality of relativity. And, unlike in 1920, he is aware that there is no freedom to accept certain parts of the theory and reject others.

Eventually, Lovecraft came to recognize relativity as a glimpse into a reality that apparently contradicted human experience and obvious notions of space and time. He undoubtedly read with interest Eddington's analysis of how "commonsense" notions of fixed space and time and the absoluteness of simultaneity became so ingrained in human perception, although they contradict the true nature of the universe as described by relativity (16–19). Lovecraft encountered the same idea in "Touch and Sight: The Earth and the Heavens"[28] from

---

28. This essay is actually the first chapter of Russell's *The ABC of Relativity* (1925), still considered one of the best non-mathematical treatments of the subject. It is not clear if HPL read it.

Selected Papers of Bertrand Russell, which Lovecraft apparently read some time in the late 1920s (Joshi, *H. P. Lovecraft: A Life* 381):

> Many of the new ideas [of relativity] can be expressed in non-mathematical language, but they are none the less difficult on that account. What is demanded is a change in our imaginative picture of the world—a picture which has been handed down from remote, perhaps pre-human, ancestors, and has been learned by each one of us in early childhood. (Russell 301)

Geometric interpretations of relativity have traditionally proven highly effective in describing relativistic ideas in non-mathematical language. Although special relativity can be expressed using basic algebra, the mathematics of general relativity is so advanced the earliest attempts to describe it in lay terms was through geometry: "Euclidian straight lines could not exist in Einstein's space. They would all be curved, and if they traveled far enough they would regain their starting point" ("Eclipse Showed Gravity Variation"); "two lines normally known as parallel do meet eventually, that a circle is not really circular, that three angles of a triangle do not necessarily make the sum total of two right angles" ("Lights All Askew in the Heavens"); and similar statements that two parallel lines do meet and Euclid is knocked out. These comments about parallel lines meeting are references to the field of non-Euclidian geometry, a branch of mathematics the roots of which are almost as old as Euclidean geometry itself. Non-Euclidean geometry is an outgrowth of dissatisfaction that Euclid's fifth postulate—which states that all non-parallel lines must eventually meet if extended indefinitely—is not sufficiently obvious to be considered a postulate, and for two thousand years attempts to prove it from other postulates failed.

By the eighteenth century, geometries absent the fifth postulate were investigated by Gauss and others, reaching a milestone under Bernhard Riemann, who systemized different geometries based on their *curvature:* given a line and some point not on the line, if the curvature is zero, then there is only one line passing through the point which is parallel to the line (Euclidean); if the curvature is positive, then there are no lines passing through the point which are parallel to the line, and if the curvature is negative, then there are an infinite number of lines passing through the point parallel to the line.[29] Einstein used these concepts for his new formulation of gravity, which was no longer considered a force tugging objects from their straight courses, but rather a distortion of space itself through which objects still followed "straight" courses, "straight" defined in non-Euclidean terms in which straight lines could bend back upon themselves describing an orbit. Overnight, one of the most obscure branches of theoretical geometry became the talk of scientists, philosophers, newspaper writers, and the man on the street. It is, therefore, quite natural that "The Call of Cthulhu"—Lovecraft's first attempt to incorporate elements of the new science into his fiction—would exploit this new concept in which the bending of light had made undeniably real, yet remained elusively beyond human comprehension and experience.

Some three years earlier, Lovecraft had attempted to capture the concept of the unnamable in "The Unnamable," but could not help actually naming the thing in realistic terms: a gelatin, a slime, eyes (*D* 207). Lovecraft's growing appreciation of relativity theory suggested that a realistic portrayal of the unnamable, or the indescribable, could be made by strictly adhering to terms of abstract mathematics. Hence, he makes no attempt actually to describe the indescribable R'lyeh, beyond suggesting that there was something wrong with its geometry, that it was somehow non-Euclidian, that angles didn't seem as they should, and that straightforward notions of horizontal and vertical perspectives were distorted. Lovecraft had found the language of the indescribable in the language of relativity.

Lovecraft continued to rely on curved space and geometric distortions to depict the indescribable in various tales over the course of the next few years. His finest attempt to integrate the concepts of relativity, however, appears in "The Shadow out of Time." On the surface, Peaslee's journey into the distant past and his encounters with beings spanning the earth's history create for him a very natural confusion between past and present. On a deeper level, Peaslee literally experiences the kinds of time distortion effects outlined by special relativity: "My conception of *time*—my ability to distinguish between consecutiveness and simultaneousness—seemed subtly disordered" (*SOT* 39). Lovecraft describes Peaslee's disorientation caused

---

29. A full account of the development of non-Euclidean geometry is found in Roberto Bonola's classic text, *Non-Euclidean Geometry*.

by learning history out of order using the language of concepts taken directly from special relativity. To drive the point home, he explicitly links Peaslee's experience to Einstein's theory: "But men in the mathematics department spoke of new developments in those theories of relativity—then discussed only in learned circles—which were later to become so famous. Dr. Einstein, they said, was rapidly reducing *time* to the status of a mere dimension" (*SOT* 40). Notice how Lovecraft is careful to qualify knowledge of relativity as "then discussed only in learned circles," since these events—approximately 1915—take place before the 1919 eclipse that made relativity famous. This placement of events in the timeline of the story are necessary so that Peaslee's period of amnesia matches Lovecraft's own withdrawal from 1908 to 1913.

On an even deeper level, Lovecraft alludes to fundamental concepts of relativity. In Peaslee's personal introduction, he states:

> Yet I would have it known that there is nothing whatever of the mad or sinister in my heredity and early life. This is a highly important fact in view of the shadow which fell so suddenly upon me from *outside* sources. . . . But the chief point is that my own ancestry and background are altogether normal. What came, came from *somewhere else*—where, I even now hesitate to assert in plain words. (*SOT* 34)

Peaslee is plagued by a *shadow* from *somewhere else*. Similar language is found in Eddington's chapter on time, of which only the most abbreviated summary can be made here. Eddington illustrates the distinction between common-sense and relativistic notions of time and space through a series of diagrams in which time follows the vertical direction and space along the horizontal. Figure 10 is his illustration showing the commonsense view: the observer is located at

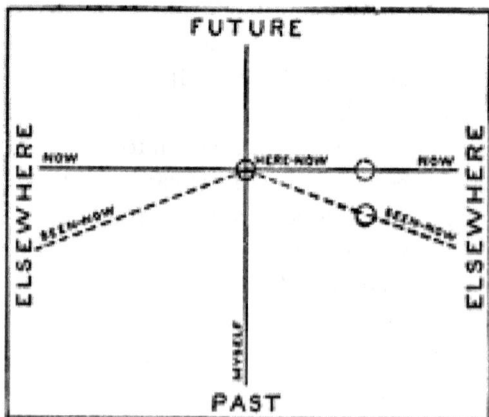

Figure 10: Commonsense View (Eddington 43)

the time-space point "Here-Now," "Now" located between past and future, "Here" between points elsewhere.

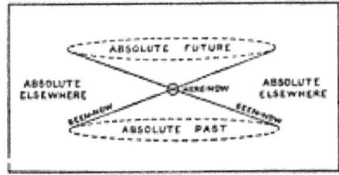

Figure 11 illustrates the relativistic view. Since all signaling is limited to the speed of light, only points in space-time (called *events*) reachable to Here-Now traveling

Figure 11: Relativistic View (Eddington 48)

at or less than the speed of light are in the past; likewise, only events reachable from Here-Now at or less than the speed of light are in the future. All other events are "elsewhere" and cannot influence or be influenced by anything at Here-Now. Most importantly, the relativistic view contains no horizontal line for "Now": the concept of "Now" does not slice across all space, and the concept of an instantaneous "Now" is ambiguous anywhere else from "Here." If an event at some point in space, say a little to the right of "Here-Now," lasts long enough to stretch vertically from the lower sloping edge of the cone to the upper sloping edge all the way through absolute elsewhere (a region Eddington also refers to as the neutral zone), the event may be reasonably considered "Now." As Eddington describes it:

> But in practice the events we notice are of more than infinitesimal duration. If the duration is sufficient to cover the width of the neutral zone, then the event taken as a while may fairly be considered to be Now absolutely. From this point of view the "nowness" of an event is like a shadow cast by it into space, and the longer the event the farther will the umbra of the shadow extend. (Eddington 49)

A shadow from elsewhere, or, in other words, a shadow from "somewhere else."

On November 9, 1931, Lovecraft attended a lecture entitled "The Size of the Universe" given by Professor Willem de Sitter (*SL* 3.437–38). Professor de Sitter was one of the foremost authorities of relativity, having published in 1917 his own solution to Einstein's equations that rivaled Einstein's. At the time Lovecraft saw him, de Sitter was engaged in a lecture tour of North America, the highlight of which was a six-part lecture, "The Development of Our Insight into the Structure of the Universe," given at the Lowell Institute in Boston in early November. This lecture covered the history of cosmological theory from the ancients to modern times. An abbreviated version entitled "The Size of the Universe" that focused on recent developments was given at many locations throughout the United States and Canada, and this is the lecture Lovecraft is referring to.[30] Unfortunately, Lovecraft says very little about the lecture itself, the contents of which can be inferred from the published version that appeared in the *Publications of the Astronomical Society of the Pacific*, while the expanded six-part Lowell Institute lecture was published in book form under the title *Kosmos*. Lovecraft, however, apparently picked up information from some source that appears in the expanded Lowell version but does not appear in the published version of "The Size of the Universe"; perhaps Lovecraft read supplemental information somewhere, or there was a question and answer session, or the version Lovecraft heard simply included material not in the published version. For example, on October 30, de Sitter gave another variant of the lecture entitled "Modern Views Regarding the Universe" that obviously contained content from "The Size of the Universe" ("Asserts Nebulae Expand—Dr. de Sitter Offers New Theory of Extra-Galactic Change," *New York Times*). Also, Lovecraft knew something of de Sitter's work, since in his letter he describes de Sitter's solar collision theory, which almost certainly did not appear in "The Size of the Universe"; Lovecraft may have learned about this theory from a report on yet another of de Sitter's lectures, given on October 26 ("De Sitter Expounds Sun Collision Theory," *New York Times*). Whatever the source, Lovecraft's imagination seems to have been impressed by the mathematical nature of several topics presented by de Sitter, including the four-dimensional mathematics of time and space, the geometry and curvature of space, and insight of the nature of the universe through pure, abstract mathematics. Three months after seeing de Sitter's lecture, Lovecraft wrote "The Dreams in the Witch House," a story that prominently features four-dimensional calculations, curvatures of space, and the power of pure mathematics. As a

---

30. De Sitter's itinerary places him at Brown University on November 9. Details of Professor de Sitter's itinerary courtesy of The Massachusetts Historical Society. An announcement of de Sitter's upcoming lecture, "The Size of the Universe," at Brown University also appears in the *New York Times*: "Will Lecture at Brown—Drs. de Sitter and Woltereck Appear at University Tomorrow."

nod to de Sitter's influence, Lovecraft even refers to him by name in the story (*MM* 264).

"Non-Euclidian Calculus" must rank as one of Lovecraft's best-remembered creations. Although, as Robert Weinberg points out in "H. P. Lovecraft and Pseudomathematics," there is no such field as non-Euclidian calculus, Weinberg is overly harsh in his assessment of the degree of creative license Lovecraft used to craft mathematical ideas of the story. Despite Weinberg's claim that "does such a name [non-Euclidean Calculus] make any real sense" (115), it is not difficult to imagine it as an application of calculus to geometric problems, including non-Euclidean problems, which is a field otherwise known as differential geometry, a topic that de Sitter mentions in his lecture (*Kosmos* 109). Lovecraft's reference to Gilman's "intuitive knack for solving Riemannian equations" (*MM* 269) suggests material that would be covered in the study of differential geometry. Weinberg's dismissal of extra-dimensionality and taking short-cuts through certain angles of space-time fails to appreciate ideas Lovecraft likely extracted from his readings: Eddington himself describes space-time as a four-dimensional manifold embedded in a ten-dimensional space (120). Eddington goes on to use an example that is particularly relevant:

> If you ask what is the distance from Glasgow to New York there are two possible replies. One man will tell you the distance measured over the surface of the ocean; another will recollect that there is a still shorter distance by tunnel through the earth. The second man makes use of a dimension which the first had put out of mind. But if two men do not agree as to distances, they will not agree as to geometry; for geometry treats of the laws of distances. To forget or to be ignorant of a dimension land us into a different geometry. Distances for the second man obey a Euclidean geometry of three dimensions; distances for the first man obey a non-Euclidean geometry of two dimensions ... By the aid of six extra dimensions we can return to Euclidean geometry; in that case our usual distances from point to point in the world are not the "true" distances, the latter taking shorter routes through an eighth or ninth dimension. To bend the world in a super-world of ten dimensions so as to provide these short cuts does, I think, help us to form an idea of the properties of its non-Euclidean geometry; at any rate the picture suggests a useful vocabulary for describing those properties. (157–58)

Professor de Sitter covered related material in far more technical language (*Kosmos* 109–10). This discussion of tunneling and short-cuts is not meant to suggest that these ideas are actually possible. Weinberg also complains: "We are also told in the story of Gilman stating that time could not exist in certain belts of space, so that one could live forever in such regions. This fact would surprise a number of scientists" (117). However, de Sitter points out:

> It is only within the solar system that our empirical knowledge of the quantities determining the state of the universe . . . extends to the second order of smallness . . . From the physical point of view everything that is outside our neighborhood is pure extrapolation, and we are entirely free to make this extrapolation as we please, to suit our philosophical or aesthetical predilections—or prejudices. (*Kosmos* 113)

Weinberg concludes his essay by claiming that while Lovecraft's

> grasp of science and mathematics might have been greater than the average layman, it was not strong enough to present a convincing picture to the careful reader. Further, Lovecraft made the cardinal mistake of speculation of the impossible. While to the non-scientist, this may not sound like much of a sin, it is the cardinal mistake of the uninformed. (117)

Weinberg makes the mistake of presuming that Lovecraft *based* the story on mathematical ideas, instead of recognizing that it was *inspired* by them, and serves as another example of a misguided attempt—in this case by an author with an academic background in mathematics—to apply modern understanding of scientific ideas too rigorously rather than considering the material which Lovecraft had at his disposal.

Perhaps one of the most interesting ideas Lovecraft carried away from de Sitter was the idea of relativity as a pure mathematical abstraction. Professor de Sitter points out that other theories are cluttered with what he calls *hypotheses*—models that explain how the theory works: the ether as the carrier of light with racks and pinions and cogwheels to do the carrying, electrons and protons as tiny particles of matter, the atom as a miniature solar system, etc. However, theories of gravity—both Newton's and Einstein's—are free from these hypotheses, and are described in pure, mathematical forms, with no attempt to explain the tugging of gravitational force (de Sitter, *Kosmos* 103–8). This influence is easily detected in a comparison between "The Whisperer in Darkness" and "The Dreams in the Witch House." "Whisperer" is full of "hypotheses": the fungus beings beat their wings against the ether and carry the brains of lesser creatures in special canisters, which are then attached to special mechanical devices to provide sight, speech, and hearing. "Dreams," however, features none of these stock features of science fiction. Keziah and Gilman access unguessed properties of the universe using only the mathematical ideas outlined by Einstein and de Sitter.

Conclusions

Without question, astronomy played a major influence in Lovecraft's life. From about the age of twelve to the end of his life, he was either reading about astronomy, observing with his own telescope, writing about astronomy, incorporating astronomical motifs into his fiction, or harmonizing the latest astronomical discoveries into his philosophical views. Although his passion for astronomy went through several distinct phases—from active observing and writing nonfiction, to a source through which he discovered, formulated, and expressed his own world view—it served as a unifying passion throughout his life. These phases do not fit into an exact chronology, but fall roughly into several broad periods: from 1902 to about 1918, Lovecraft pursued astronomy as a career discipline; from about 1915 to about 1925, he used his classical (pre-twentieth-century) astronomical background as mood and plot elements in fiction; from about 1925 to the end of his life, he used the latest astronomical discoveries as a means to express his world view through his fiction. A brief summery of each of these phases helps to define astronomy's influence on Lovecraft's life.

As is well known from his correspondence, as a young adult Lovecraft fully expected to find a career in astronomy and worked hard to prepare himself for it. These efforts hit a major snag when he dropped out of high school and failed to attend college. Lovecraft's less than perfect grasp of mathematics undoubtedly played some role in this setback, but other factors almost certainly played a part. While astronomy provided Lovecraft a source of discovery and boyhood wonder, as he matured it probably dawned on him that the days when William Herschel could point his telescope to the sky from his backyard and make spontaneous discoveries were long gone. Instead,

modern astronomy was quickly transforming into a field where discoveries were made only after long, tedious observations that increasingly made use of photography, and fewer astronomers themselves
actually gazed through telescopes. For a boy who never dealt well
with tedium or drudgery, this was probably increasingly disillusioning. Lovecraft also may have been disappointed to find that astronomers like Percival Lowell and William H. Pickering—men who
explored some of astronomy's most exciting phenomena, such as the
active volcanoes on the moon, melting icecaps on Mars, and unknown planets beyond Neptune—were more or less ignored by the
mainstream of the astronomical community, who after about 1910
rejected the existence of Martian canals and focused on topics outside
the solar system (Plotkin 115).[31] Years later, Lovecraft alluded to
Lowell's ostracizing: "Poor chap! His better known observations &
speculations never fared well in the scientific world" (SL 3.136). Professional astronomy simply lacked the excitement that amateur astronomy had offered.

   It is hard, however, not to speculate about what if Lovecraft
might have been able to pull himself together after 1914 and find
some sort of career in astronomy. At the time, astronomy had its
share of professionals with non-traditional backgrounds: Harlow
Shapely had started as a crime reporter, but when he decided to obtain some formal education, he discovered the journalism course he
wanted was unavailable, so he settled on astronomy because it came
first in the course catalog (Gribbin 42–43). Herber Curtis—Shapley's
chief rival in the island universe controversy—was a professor of classics who became interested in astronomy and simply switched into
that field when an opening appeared (Gribbin 46). George Ellery
Hale—one of the principal architects in establishing America as the
center of the astronomical world—held only honorary doctorates, although his father having donated great sums of money to the field

---

31. Privately, Pickering defended his decision to publish his "Reports on
Mars" in the amateur-oriented *Popular Astronomy* instead of a professional
journal such as the *Harvard College Observatory Annals* "because none of
those who are interested in them would find them. One might as well publish in a botanical journal. . . . The Annals are read only by astronomers (professionals), and very few professionals care a rap about either Mars or the
Moon" (Plotkin 112).

probably helped. Percival Lowell also relied somewhat on his fortune rather than his academic background for his influence. Edwin Hubble's right-hand man, Milton Humason, was, like Lovecraft, a high school dropout and only one year younger than Lovecraft. After working for a time as a mule driver on Mount Wilson, Humason worked his way up to a janitor of the observatory, to night assistant, to assistant astronomer, to full astronomer, never having received any formal training beyond his few years of high school. He earned his reputation through his skill at handling telescopic instruments, but marrying the observatory engineer's daughter probably helped (Gribbin 65–67). Lovecraft, of course, had no fortune, nor was he likely to marry into opportunity, but he was obviously intelligent, very likable, and could have milked his connections to Winslow Upton and others at Ladd Observatory.

Even if Lovecraft had gotten his act together, however, he simply may not have had the perspective of a good scientist. Lovecraft relied on his library of astronomy books—many of them quite old—to form the basis of his astronomical background, and espoused many of the ideas therein long after they had been abandoned by the rest of the scientific community. In my opinion, these books were treated not so much as family heirlooms by Lovecraft, but actually as part of his *identity*, and scientific advances that invalidated them, therefore, threatened this identity. Lovecraft's primary concern with relativity theory was to reconcile it with his philosophical views; this he accomplished by presuming that the space in the vicinity of earth *"isn't big enough* to let relativity get in its major effects" (*SL* 2.265). While scientists like Eddington and de Sitter grappled with the new philosophical implications of relativity theory—is space finite or infinite? what is the meaning of the expansion of the universe? what role does our consciousness play with our perception of time?—Lovecraft was busy trying to marginalize the new theory to fit the old philosophy. While this may have been brilliant for his philosophy (Joshi, *H. P. Lovecraft: A Life* 481), it amounts to little more than regarding the earth as "philosophically" flat, because that's the way tiny mortals perceive it, or "philosophically" at the center of the universe with everything moving around it, because precise observations are required to show any deviation from Ptolemaic theory. Lovecraft failed to appreciate that *all* effects of gravity and inertia—whether over vast or small distances, or in intense or weak gravitational fields—are "major effects" of relativity, and that every experiment that ever demonstrated the accuracy of Newton's laws also demonstrated the accuracy of Einstein's. Newton, in fact, could not even explain the fundamental experiment of physics: why two objects of different weights fall at the same rate.[32] Lovecraft has, in effect, followed in the footsteps of the Florentine astronomer Sizzi, "who thus argued against the existence of Jupiter's satellites: 'Moreover', quoth this sage in the course of his argument, 'the satellites are invisible to the naked eye, and therefore can exert no influence on the earth, and therefore would be useless, *and therefore do not exist!*'" (*SL* 1.45).

Another factor that would have worked against a professional career in astronomy for Lovecraft was his extreme aversion to cold. Observational astronomy is not a fair-weather activity, and as fate would have it, winter observation offers certain advantages over summer: the nights are longer, the air is clearer, and the planets are better placed for observation.[33] The changing of the seasons from winter to spring is therefore a bittersweet event for most observational astronomers, yet Lovecraft calls it "the happiest astronomical event of the year" (*CE* 3.177). Although Lovecraft describes developing a permanent curvature of his neck from awkward observing (*SL* 1.38), he never describes having suffered from the effects of cold during his childhood observations. From the few scraps available from his astronomical notebook, he did make observations in February: on the 1st in 1912, and the 26th in 1914 (*CE* 3.332). Neither is in the dead of night, but immediately after sunset: the February 1st entry is recorded at 6:30 P.M., and the 26th describes the thin crescent moon, which was only a day old on that date and set very soon after

---

32. Newton provided a rational explanation of how the weight of an object was proportional to the gravitational field, and how the force applied to an object was proportional to the acceleration it experienced, but it was a complete mystery as to why these proportionalities (called *mass*) of these two seemingly unrelated phenomena would be identical and therefore cancel out. Under Einstein, there is no mystery because gravity and inertia are *exactly the same thing*. See de Sitter, "Size of the Universe" 100–101.

33. The planets follow the same path (called the *ecliptic*) through the sky as the sun; when the sun traces a high arc through the sky (summer), the part of the ecliptic opposite the sun (the part visible at night) traces a low arc. Likewise, when the sun traces a low arc (winter), the part of the ecliptic visible at night (and any planets situated on it) traces a high arc.

sundown. In September 1914, he observed Delavan's comet in the early pre-dawn hours (CE 3.125, 332). He also describes viewing Borelli's comet in August 1903, and Halley's in 1910 (SL 5.282), which reached its best placement on April 20. His later outdoor observations described in his letters are never in winter: in 1933, he described observing the conjunction of Mars and Jupiter in early June (SL 4.203); during his 1934 summertime visit to Nantucket he observed Saturn from the Maria Mitchell Observatory (SL 5.102); in March 1935 Venus, and the moon in early March (SL 5.128), and later in August he observed a lunar rainbow (SL 5.192–93); in July 1936 he observed Peltier's comet from Ladd Observatory (SL 5.282). His few winter observations are limited to the view from his westward facing windows at 66 College Street: in November 1933, he observed the conjunction of Venus and the moon (SL 4.328), and in February 1935 he observed a very thin crescent moon from there. He claims to have been ready to view the occultation of the Pleiades on February 10, but clouds interfered (SL 5.107).[34] The obvious pattern here is that in his youth he claims "not one clear night passed without long observation on my part" (SL 1.8), and his observation notebook places him outdoors in seasons including winter; but after 1914, his outdoor observations of the sky are limited to spring, summer and fall. I suspect his sensitivity to cold did not develop until his breakdown in 1908, and the onset of this problem discouraged his pursuit of astronomy as much as any of the other factors.

During the second phase, running roughly between 1915 and 1925, Lovecraft returned to fiction writing and developed the astronomical motifs that define his style. His earliest tales—"The Beast in the Cave" (1905) and "The Alchemist" (1908)—do not incorporate any astronomy, although they were written well into the period of Lovecraft's interest in that field. It is not until his interest in science gave way to literature that he began to exploit astronomical references: both "The Tomb" and "Dagon" (1917) use the moon as background mood symbols, but in "Polaris" (1918), astronomical imagery and concepts like procession are woven into the fabric of the story. Likewise, Nova Persei figures into the climax of "Beyond the Wall of Sleep"

---

34. This event would have been at about 7 P.M., and taken place close to the zenith, so probably not visible from his west window. We will never know if he would have actually ventured outdoors.

(1919). Thereafter, in all but a few stories, the stars, moon, aurora, and eclipses become familiar staples in Lovecraft's fiction, and some works—such as "The Festival" (1923)—exhibit a realism that would have required reference works and a planisphere. What characterizes the stories of this period is that all the background source material required to achieve the level of realism exhibited was lifted from Lovecraft's collection of old astronomy books.

The third phase commences more or less with Lovecraft's return to Providence in 1926: during this phase, new ideas inspired by contemporary developments in physics and cosmology begin appearing as fictional devices. The transition between these phases is not perfectly smooth: "The Shunned House" (1924) refers to a "newer science which includes the theories of relativity and intra-atomic action" (*MM* 252), while astronomical imagery in "The Shadow over Innsmouth" (1931) is limited to lunar mood effects, more typical of the second phase. Nonetheless, the shift is pronounced: "The Call of Cthulhu" (1926), "The Colour out of Space" (1927), "The Dunwich Horror" (1928), "The Whisperer in Darkness" (1930), *At the Mountains of Madness* (1931), "The Dreams in the Witch House" (1932), and "The Shadow out of Time" (1934–35)—among Lovecraft's most iconic tales—all owe a great deal of their motifs and imagery to the new scientific ideas he was absorbing during their creation. The discovery of Pluto, in fact, occurred during writing "The Whisperer in Darkness" and prompted Lovecraft to integrate it as part of his revisions. All these stories are bound together with concepts such as the existence of regions of space unlike our own, non-Euclidean geometry, and paradoxes in time, all of which can be traced back to concepts from relativity theory. Even some of the lesser "cosmic" tales of this period make use of the new science: *The Case of Charles Dexter Ward* (1927) contains Lovecraft's earliest explicit fictional reference to Einstein (*MM* 161), and "The Thing on the Doorstep" (1933) refers to "complex angles that lead through invisible walls to other regions of space" and objects "whose insane curves and surfaces answered to no conceivable purpose and followed no conceivable geometry" (*DH* 285–86). Joseph Curwen's arrival in the future to meet his descendents may have been inspired by a relativistic time paradox, like that suggested by R. D. Carmichael, in which, after a long journey, a man might return to his starting point to find his kin had given place to new generations.

This third phase of Lovecraft's relationship with astronomy showed signs of winding down after writing "The Shadow out of Time": his next—and last—major tale, "The Haunter of the Dark" (1935), contains no astronomical elements beyond old manuscripts containing astronomical symbols (*DH* 100–101). Perhaps Lovecraft had exhausted relativity themes and was looking for some new influence. During this short period, Lovecraft, for the first time in almost twenty years, showed renewed interest in more than casual observational astronomy, re-equipping his planisphere with new planetary data and describing astronomy as an early interest cropping up again (*SL* 5.412); he also attended a meeting of an amateur group called "The Skyscrapers" and prepared to write revised editions of his introduction to astronomy articles for a local paper in DeLand, Florida (*SL* 5.422). Unfortunately, Lovecraft's untimely death precludes any possibility of knowing where this thread may have led.

Assessment of Lovecraft's scientific background and the influence it had on his fiction is complicated by several factors: scientific progress since Lovecraft's time has rendered obsolete many mainstream scientific ideas to which he subscribed, requiring careful scrutiny to separate Lovecraft's own misinterpretations from sound theory which has subsequently been discarded. Another obvious complication is the nature of science itself, which many readers and critics find intimidating. In his memoir, "Lovecraft and Science," Kenneth Sterling describes Lovecraft's interest in the physical sciences as unusual, "a field decidedly alien if not indeed repulsive to most men of letters" (425). A sobering remark, since much of what we know of Lovecraft—either directly or indirectly—is through men of letters. Some of Sterling's other remarks are even more insightful, if inadvertently. As an example of Lovecraft's wide range of knowledge, Sterling relates a conversation between them on "how great an area of the moon's surface" could be seen with the 200-inch telescope then under construction; using the diameter of the moon and its distance from the earth, Lovecraft supposedly computes the size of the area (423). The problem with this anecdote is that a telescope is used to discern small areas, not great ones: the entire area of the moon can be seen without any telescope. Presuming Sterling actually meant how *small* an area could be seen, the next problem is that the diameter of the moon is really irrelevant to the question. Unfortunately, Sterling does not relate what Lovecraft's answer was, so there is no way of knowing if he came to the right answer. Did Sterling's imperfect memory garble the conversation, or was Lovecraft was just blowing smoke at an impressionable fifteen-year-old? Lovecraft has been described as an author who ignored major facets of science that were known to most intelligent persons of his time as well as a self-educated genius who could draw on knowledge from a vast range of fields and make scientific calculations off the cuff without breaking a sweat. The real Lovecraft lies somewhere in between.

Appendix: A Survey of Astronomical References in Lovecraft's Fiction

AURORA: "Celephaïs" (D 87), "The Rats in the Walls" (DH 34), "The Call of Cthulhu" (DH 135), and "The Strange House High in the Mist" (D 284).

ECLIPSE: "The Other Gods" (D 128, 131, 132).

THE MOON: "The Tomb" (D 4, 11), "Dagon" (D 16, 17, 18, 19), "Polaris" (D 20, 21, 22), "The Transition of Juan Romero" (D 340), "The White Ship" (D 37, 39–40), "The Doom That Came to Sarnath" (D 43, 46, 47, 48, 49), "The Statement of Randolph Carter" (MM 301, 302, 303, 305), "The Terrible Old Man" (DH 273), "The Tree" (D 50), "Facts concerning the Late Arthur Jermyn and His Family" (D 74), "The Street" (D 345, 347, 349, 350, 352), "Celephaïs" (D 84, 87), "The Picture in the House" (DH 116), "The Nameless City" (D 98, 99–100, 101, 106, 108), "The Quest of Iranon" (D 111, 112, 115, 117), "The Moon-Bog" (D 118, 119, 121, 122, 123, 125), "The Outsider" (DH 48, 49, 52), "The Other Gods" (D 129), "The Music of Erich Zann" (DH 86, 91), "Herbert West—Reanimator" (D 146, 147, 148), "The Hound" (D 173, 175, 177), "The Lurking Fear" (D 196, 197), "The Unnamable" (D 205), "The Festival" (D 212), "Under the Pyramids" (D 226, 227, 232), "The Horror at Red Hook" (D 253, 255, 262, 265), "He" (D 266, 267, 271, 274, 275, 276), "In the Vault" (DH 8, 9, 10), "The Call of Cthulhu" (DH 154), "Pickman's Model" (DH 17), "The Silver Key" (MM 408), The Dream-Quest of Unknown Kadath (MM 309, 310, 312, 314, 319, 322, 326, 350, 351, 399), The Case of Charles Dexter Ward (MM 136, 220), "The Colour out of Space" (DH 61, 64, 73, 74, 75, 76, 77, 78, 79), "The Whisperer in Darkness" (DH 211, 229, 231, 232, 233, 234, 235, 249, 257, 271), "The Shadow over Innsmouth" (DH 319, 347, 349, 350, 351, 352, 353, 354,

355, 356, 357, 358, 359, 360), and "The Shadow out of Time" (*SOT* 45, 69, 70, 72, 73, 74, 75, 76, 87, 89, 90).

PLANETS: "The Doom That Came to Sarnath" (*D* 46).

STARS: "Polaris" (*D* 20, 21, 23, 24), "Beyond the Wall of Sleep" (*D* 33, 34, 35), "The Doom That Came to Sarnath" (*D* 34), "The Street" (*D* 345, 351), "Celephaïs" (*D* 84), "The Nameless City" (*D* 99), "The Quest of Iranon" (*D* 117), "The Outsider" (*DH* 48), "Hypnos" (*D* 166), "The Festival" (*D* 208, 209, 212), "The Horror at Red Hook" (*D* 257), "He" (*D* 266), "The Silver Key" (*MM* 417), "The Strange House High in the Mist" (*D* 277), *The Dream-Quest of Unknown Kadath* (*MM* 307, 314, 320, 322, 327, 334, 351, 357, 392, 393, 401, 402, 406), *The Case of Charles Dexter Ward* (*MM* 141), "The Colour out of Space" (*DH* 56, 57, 78), "The Dreams in the Witch House" (*MM* 275, 289), and "The Shadow out of Time" (*SOT* 45).

NONE: "The Beast in the Cave," "The Alchemist," "The Cats of Ulthar," "The Temple," "From Beyond," and "Cool Air."

Works Cited

"A New Physics, Based on Einstein." *New York Times* (25 November 1919): 17.

"Accepts Einstein Gravitation Theory." *New York Times* (11 November 1919): 17.

Allen, Richard Hinckley. *Star-Names and Their Meanings* [retitled *Star Names: Their Lore and Meaning*]. 1899. New York: Dover, 1963.

Alter, Dinsmore. "A Statistical Study of the Solar Atmosphere with Application to the Evolution of Planets." *Astrophysical Journal* 79 (1934): 498–510.

"Assaulting the Absolute." *New York Times* (7 December 1919): X1.

"Asserts Nebulae Expand—Dr. de Sitter Offers New Theory of Extra-Galactic Change." *New York Times* (31 October 1931): 19.

Baldwin, R. B. "An Overview of Impact Cratering." *Meteoritics* 13 (31 December 1978): 364–79.

Bartusiak, Marcia. "Meeting the Multiverse." *Harvard Magazine* (November–December 2005): 19–22.

Bateman, H. "The Form of the Ether." *Publications of the Astronomical Society of the Pacific* 34, No. 198 (1922): 94–107.

Beckwith, Henry L. P., Jr. *Lovecraft's Providence and Adjacent Parts.* 1979. Rev. ed. Hampton Falls, NH: Donald M. Grant, 1990.

Bohm, David. *The Special Theory of Relativity.* New York: W. A Benjamin, 1965.

Bonola, Roberto. *Non-Euclidean Geometry.* Tr. H. S. Carslaw. 1912. New York: Dover, 1955.

Boss, Lewis J. "Convergent of a Moving Cluster in Taurus." *Astronomical Journal* 26, No. 604 (1908): 31–36.

Brush, Stephen G. "A Geologist among Astronomers: The Rise and Fall of the Chamberlin-Moulton Cosmogony." *Journal of the History of Astronomy* (1978): 1–41, 77–104.

Burleson, Donald R. *H. P. Lovecraft: A Critical Study.* Westport, CT: Greenwood Press, 1983.

Burnham, Robert, Jr. *Burnham's Celestial Handbook.* 1966. New York: Dover, 1978.

Burritt, Elijah H. *The Geography of the Heavens and Class-Book of Astronomy: Accompanied by a Celestial Atlas.* New York: Mason Brothers, 1856.

Campbell, W. W., and R. Trumper. "Observations on the Deflection of Light in Passing Through the Sun's Gravitational Field." *Lick Observatory Bulletin* No. 346 (June 1923): 41–54.

Carmichael, R. D. "Einstein's Third Victory." *New York Times* (28 March 1920): X11.

———. "Given the Speed, Time Is Naught." *New York Times* (7 December 1919): 18.

Coles, Peter. "Einstein, Eddington and the 1919 Eclipse." *Historical Development of Modern Cosmology, ASP Conference Proceedings.* Vol. 252. San Francisco: Publications of the Astronomical Society of the Pacific, 2001. 21–41.

de Sitter, W. "Einstein's Theory of Gravitation and Its Astronomical Consequences. Third Paper." *Monthly Notices of the Royal Astronomical Society* 78 (November 1917): 3–28.

———. *Kosmos.* Cambridge, MA: Harvard University Press, 1932.

———. "The Size of the Universe." *Publications of the Astronomical Society of the Pacific* 44, No. 258 (April 1932): 89–104.

"de Sitter Expounds Sun Collision Theory." *New York Times* (27 October 1931): 27.

Derleth, August. *The Lurker at the Threshold.* In *The Watchers out of Time and Others.* Sauk City, WI: Arkham House, 1974.

"Don't Worry over New Light Theory." *New York Times* (16 November 1919): E1.

"Eclipse Showed Gravity Variation." *New York Times* (9 November 1919): 6.

Eddington, A. S. *The Nature of the Physical World.* New York: Macmillan, 1928.

Einstein, Albert. *Ideas and Opinions.* New York: Wings Books, 1954.

———. "Time, Space, and Gravitation." *Science* (2 January 1920): 8–10.

"Einstein Expounds His New Theory." *New York Times* (3 December 1919): 19.

"Einstein's Theory Discussed Here." *New York Times* (2 December 1919): 12.

Ely, Owen. "What Is the Ether?" *Popular Astronomy* 18 (November 1910): 525–32.

Fernie, J. D. "The Historical Quest for the Nature of the Spiral Nebulae." *Publications of the Astronomical Society of the Pacific* (December 1970): 1189–1230.

Gribbin, John R. *In Search of the Big Bang: Quantum Physics and Cosmology.* New York: Bantam Books, 1986.

Hagerstown Town and Country Almanack. Hagerstown, MD: T. G. Robertson, Bookseller, 1862.

Haught, John F. *Science and Religion: From Conflict to Conversation.* New York: Paulist Press, 1995.

Holmes, Charles Nevers. "Polaris." *Popular Astronomy* 24 (December 1916): 633–38.

Hoskin, M. A. "The Great Debate: What Really Happened." *Journal for the History of Astronomy* (1976): 169–82.

"Jazz in the Scientific World." *New York Times* (16 November 1919): X8.

Jevons, William Stanley. *Investigations in Currency and Finance.* New York: Macmillan, 1884.

Jeans, Sir James. *The Universe Around Us.* New York: Macmillan, 1929.

Joshi, S. T. *H. P. Lovecraft: A Life.* West Warwick, RI: Necronomicon Press, 1996.

———. *Primal Sources: Essays on H. P. Lovecraft.* New York: Hippocampus Press, 2003.

Kepler, Johannes. *Epitome of Copernican Astronomy.* Tr. Glenn Wallis. (Great Books of the Western World, Vol. 16.) Chicago: Encyclopedia Britannica, 1952.

Kidwell, Peggy Aldrich. "Elija Burritt and the 'Geography of the Heavens.'" *Sky & Telescope* 69, No. 1 (Jan 1985): 26–28.

Leiber, Fritz, Jr. "Through Hyperspace with Brown Jenkin: Love-craft's Contribution to Speculative Fiction." 1966. In S. T. Joshi, ed. *H. P. Lovecraft: Four Decades of Criticism.* Athens: Ohio University Press, 1980. 140–52.

"Light and Logic." *New York Times* (16 November 1919): X1.

"Lights All Askew in the Heavens." *New York Times* (10 November 1919): 17.

"Lodge Pays Tribute to Einstein Theory." *New York Times* (9 February 1920): 3.

Lorentz, H. A. "Dutch Colleague Explains Einstein." *New York Times* (21 December 1919): 20.

Lovecraft, H. P. *The Shadow out of Time.* Ed. S. T. Joshi and David E. Schultz. New York: Hippocampus Press, 2001. [Abbreviated in the text as *SOT.*]

———. *Letters to Alfred Galpin.* Ed. S.T. Joshi and David E. Schultz. New York: Hippocampus Press, 2003.

Martin, Martha Evans. *The Friendly Stars.* New York: Harper & Brothers, 1907.

Newcomb, Simon. *Popular Astronomy.* New York: Harper & Brothers, 1880.

———. *Astronomy for Everybody.* Garden City, NY: Garden City Publishing Co., 1902.

Perridas, Chris. "Constellation Felis: Is It Slyly Mentioned in 'The Dreams of the Witch House'?" *Chris Perridas: H. P. Lovecraft & His Legacy,* October 2006. <http://chrisperridas.blogspot.com/2006/10/constellation-felis-is-it-slyly.html> Accessed June 14, 2008.

Pickering, William H. "Aberration and Relativity." *Popular Astronomy* 30 (June 1922): 340–43.

———. "Shall We Accept Relativity." *Popular Astronomy* 30 (April 1922): 199–203.

———. "The Theory of Relativity." *Popular Astronomy* 28 (June 1920): 334–44.

Plotkin, Howard. "William H. Pickering in Jamaica: The Founding of Woodlawn and Studies of Mars." *Journal for the History of Astronomy* (May 1993): 101–22.

Rufus, W. Carl. "Relativity in Astronomy." *Popular Astronomy* 26 (March 1918): 160–65.

Russell, Bertrand. *Selected Papers of Bertrand Russell.* New York: Modern Library, 1927.

Ryabov, Y. *An Elementary Survey of Celestial Mechanics.* Tr. G. Yan-
    kovsky. 1959. New York: Dover, 1961.

Shapley, Harlow. *Starlight.* New York: George H. Doran Co., 1926.

Sherrill, Thomas J. "A Career of Controversy: The Anomaly of T. J. J.
    See." *Journal for the History of Astronomy* (February 1999): 25–50.

Sterling, Kenneth. "Lovecraft and Science." 1944. In Peter Cannon, ed.
    Lovecraft Remembered. Sauk City, WI: Arkham House, 1998.

Swenson, Loyd S. "The Michelson-Morley-Miller Experiments Before
    and After 1905." *Journal for the History of Astronomy* 1 (1970): 56–
    78.

Tirion, Will, Barry Rappaport, and George Lovi. *Uranometria* 2000.0.
    Volume I. Richmond, VA: Willmann-Bell, 1987.

Trimble, Virginia. "The 1920 Shapley-Curts Discussion: Background,
    Issues, and Aftermath." *Publications of the Astronomical Society of
    the Pacific* 107 (December 1995): 1133–44.

Weinberg, Robert. "H. P. Lovecraft and Pseudomathematics." 1971. In
    Darrell Schweitzer, ed. *Discovering H. P. Lovecraft.* Rev. ed. Mer-
    cer Island, WA: Starmont House, 1987. 113–17.

"Will Lecture at Brown." *New York Times* (8 November 1931): N20.

Wilson, Edmund. "Tales of the Marvellous and the Ridiculous." 1945.
    In S. T. Joshi, ed. *H. P. Lovecraft: Four Decades of Criticism.* Ath-
    ens: Ohio University Press, 1980. 46–49.

Young, R. K. "The Drift of the Ether." *Journal of the Royal Astronomi-
    cal Society of Canada* 20 (1926): 1–14.

The Sickness unto Death in H. P. Lovecraft's "The Hound"

James Goho

Lovecraft's stories have often been condemned for dreadful writing, particularly by mainstream literary critics such as Edmund Wilson, who called Lovecraft a writer of "bad taste and bad art" (287). Very recently, Laura Miller and Stephen Schwartz expressed outrage that Lovecraft was included in the Library of America while lamenting that Wilson was not. Schwartz's indignation at Lovecraft's inclusion is reflected in the title of his review, "Infinitely Abysmal." He writes, "[Lovecraft's] stories always evince overwriting of a kind that disappeared with the pulp genre in which it flourished" (75). Schwartz calls Lovecraft's descriptions "absurd confabulations" (75). Comparison with Borges, he says, "is ridiculous" (76).[1] This is extreme literary elitism.[2]

"The Hound" (*D* 171–78), in particular, has been criticized as absurd and overwritten, suffering from "adjectivitis" and gibberish.[3] Even sympathetic criticism has characterized the story as a self-parody.[4] Mariconda notes that Lovecraft himself referred to the story

---

1. Borges's admiration for HPL is attested by "There Are More Things," a story in the mode of and dedicated "To the memory of H. P. Lovecraft" (471).

2. Dirda, on the other hand, contends that the Library of America volume helped HPL reach "from beyond the grave to claim his rightful place as a grand master of visionary fiction" (2). This task has been worked at for many years by such notables as August Derleth, James Turner, and S. T. Joshi.

3. Schweitzer suggests that "The Hound" gibbers from start to finish. Not all critics feel this way about the story. Jeffery calls the story HPL's "master work" (18), but perhaps this is tongue-in-cheek.

4. Joshi in *H. P. Lovecraft: A Life* and elsewhere has argued for the perspective of self-parody, or at least parody of blood and guts horror. Mariconda in "'The Hound'—A Dead Dog?" calls the story a "thinly disguised literary joke" (46) and a parody. It is true I think that HPL is having fun in the story but I

as a "dead dog," perhaps confirming the critical perspective. The remark, however, may be ironic, similar to Mary Shelley calling *Frankenstein* her "hideous progeny" (xxv). Besides, Lovecraft despaired about much of his literary work.[5] Artists themselves are not always the best critics of their work, even so confident a writer as James Joyce expressed occasional self-doubts.[6]

Nonetheless, "The Hound" is a sound pillar supporting Lovecraft's literary status. The story is at the core of his art and shows Lovecraft experimenting with form, style, plotting, and characterization. He marshals the common tools of horror stories, such as foreshadowing, building suspense through mood, and returning characters to a disturbing place, as if he is using them up and squeezing what he can out of old techniques. What's more, he is also having fun, a bleak fun surely. This article explores the story through several intersecting lenses. As with much of Lovecraft, the story appeals in a fundamental visceral manner, the way all true weird tales appeal as they evoke a primal sense of unwanted touching or being touched by an indefinite menacing something from a strange otherness. We find so much in "The Hound" about the experience of horror, about the language of horror stories creating mood and atmosphere (the language haunts readers more than the plot), and even about the American tradition of adventure stories. Lovecraft was beginning to cut the new wood of horror in this story. That is why some of the language seems crooked and the images splintered, but it is a gateway into his more mature body of work where the themes are elaborated on a bigger stage. Still, the story unearths a sense of true dread.

The language itself is the fundamental gateway to understanding the

---

am not convinced that HPL would mock his own style this early in his "professional" writing career. There is parody, I think, for example to the trait of literary allusion. But more important is the undertow of despair that finally takes the story into the depths of real horror, into dread.

5. Mariconda in "'The Hound'—A Dead Dog?" traces HPL's increasing dissatisfaction with "The Hound." Cannon also notes HPL's dismissal of this story, but he thinks the story has some merit due to "its vivacity alone" (33).

6. At the end of *Finnegans Wake*, Joyce writes: "is there one who understands me" (627). And in a letter to Viscount Carlow, Joyce wrote of *Finnegans Wake*, "I think I can see some lofty thinkers and noble livers turning away from it with a look of pained displeasure" (*Letters* 395).

story. It is the exemplar of the baroque language of horror—perhaps the only language to use in exploring the sickness unto death or in confronting authenticity in the experience of dread. That is the core bravery of the story: it is not fear but dread that Lovecraft confronts. And the message is that in the end even language cannot protect us. Eventually words fail in the story as they cannot describe phenomena, instead referring to "less explicable things," "that I must not speak," and that which is "utterly impossible to describe." The odd sentence, "Bizarre manifestations were now too frequent to count," is another example of the corroding and breakdown of language. By the last paragraph, language becomes confused, inarticulate, and chaotic, ending in a silent gunshot off stage.

A third way of exploring the story is through Kierkegaard's concepts of dread and despair. The heroes suffer through the "sickness unto death." They experience the moral chaos of dread, the end of good and evil, where dread is ultimately a confrontation with a person's nothingness in the world. And the heroes fall prey to the sickness. But Lovecraft worked through this in his own life by revolting against dread. In a sense, Lovecraft is a metaphysical rebel as described by Camus in *The Rebel*. He rebels against the situation of life, against the world we inhabit. Houellebecq argues that Lovecraft's art was a rebellion against realism, against the facts of existence. Lovecraft "conquers his own existence" (Camus, *The Rebel* 103), by writing. Lamont believes that "becoming a writer is about becoming conscious" (225). Lovecraft was heroic in an existential sense by knowing the anguish of life, yet persisting in the face of hopelessness through writing. In *The Myth of Sisyphus*, Camus argues that the core philosophical question is whether to commit suicide or not in the face of the absurdity of life. Lévy suggests that Lovecraft fought with suicide and survived at least in part through his dreams, which he later transformed into art. In "The Hound," along with other stories, Lovecraft explores the idea of suicide as a response to knowledge of the world. The unnamed hero succumbs to the sickness unto death and takes his own life; Lovecraft soldiered onwards.

In addition, it is helpful to read the story and the experience of dread through the perspective of the double. There are multiple layers of this theme in the characters, the action, and in the act of reading itself. Throughout the story the reader is a double as he or she is directly addressed by the narrator. We become co-conspirators in the crime of avoiding the truth of our existence in our very reading of the story if we become lost in the thickets of words. We are not just passive observers of the story's events but real agents in its creation as we respond or not to the messages about dread. Lovecraft is an artist of substantial literary presence, and this article explores his talent in the writing of "The Hound."

The story starts with the unnamed narrator, hard gun in hand, fondly anticipating suicide after the killing of St. John, his companion. And death may be an ethical end for his sickness, reified as "the black, shapeless nemesis." This is dread. This expression is similar to the "black seas of infinity" (*DH* 125) and that "dark terror which will never leave" (*DH* 149) in "The Call of Cthulhu." In the poem, "The Going," Hardy conveyed the same overwhelming dread, "in darkening darkness / The yawning blankness / Of that perspective sickens me" (80). Lovecraft is part of this tradition in literature; he wrote weird tales and poetry to express his anguish; Hardy wrote mainstream novels, stories, and poems. Lovecraft in pulp magazines and in his letters explored the same frontiers of thought. Berruti notes Lovecraft's use of obscurity as an image for "outsideness," which Berruti describes "as the pervasiveness of the horror and the ineluctability of its menace" (372).[7] This is one way of apprehending the concept of dread. In "The Hound," this image of darkness is the real menace, for example, as the premonition of death, when, "a large, opaque body darkened . . . [their] library window." It is with the "blackest of apprehensions" that they realize the language of the chattering outside their library door is Dutch. The narrator arrives at the scene of St. John's screams to "see a vague black cloudy thing silhouetted against the rising

---

7. The concept of "outsideness" is not exactly the same as the concept of "dread" elucidated by Kierkegaard although there are intersections. Outsideness is similar to alienation where we feel separated from the world and it evades our limited understanding and it does not respond to our needs. Perhaps it is the unutterable and indescribable. Berruti writes that the experience is that "of the limit, of the threshold: on the edge, along the razor blade, one hovers between life and death, between sanity and madness" (382). It brings one to the edge of suicide. The story "Facts concerning the Late Arthur Jermyn and His Family" starts: "Life is a hideous thing" (*D* 73). There the outsideness is embedded in a sordid evolutionary history where the link to apes is much closer than one would think. We are not made in the image of God but are adrift in an alien universe.

moon." Later he witnesses "a black shape obscure one of the reflections of the lamps in the water." In the last paragraph, the unnamed narrator succumbs to the "night-black." It is this overwhelming image of darkness—a symbol of dread—that engulfs his existence.

This presence of something that is almost not there but also everywhere arises from the tomb—the ghoul (underneath the ground, perhaps from hell), from the surface of the earth itself—the gigantic hound, and down from the sky—"the stealthy whirring and flapping of those accursed web-wings circles closer and closer." There is no escape; it is everywhere. It is a suffocating, smothering atmosphere; one is numbed by the thick beating of the reptilian wings, overcome by the "stenches of the uncovered grave," deafened by the unrelenting baying, and blinded by the "black, shapeless Nemesis."

Lovecraft attacks all our senses, although there is a special ringing reek to this story—roused by the repeating gong of the baying monster. The story attacks our ears, unrelentingly. Moreover, there is that intense unease at the dead human body; no one, willingly, is going to touch the thing "covered with caked blood and shreds of alien flesh and hair." And yet, perhaps the heroes would as Lovecraft alludes to the cannibalism of the dead when, on the first opening the grave, the heroes "feasted" and in the description of the corpse of St. John laid out like a chewed cut of beef. There is the core of traditional horror in the story, but it is the consuming cosmic nothingness that gives it the biting edge.

In "Supernatural Horror in Literature," Lovecraft writes that he wanted to evoke in readers "a profound sense of dread, and of contact with unknown spheres and powers, a subtle attitude of awed listening, as if for the beating of black wings or the scratching of outside shapes and entities on the known universe's utmost rim" (D 368–69). The moments of "awed listening" that we all avoid, turning away from the buzzing night forest, by turning up the TV, drinking, or praying. In "The Hound" Lovecraft articulates this avoidance from the dark night of the soul, an avoidance that will ultimately fail.

It is the language of the story that sticks with people; language that is over-the-top. Indeed, some find the language annoying and childish, but it is also exhilarating and enchanting. And contrary to the claims of mainstream criticism, Mariconda, in "H. P. Lovecraft: Consummate Prose Stylist," and Berruti have demonstrated that Lovecraft altered his style to suit the subject matter of his stories.

Joshi argues that Lovecraft "was almost always the master, rather than the slave, of his style" ("Introduction" xix). The self-affected style of "The Hound" purposely draws attention to the un-naturalism of the story and the spoiled-brat heroes. The rhetorical excess reflects the excess of the protagonists. The language expressly shows itself through word flourishes and hyperbole. But there is more to the language than baroque extravagance. Lovecraft's language serves a clear purpose as the "purple prose" itself expresses the substance of the story. "The Hound" is packed with adjectives, replete with qualifiers as if there are not enough words to describe the experiences of the characters, abounding with repetitions like incantations against evil. Perhaps by writing enough, the dread will pass by. But it is not to be. You can feel Lovecraft combating with the form and substance of horror in "The Hound," in the full, exuberant flowering of words. In the story, the words and phrases are artifices, fortifications against the tenebrous hours of darkness.

Among other things, "The Hound" is a study in using rhetoric to cope with horror. The language is its glory. The language is appropriate to the hysterical situation and the annoying main characters who may strike readers as immature, naughty boys. All through his writing career Lovecraft struggled with symbols and shadow to express his dark insights. The repetitions are necessary, the allusions to the canon of weird tales are central, and the alliteration and formulaic phrasings invoke the muses of horror.[8] This story is a nightmare. It followed on a visit by Lovecraft and his friend Rheinhart Kleiner[9] to a graveyard. Lovecraft stole away with a small chunk of a gravestone which he promised to put under his pillow—a charm to rouse the muses or demons of sleep.

However, the artifices of rhetoric fail to keep the dread at bay. Lovecraft uses many such devices in the story. From the first paragraph, onomatopoeia ("whirring," "flapping," and "baying") and anaphora (repetition of the same word or phrase in successive clauses:

---

8. The phrase "baying of some gigantic hound" and its component words are used in a traditionally oral manner where key phrases and words are used as mnemonics. "Hound" is used 8 times, "baying" 14 times, and the phrase "some gigantic hound" 5 times. Some of the words in the story, such as "baying," "flapping," "gigantic hound," function as a soundtrack does in horror movies to pump up the tension.

9. In his letters, HPL called Kleiner "St. John."

"It is not a dream—it is not, I fear . . .") are used to signal the deployment of rhetorical devices. Overall, the story is a prime example of synathroesmus (piling up of adjectives), although the paragraph describing the first visit to the grave of the ghoul is the highlight sequence, and pleonasm (a word or phrase that, if omitted, would not change the meaning). Other examples include hyperbaton (reversal of normal word order), "Statues and paintings there were"; neologism, *"Necronomicon"*; allliteration, "dripping death aside a Bacchanale of bats from the night-black ruins of buried temples of Belial"; tautology, "unknown and unnamable drawings"; oxymoron, "articulate chatter"; and allusion, "I heard a knock at my chamber door," alluding to "The Raven." Yet rhetoric cannot keep the dread away.

An overwhelming sense of existential despair, disgust, and dread permeates the adventures of the heroes.[10] It is a case study of the sickness unto death spelled out by Kierkegaard. In *Either/Or*, Kierkegaard describes two ways for humans to live, the aesthetic or the ethical. The aesthetic existence leads to hedonism, consisting of a search for gratification and a nurturing of mood. The aesthetic person must always seek novelty in an effort to stave off world-weariness and an all-pervading melancholy; but in the end he has only boredom and despair. The heroes in "The Hound" live the aesthetic life and try to escape ennui by indulging in the grotesque and morbid, hoping to enliven their existence through a continuous spiral deeper into degradation and corruption as they hunt for satiation of their feeling of nothingness. They live in a sort of death-coma, as Kierkegaard might say. Although the heroes recognize dimly the emptiness of their aesthetic life, they cling desperately to it. Kierkegaard's argument is that this emptiness arises from the fact that we have within us something else, which will not be satisfied by a sensory life. This is the eternal. For Kierkegaard, we are a synthesis of body and spirit, of temporal and eternal, of necessity and freedom. The aesthetic life, however, emphasizes the corporeal, the temporal, and the finite. This leads to a desperate search for endless gratification. The aesthetic way of life leads to dread or angst. In contrast, the ethical life is based on adhering to

10. This feeling of existential loneliness infuses other stories, particularly "The Outsider" and *At the Mountains of Madness*. In both of these the sense of separation from others and from the universe is intense. The heroes inhabit a space of solitudes and unbearable loss—they are exiles, as perhaps we all are.

moral codes and living in a spirit of fellow-feeling. It is possible to achieve the ethical life by following cultural moral precepts. There is also a third way of living, the true way, the religious way of life, when we make a leap of faith beyond despair by acknowledging our sin and embracing belief in God. But if we have felt dread, yet obstinately persist in an existence in the sensory sphere, we will end in despair.

Despair is the sickness unto death. The narrator seems to be moving toward the ethical life as he retells the adventure. He speaks of the moral failure of their exploits and calls to God.[11] However, the heroes confront dread, persist in their worldly adventures, and end in despair, in the death desire as described by Kierkegaard in *The Sickness unto Death*. A way of thinking about this matter is to consider that people tend to deal with this anxiety by obsessively focusing on physical apparitions and fantasies rather than the dread itself. Dread is not like fear; it lacks any determinate object and is something we all feel. "There lives not one single man . . . in whose inmost parts there does not exist a disquietude, a perturbation, a discord, an anxious dread[12] of an unknown something, or of a something he does not even dare to make acquaintance with" (Kierkegaard, *The Sickness unto Death* 155). No wonder—as it is so overwhelmingly awful, like a cold darkness spilling eternally into your bedroom, or night falling through your tall dark windows like coffins. We objectify dread to escape the valley of existential loss as long as we can. Mistakenly, we displace the anxiety to an external object and hope that dread can be managed by getting rid of the object—but when this fails the fear reverts to the original dread. This is the horror of human existence that Lovecraft experienced and tried to dissolve in his writings.

---

11. In *H. P. Lovecraft: The Decline of the West*, Joshi details the narrator's change in ethical posture.

12. Kierkegaard's concept of dread is confusing, complex, and manifold. A key element is that dread or angst is a feeling that has no definite object; it is different from the fear that comes from an objective threat (for example, a mugger, a grizzly bear in the wilds). In a sense dread is a sign that we have the eternal or the desire for the eternal within us but something is missing. Kierkegaard suggests that the solution to dread is finding a connection to the power that established us as humans, namely with God. By truly linking with the source of everything in the universe, we can be fully realized. Dread is a sin when we do not connect with God, which we do through faith. Of course there is no rational basis for this and Kierkegaard glories in it.

The heroes objectify dread into a thing that seems like a gigantic hound, or at least the narrator does. However, it is more than a black dog barking in their heads. In the story, the quest for escape from ennui leads the heroes to grave-robbing. In this expedition, they find more than they bargain for as out of their frenzied digging arises the monster, the objectification of dread, the false hope to transform it into fear. In a sense, they unearth the other and see their personal hell. The "sickness unto death" infects the entire story and erupts in many words and phrases: "soul-upheaving stenches of the uncovered grave," "dissonances of exquisite morbidity and cacodaemoniacal ghastliness," "features . . . savouring at once of death, bestiality, and malevolence," "vexed and gnawed at the dead," "wind moaned sad and wan," "gibber out insane pleas," "queer combination of rustling, tittering, and articulate chatter," and "madness rides the star-wind." These strange phrases are attempts by the narrator to describe his illness and his dread.

In "The Uncanny" Freud describes an encounter with dread, where the known causes terror precisely because it is known, but somehow now twisted into the unfamiliar and disruptive of the normal. The uncanny is "that class of the terrifying which leads back to something long known and to us, once familiar" (370–71). The uncanny arises from the unclear boundaries between the living and the dead and the figure of the double. Both of these resonate throughout "The Hound." The narrator and St. John are old hands at the boundaries of life and death and know decay and corruption; indeed, that is their rapture. Even the icon of dread in the story, the amulet, "was not wholly unfamiliar" to the pair. Alien to most but not to these two, who have read the *Necronomicon*. However, this does not protect them from a fiend of the grave. But more important is the notion of the double, for the narrator and St. John are doubles. St. John is the purported leader, but this is hard to believe as the narrator does not seem like the tagalong type. The double is one mode of the uncanny. It can be considered part of the longing for immortality. Freud, reflecting on the work of Otto Rank, thought of the double as a characteristic of the "primary narcissism" (Freud 387) of childhood. The double, in a sense and at this early stage, protects against the loss of the ego. Later, the double functions as the conscience. Rank saw the double reversing as it continued to develop into an uncanny otherness within the self and eventually becoming a thing of terror, a bringer of death. So the double becomes a "vision of terror" according to Freud, just as, after the collapse of a religion, "the gods took on daemonic shapes" (389). In "The Hound" Lovecraft expresses the horror through the double; for who is St. John and who is the unnamed narrator, but two of the same, partners in crime? A reader gains a vague notion of the narrator but St. John is only a shadow figure, befitting a double. And when the double dies, the original is sure to follow.

However, the real double is the "one buried for five centuries, who had himself been a ghoul in his time." Lovecraft deploys the dislocating effect of the known transforming into a monstrous unknown, yet still familiar presence in the story. Dirk W. Mosig explicates this disturbing effect of many of Lovecraft's stories. There are other layers of doubles in this weird tale. The protagonists are both predators and prey. The ghoul in the grave was a fellow despoiler of graves, who also "had stolen a potent thing from a mighty sepulchre." The scene at the grave is repeated explicitly representing the intrusion of the past into the present. Opening the grave opens the past and unleashes the horror; it is as if the monstrous events will occur eternally, for there is no salvation. The characters in the story are struck by dread, but the real cosmic dread is that we, as readers, are drawn into the same recurring horror story.

Reason collapses under the weight of dread. This is Lovecraft's philosophical perspective. There is a difference between the narrator of "The Hound" and Lovecraft: the narrator gives up but Lovecraft, in the grip of despair, persisted. Lovecraft saw the universe as awful, like Pascal, who, when thinking of the starlit night sky, wrote, "The eternal silence of these infinite spaces frightens me" (211). That is the universe Lovecraft experienced and tried to articulate in his writings. Indeed, in "The Call of Cthulhu," Thurston speaks in a tone similar to Pascal of the horrible possibility that knowledge "will open up . . . terrifying vistas of reality" (*DH* 125). In "For the Time Being: A Christmas Oratorio," W. H. Auden also describes this alien landscape, where "We are afraid / Of pain but more afraid of silence; for no nightmare / Of hostile objects could be as terrible as this Void" (352). For Kierkegaard there is an escape with a leap of faith. This leap is awakened by our longing for and recognition of the essential need for religion. We can obliterate our dread and the manifestations of this dread in apparitions through God. Fear of nothingness and despair at our limitations can be overcome. But Lovecraft would not traffic with a God. Nietzsche had already broadcast that "God is dead" (35).

Moreover, the horrors of World War I spotlighted the emptiness of the idea of a personal God. Nietzsche, of course, did not think there was a God to die but he argued that the idea was bankrupt in a scientific world. In a sense, the concept of God had no meaningful explanatory role in the world. Talking about God was talking nonsense. It was time for humans to grow up and throw away the thoughts of children. Lovecraft does have some fun with the notion of appealing to God in the story. The second paragraph starts, "May heaven forgive the folly and morbidity which led us both to so monstrous a fate!" Of the particularly noxious tomb-loot, the narrator exclaims, "thank God I had the courage to destroy it long before I thought of destroying myself!" In the last scene at the ghoul's grave, when the narrator says, "I know not why I went thither unless to pray, or gibber out insane pleas," Lovecraft compares praying to gibbering and mocks the false hope of religion.

Lévy argues that Lovecraft gave up on religion knowing the bleak cosmos and tried in his writing to forge a meaningful life in spite of the fact of nothingness. Houellebecq writes that Lovecraft lived an "exemplary life," that his "only animus was literature and dreams" (89). He was a "man without hope" (Lévy 31), the true existential man, who felt always the absurdity of life. Lovecraft was authentic and expressed his existential understanding of himself in a hostile world. For Lovecraft, the unknown comes from within one's own head and the hostile universe we inhabit and try to ignore. The true weird tale needed more than a murder or clacking bones or ghostly forms—more than mere fear. Fear is, in a sense, comprised of tangible things—like slasher movies, drooling zombies, or the fear of death. Dread on the other hand is more formidable because it has no objective source. There is not a sane method to overcome the sense, the feeling of nothingness.

In "The Hound" the unnamed narrator is trying to flee from everything, including the reader, and uses language to shape-shift and distort his story. Always he turns away from the real truth of dread, using words to keep the night at bay and to confuse us—the readers. But that is part of the agony he goes through, and perhaps it is so awful that none of us could stomach it—not the actual sense of cosmic loneliness. Lovecraft chronicles this objectification of dread and hopelessness of doing so in "The Hound." But the objectification of dread in a fear object is a temporary measure. The emotions in the story move from ennui, to excitement, to fear, to horror; then full-blown dread.

And at the conclusion of the story, language breaks down entirely when the narrator faces the unexplainable despair elucidated by Kierkegaard. Finally, the narrator is engulfed and he can no longer use the magic of words to keep it away. The fear object becomes more intense throughout the story from the faint but mounting sounds of the beast; to marks left by the dead monster outside a door, underneath a window; to a savaged, mutilated, dead friend; to the dread object itself, characterized as some "dead, fleshless monstrosity." In "The Hound" there are no mild-mannered black dogs of suburban depression but a real howling madness. No Zoloft will work here.

But Lovecraft does have fun with the story. It is a takeoff on the grand English tradition of tomb-looting and museum building. This colossal social edifice of stealing the relics of the dead is twisted on its head, or perhaps illuminated for what it really is. As Lovecraft always reminds us, cemeteries are not dead; malignant, decayed, abominable, yes, but not dead; the heroes eventually learn this the hard way. In the story, their museum is a re-creation of the tomb, of death. They lug trophies from the dead back to their chamber of horrors in England. They savor their sordid Elgin Marbles "far, far underground" like a tomb itself. And the narrator "cannot reveal the details of . . . [the] shocking expeditions, or catalogue even partly the worst of the trophies adorning the nameless museum." This is a sick archaeology, a twisted science to know death. And as the heroes seem to have no means of supporting themselves, perhaps they are in the market of selling pilfered grave goods, literally living off the dead. The heroes suffer the sickness unto death, but do not evoke a lot of sympathy from readers because they seem too wearisome, just bad little boys.

The heroes—are they brothers, twins, lovers? Doubles? The double seems the most likely. "The Hound" is a story of two men on an adventure, a common theme in American literature. Leslie Fiedler, in *Love and Death in the American Novel*, suggested that much of American literature focused on male bonding through adventure, often in undefiled nature, and that it was essentially a boys' literature. Lovecraft's "The Hound" is a sick adventure of two men who sometimes seem like juveniles in a defiled world, and finally in this tale we find out where all that really ends. This is not a boy's tale of the wilderness but an adult's descent into sickness, madness, murder, and suicide. From the hairy earth, the heroes have dug up their own death. Lovecraft has dared to express the truth about this stream of American writing.

In this story the narrator dares not say his own name—but howls at the outrages of life, of the earth, of the universe.[13] At the end, the narrator recognizes his own sickness, his own sin, his own monstrousness; he has become another monster, "the unnamed," the double of the "unnamable." Even language cannot ward off the ennui, the darkness, the awfulness of existence, and so there is really only one last act. He succumbs to sickness and death and is overwhelmed by the darkness of Belial.[14] The unnamed transforms into the unnamable realizing the nightmare of the sickness. For ultimate dread really is unnamable. But perhaps he is redeemed, a little, by plugging himself; he refuses to go back to regular culture and conventional morality for he has seen the truth, and he will not pray.

So, what is "The Hound"? What is the hound itself? Only a silly garish undead, a feeble image of infantilism? No. It is the reification of dread. We hear the real anguish, the howls of dread from the hero; perhaps more than we really want to hear or understand. Yes, as a story it has faults, there may be more than we want in adjectives but also less than we want in the elaboration of the chilling cosmic terror that Lovecraft explores in his later work. The baroque language is maybe too florid and it fails finally at the end—as it must. The heroes or doubles are silly schoolboys, playing with forces too big for them to handle. The narrator succumbs to the sickness unto death. The action is full of repetition. The literary allusions may be too obvious and overdone, particularly the ongoing references to the baying hound. Yet there is a power in the story that creates unease; we sense

---

13. As the power and impotence of language are themes in this story, it seems appropriate that the narrator's name is not revealed. It is as if there is a disembodied voice crying out against the terror of life, not sure if there will be listeners.

14. Joshi pointed this out in his notes to "The Hound" in *The Call of Cthulhu and Other Weird Stories*. Belial is described in II Corinthians 6:15 as akin to darkness: "what communion hath light with darkness? And what concord hath Christ with Belial?" In the Dead Sea Scrolls, Belial leads the hordes of darkness against the army of light, "his rule is in Darkness" (136). In *The Jewish Encyclopedia*, the meaning of the word is elucidated and one of the references is as "the spirit of darkness" in the Testaments of the Twelve Patriarchs (Levi xix; Joseph vii, xx). In a sense Belial is darkness. This speaks again to the real dread in the story—not the "hound" but the overwhelming universe expressed as darkness.

an undertow tugging at us, dragging us down into the night ocean of dread. Lovecraft captures us with his magic language and in doing so has portrayed an episode in the experience of dread. Kierkegaard wrote: "If there were no eternal consciousness in a man, if at the foundation of all there lay only a wild seething power . . ., if a bottomless void never satiated lay hidden beneath all, what would life be but despair" (*Fear and Trembling* 30). Lovecraft knew this to be the truth of existence and there was no salvation through Christian rapture. In "The Hound," we have been blessed with a brief glimpse into the sickness and death that envelops us all. The "unnamable" is the sickness unto death and Lovecraft has broken down the walls of infinity for a moment, allowing us an instant of awed listening.

Works Cited

Auden, W. H. "For the Time Being: A Christmas Oratorio." In *Collected Poems*. Ed. Edward Mendelson. New York: Vintage, 1991. 347–400.

Berruti, Massimo. "H. P. Lovecraft and the Anatomy of Nothingness: The Cthulhu Mythos." *Semiotica* 150 (2004): 363–418.

Borges, Jorge Luis. "There Are More Things." In *Collected Fictions*. Tr. Andrew Hurley. New York: Viking, 1998. 437–42.

Camus, Albert. "The Myth of Sisyphus." In *The Myth of Sisyphus and Other Essays*. Tr. Justin O'Brien. New York: Vintage, 1955. 1–102.

———. *The Rebel*. Tr. Anthony Bower. New York: Vintage, 1956.

Cannon, Peter. *H. P. Lovecraft*. Boston: Twayne, 1989.

Dead Sea Scrolls. Tr. and Ed. Geza Vermes. London: Folio Books, 2000.

Dirda, Michael. "The Horror, the Horror! H. P. Lovecraft Enters the American Canon." *Weekly Standard* (010/23, 2005), retrieved August 2005 from http://www.theweeklystandard.com/Content/ Public/ Articles/000/ 000/005/285tmhfa.asp

Fiedler, Leslie. *Love and Death in the American Novel*. New York: Criterion, 1960.

Freud, Sigmund. "The 'Uncanny.'" In *Collected Papers*. Vol. IV. Ed. Ernest Jones. Tr. Alix Strachey. London: Hogarth Press, 1950. 368–407.

Hardy, Thomas. *A Selection of His Finest Poems*. Oxford: Oxford University Press, 1994.

Houellebecq, Michel. *H. P. Lovecraft: Against the World, Against Life*. Tr. Dorna Khazeni. San Francisco: Believer Books, 2005.

Jastrow, M. Jr.; Levi, G. B.; and Jastrow, M. "Belial." In *The Jewish Encyclopedia*. 1901–06. 658–59.

Jeffery, Petal. "St. John's Assassin Bites Back." *Crypt of Cthulhu* No. 87 (Lamas 1994): 17–18.

Joshi, S. T. *H. P. Lovecraft: The Decline of the West*. 1990. Berkeley Heights, NJ: Wildside Press, 2001.

———. *H. P. Lovecraft: A Life*. West Warwick, RI: Necronomicon Press, 1996.

———. *A Subtler Magick: The Writings and Philosophy of H. P. Lovecraft*. 1996. Berkeley Heights: NJ: Wildside Press, 1999.

———. "Introduction." *The Call of Cthulhu and Other Weird Stories*. By H. P. Lovecraft. New York: Penguin, 1999. vii–xx.

Joyce, James. *Finnegans Wake*. New York: Viking Press, 1959.

———. *Selected Letters of James Joyce*. Ed. Richard Ellmann. London: Faber & Faber, 1978.

Kierkegaard, Søren. *Either/Or*. In *A Kierkegaard Anthology*. Ed. Robert Bretall. Tr. David F. Swenson, Lillian Marvin Swenson, and Walter Lowrie. New York: Modern Library, 1946. 19–108.

———. *Fear and Trembling and The Sickness unto Death*. Ed. and tr. Walter Lowrie. Garden City, NY: Doubleday, 1954.

Lamont, A. *Some Instructions on Writing and Life*. New York: Anchor/Doubleday, 1994.

Lévy, Maurice. *Lovecraft: A Study in the Fantastic*. Tr. S. T. Joshi. Detroit: Wayne State University Press, 1988.

Mariconda, Steven J. "'The Hound'—A Dead Dog?" In *On the Emergence of "Cthulhu" and Other Observations*. West Warwick, RI: Necronomicon Press, 1995. 45–49.

———. "H. P. Lovecraft: Consummate Prose Stylist." In *On the Emergence of "Cthulhu' and Other Observations*. West Warwick, RI: Necronomicon Press, 1995. 7–13.

Miller, Laura. "Master of Disgust." *Salon.com*. Retrieved May 12, 2005 from http://www.salon.com/books/feature/2005/02/12/lovecraft

Mosig, Dirk W. *Mosig at Last: A Psychologist Looks at H. P. Lovecraft*. West Warwick, RI: Necronomicon Press, 1997.

Nietzsche, Freidrich. *Thus Spake Zarathustra*. Tr. Thomas Common. Rev. and ed. H. James Birx. Amherst, NY: Prometheus Books, 1993.

Pascal, Blaise. *Pensées*. In *The Provincial Letters, Pensées, and Scientific Treatises*. Ed. Robert Maynard Hutchins. Tr. W. F. Trotter. Chicago: Encyclopedia Britannica Great Books, 1952. 171–352.

Rank, Otto. "The Double as Immortal Self." In *Beyond Psychology*. 1941. New York: Dover, 1958. 62–101.

Schwartz, Stephen. "Infinitely Abysmal." *New Criterion* (May 2005): 75–76.

Schweitzer, Darrell. "Lovecraft and Lord Dunsany." In *Discovering H.P. Lovecraft*. Ed. Darrell Schweitzer. Holicong, PA: Wildside Press, 2001.

Shelley, Mary. *Frankenstein*. 3rd ed. 1831. London: The Folio Society, 2004.

Wilson, Edmund. "Tales of the Marvellous and the Ridiculous." In *Classics and Commercials: A Literary Chronicle of the Forties*. New York: Farrar, Straus, 1950. 286–90.

Briefly Noted

Barnes & Noble has arranged with S. T. Joshi to present an enormous omnibus of H. P. Lovecraft's complete original fiction, due out this fall. The volume will contain every original tale written by Lovecraft, including even his juvenilia; no revisions or collaborations, with the exception of "Under the Pyramids" and "Through the Gates of the Silver Key," will be included. Among the treasures of the volume will be the first appearance in print of a "long" version of Lovecraft's juvenile tale "The Mysterious Ship" (1902). We cannot say that this version is much better than the "short" version that has been available since 1959, but it is of some interest nonetheless. The volume is not annotated aside from brief headnotes to each story written by Joshi. It also includes "Supernatural Horror in Literature." It is hoped that this omnibus, using Joshi's corrected texts, will be preferred to *The Necronomicon: The Best Weird Fiction of H. P. Lovecraft*, a volume issued in January by Victor Gollancz of London. The volume does not print Lovecraft's entire corpus of fiction and uses a curious mélange of uncorrected texts. Another British publisher, Wordsworth, has issued two volumes in what purports to be a multi-volume edition of "Collected Stories": *The Whisperer in Darkness* (February 2007) and *The Loved Dead* (May 2007). But these editions also use uncorrected texts.

Queer Tales?
Sexuality, Race, and Architecture in "The Thing on the Doorstep"

Joel Pace

If history and time could ever be rearranged so that Dr. Sigmund Freud could have paid a house call to the residence in which Howard Phillips Lovecraft spent his final years, the small house near the top of Providence's College Hill would not have had a room large enough to accommodate all the scholars who would wish to be flies on the wall. In the absence of such a meeting, critics have regarded the topic of sexuality in Lovecraft's fiction as flypaper: they've been initially attracted to it, yet often find themselves stuck—not able to budge one way or another due to lack of pertinent plots, dialogue, and characters in stories. Researchers are trapped by the irony that an author whose surname as well as the lurid covers of *Weird Tales*, the magazine in which his stories were published, would suggest otherwise crafted tales that tread gently around topics of love and lovemaking.[1] As S. T. Joshi points out in *H. P. Lovecraft: A Life:* "One must look very hard even to find hints of sex in the fiction" (582). Any analysis of sexuality in Lovecraft's fiction must also consider his life, which Joshi notes is similarly asexual (581), but may help us gain an understanding of the spirit of the issue as expressed in the stories. It is generally accepted that Lovecraft was not much interested in women. His short-lived marriage to Sonia H. Davis (then Greene) was affected by his inability to live in a way beneficial to the overall good of their union. It is important to realize, however, that Lovecraft wanted the marriage to work, as is easily gleaned from his letters and also Davis's 1948 memoir, *The Private Life of H. P.*

---

1. Sexuality and racial otherness are combined in the April 1929 cover of *Weird Tales*, which illustrates Seabury Quinn's "The Devil's Rosary."

Lovecraft. He did come into contact with women in a professional capacity; however, experientially women were not love interests for Lovecraft and he did not know how to treat them as such. Other than Sonia, there is little evidence of a premarital sweetheart or any other woman very close to him—save, of course, his mother and aunts, about his relationship with whom much has been written. If Lovecraft were ever to find himself stretched out on Dr. Freud's couch, he may indeed, with no little coaxing from the overly interested doctor, trace his problematic relationships with women back to his mother, who by twists and turns inspired and vexed him.

Another seeming barrier to the analysis of sexuality in the works of Lovecraft is the absence of female characters. There is, however, one story in which a woman figures prominently: "The Thing on the Doorstep" (1933; *DH* 276–302). Joshi, the preeminent Lovecraft scholar of our time, dwells on this story in a discussion of Lovecraft and sexuality:

> Not a word is said of Edward and Asenath Derby's sexual relations in "The Thing on the Doorstep," perhaps because they are irrelevant to the story; but nothing is even said about the anomalies of sex reversal. Ephraim Waite takes over the body of his daughter Asenath: what are his sentiments when he becomes a woman, and especially when he marries Derby? If, as this story suggests, Lovecraft regarded the mind or personality (rather than the body) as the essence of an individual, is this marriage homosexual? What does Derby feel when his mind is thrown into the rotting body of his wife? If someone were to write a story on this basic premise today, it is unlikely that such issues would be avoided. (*Lovecraft: A Life* 582)

In "The Innsmouth 'Thing': Monstrous Androgyny in H. P. Lovecraft's 'The Thing on the Doorstep,'" Kálmán Matolcsy, one of the only other critics to discuss sexuality in Lovecraft, offers an illuminating reading of the story. This otherwise excellent article does not explicitly mention or discuss the homoerotic overtones that are clearly present in the tale. Even if Lovecraft himself attempted to skirt such issues in his own work, they would not have been off limits to his contemporary readers, especially when we consider the number of gay or bisexual men among his friends and correspondents: R. H. Barlow, Hart Crane, August Derleth, Gordon Hatfield, and Samuel Loveman. Similarly, as Joshi notes, the presence of sexuality in the works of other authors did not go unnoticed by Lovecraft either. In a 4 January 1930 missive to Maurice W. Moe, the author literally did count the ways in which love (*eros*) could find its way into art and literature, which suggests that he may have used these very same means, in addition to some of his own, to bring eroticism subtly into his own works:

1. Impersonal and serious descriptions of erotic scenes, relationships, motivations, and consequences in real life.
2. Poetic—and other aesthetic—exaltations of erotic feelings.
3. Satirical glimpses of the erotic realities underlying non-erotic pretences and exteriors.
4. Artificial descriptions or symbols designed to stimulate erotic feelings, yet without a well-proportioned grounding in life or art.
5. Corporeal nudity in pictorial or sartorial art.
6. Erotic subject matter through the medium of wit and humour.
7. Free discussion of philosophic and scientific issues involving sex. (*SL* 3.103)

To illustrate these tenets, Lovecraft drew examples from earlier writers, such as Whitman and the Marquis de Sade. Interestingly, Lovecraft ruminated on this topic toward the end of his life and did not publish "The Thing on the Doorstep" until after he had thus codified his own views against censoring sexual content in literature and art.

If the word "satirical" were removed from item number three, it would almost entirely explain the implicit sexuality of the married relationship between Edward Derby and Asenath/Ephraim Waite, notwithstanding the possible presence of satirical aspects to this relationship. It is not outside the realm of possibility that the reader is meant to understand that this married couple is sexually active, which as Joshi points out would mean that Edward is having sex with his wife's father, who has taken over Asenath's body. It is interesting that in maxim number two, Lovecraft leaves room for "other aesthetic" exaltations of erotic feelings. Lovecraft's writing was based in the aesthetics of the Gothic, a genre that is rife with the veiled expression of the erotic (especially society's taboos, such as same-sex eroticism, incest, and necrophilia, all exemplified to a degree in "The Thing on the Doorstep"). In addition to examining sexuality in Lovecraft's life, we must also examine its presence in the gothic works with which he was familiar.

Another element crucial to an examination of sexuality in the life, works, and reading of Lovecraft is a consideration of race, as it is inextricably linked to sexuality in the works of Lovecraft and early Gothic writers, such as M. G. Lewis, Samuel Taylor Coleridge, Thomas De Quincey, Edgar Allan Poe, and Mary Shelley. The border states that Lovecraft's characters and those of his predecessors occupy are often spaces between societal oppositions of not only straight and gay, man and woman, but also Anglo-American and racially "other." An examination of sexuality (and race) also necessitates some form of psycho-analytic analysis of Lovecraft's life and works; in Gothic and horror, the most common metaphor for the mind is architecture, the ruined structure's hidden passageways and underground spaces symbolizing hidden compartments and liminal spaces of the mind, the hiding places of forbidden desires. As the title of "The Thing on the Doorstep" suggests, the story uses architecture to express a border-state, the existence of some-thing on the threshold of man and woman, human and beast, natural and super- (preter- and un)natural, Anglo-American and racial "otherness." Architecture takes on special significance with regard to race, sexuality, and the mind in a time when the racist science of phrenology still held sway over society and sought to dehumanize the people outside of the norms determined by those in power. Another Gothic trope that allows for expressions of sexual fantasies is dreaming, often involving an exoticized and eroticized racial otherness as well as nightmares expressing sex and race-related fears.

I

Queer Tales of Rhode Island and Providence Plantations: Sexuality, Race, and Place in Lovecraft's Life

Before we delve into architecture as a trope for expressions of sexuality and race in "The Thing on the Doorstep" and the Gothic works that influenced it, let's go into his closet—not necessarily to out him or to find skeletons—and his wardrobe, not to find a lion or a witch, but to examine the most oft-discussed aspect of Lovecraft's childhood: his mother's dressing him (as was the custom of the day for children of both genders) in a gown and keeping his hair shoulder length. Sonia

Davis's 1948 memoir provides information that critics interpreting Lovecraft from a Freudian perspective have made much of:

> It was . . . at this time the fashion for mothers to start "hope-chests" for their daughters even before they were born, so that when Mrs. Winfield Scott Lovecraft was expecting her first child she had hoped it would be a girl; nor was this curtailed at the birth of her boy. . . . As a baby Howard looked like a beautiful girl. He had, at the tender age of three years, a head of flaxen curls of which any girl would have been proud. . . . These he wore until he was about six. When at last he protested and wanted them cut off, his mother had taken him to the barber's and cried bitterly as the 'cruel' shears separated them from his head. (8)

Additionally, his mother dressed him in frocks for many years, so to all outward appearances he was a girl. As R. H. Barlow notes, Lovecraft was known to state "I'm a little girl," as he would insist to his relative Annie Gamwell (*On Lovecraft and Life* 18). One last bit of important biographical information comes from a letter of Whipple Phillips in which he writes young Lovecraft about his travels, noting to the boy: "I will tell you more about what I have seen if you are a good boy and *wear trousers.*"[2] At the very least, these incidents signal that, as a child, Lovecraft self-identified as a member of the opposite sex.

Given this background, Lovecraft's later homophobia can be seen as his means of self-definition to correspond to his scripted gender role while distancing himself from the early liminal space he occupied. On 16 February 1933, he waxes prejudicially on same-sex attraction in a letter to August Derleth: "So far as the case of homosexualism goes, the primary and vital objection against it is that it is naturally (physically and involuntarily—not merely 'morally' or aesthetically) repugnant to the overwhelming bulk of mankind" (*Essential Solitude* 545–46). Similarly discriminatory are his adverse reactions to meeting a gay man in Cleveland in 1922 and his musings on Oscar Wilde. In a 20 January 1927 letter to August Derleth, he wrote:

> As a man, however, Wilde admits of absolutely no defence. His character, notwithstanding a daintiness of manners which imposed an ex-

2. Manuscript in John Hay Library. For more information on this aspect of HPL's life see S. T. Joshi's *H. P. Lovecraft: A Life* (1996), 42, 280, 581–82.

terior shell of decorative decency and decorum, was as thoroughly rotten and contemptible as it is possible for a human character to be. . . . So thorough was his absence of that form of taste which we call a moral sense, that his derelictions comprised not only the greater and grosser offences, but all those petty dishonesties, shiftinesses, pusil-lanimities, and affected contemptibilities and cowardices which mark the mere "cad" or "bounder" as well as the actual "villain." It is an ironic circumstance that he who succeeded for a time in being the Prince of Dandies, was never in any basic sense what one likes to call a *gentleman. (Essential Solitude* 64–5)

The difference between Wilde's exterior and interior, in Lovecraft's eyes, calls to mind the same border state of Asenath Derby, from "The Thing on the Doorstep," who is not what she appears to be.

The decorum and manners of characters in Lovecraft's stories are thin veneers for the horrors lurking below the surface, and this con-nection links Edward Derby and Asenath Waite to Oscar Wilde: Lovecraft saw Wilde's "daintiness of manners" as a threadbare cover-ing for his "rotten" aspects. In Lovecraft's stories an outward decorum attempts to function as a border keeping characters within their gen-der roles in the face of horror. When the thing comes to the doorstep *and enters into the threshold*, the narrator Dan Upton hopes his "wife would not wake to confront it." As Peter Cannon states in a footnote to this passage:

In Lovecraft a husband's natural instinct is to protect his wife from horror. In "The Dunwich Horror" Dr. Armitage warns his wife off when her eyes wander toward the notes he's been taking on Wilbur Whateley's diary, while in *The Case of Charles Dexter Ward* Theo-dore Howland Ward carries his wife downstairs, after she's fainted, to spare her hearing more of the strange noises coming from behind the door of their son's laboratory. (*More Annotated Lovecraft* 274)

Kálmán Matolcsy also comments on the ways in which "manners maketh [wo]man" in the story:

Asenath's figure, her overflowing and diffuse body is counterbalanced in "Doorstep" by Daniel Upton's spouse, a constrained, somewhat re-stricted, genuine angel of the house, about whose purity no doubt is raised. [. . .] The fact that she does not see Asenath's decomposing body—Daniel's wife is always shunned, evanescent, and ethereal (she never appears in body throughout the story)—offers an instance of the gendered version of the Lovecraftian 'cosmicist' thesis, that is, witnessing the horror equals knowing it, knowledge is always harmful, and both knowledge and harm are closely tied to gender. (172)

As in Wilde's *The Importance of Being Earnest*, the conventions of decorum in "Doorstep" cover up the shocking truth of infidelities underlying heterosexual marriage arranged by status and class rather than love, and so Derby has a hard time, during etiquette-controlled conversations with Upton, telling him the truth about his marriage to Asenath. The notion of decorum as a framework for solidifying gender roles and covering up horrors throws a new light on a seemingly meaningless and off-handed detail in the penultimate paragraph of "Doorstep": "The butler, tougher-fibred than I, did not faint at what met him in the hall in the morning. Instead, he telephoned the police. When they came I had been taken upstairs to bed, but the—other mass—lay where it had collapsed in the night. The men put handkerchiefs to their noses." What is most interesting, though, about the connection between Wilde and "The Thing on the Doorstep" is that Lovecraft mentions several times in the story that Edward Pickman Derby takes up with the Miskatonic University Decadents, American aesthetes who slavishly follow Wilde's aesthetic in literature and dress:

> He began to mingle in the more "advanced" college set despite his middle age, and was present at some extremely *wild* doings—on one occasion paying heavy blackmail (which he borrowed of me) to keep his presence at a certain affair from his father's notice. Some of the whispered rumours about the *wild* Miskatonic set were extremely singular. (Emphasis added)

In order to understand the potency of Lovecraft's puns on the surname of the most notorious decadent of his day, we must remember that Wilde was an accomplished and erudite writer of "middle age," who spent his time with young aesthetes at Oxford University. The parallels do not end there, as Derby's "paying heavy blackmail" to keep "a certain affair" from his father not only recalls Wilde's being blackmailed by the male prostitutes of London with threats to expose his letters to his lover, the Magdalen College student Bosie (Lord Alfred Douglas), but also Bosie's attempts to keep his relationship from his father.

Lovecraft's strong reaction to Wilde's life becomes even more complex when we take into consideration Lovecraft's time spent among youthful aspiring authors who fêted him in much the same way that Wilde was courted by Bosie's set. Another frame of reference and reflexivity is added as we recall that Lovecraft addresses his condemnation of Wilde to August Derleth, a young, bisexual aspiring author who greatly admired Lovecraft's stories. Another frame within a frame is present in the architecture of the plot line's story within a story. In narrating this twice-told tale, Upton who dotes on his friend Derby, an aspiring author eight years his junior:

> As he [Derby] grew to years of manhood he retained a deceptive aspect of boyishness. Blond and blue eyed, he had the fresh complexion of a child; *and his attempts to raise a moustache were discernible only with difficulty. . . .* He was of a good height, and his *handsome face* would have made him a notable gallant had not his shyness held him to seclusion and bookishness. . . . His *Poe-like talents* turned more and more toward the *decadent,* and other artistic sensibilities and *yearnings were half-aroused in him.* (Emphases added)

The connection of this passage to Lovecraft's life and his description of one of his own devotees is made by Cannon who notes (in a footnote to the text quoted above) that soon

> after meeting Frank Belknap Long, in New York City in the spring of 1922, Lovecraft wrote in a letter: "Long . . . is an exquisite boy of twenty who hardly looks fifteen. He is dark and slight, with a bushy wealth of almost black hair and a delicate, beautiful face still a stranger to the gillette. I think he likes the tiny collection of lip-hairs—about six on one side and five on the other—which may with assiduous care some day help to enhance his genuine resemblance to his chief idol—Edgar Allan Poe. (244; *SL* 1.180)

Derby's turning to the decadent and experiencing "yearnings . . . half-aroused" is described in language with obvious connotations. The parallels to Wilde and Bosie as well as the language are too suggestive to rule out a homoerotic element in this passage, but wouldn't Lovecraft's aesthetics forbid such latent content? Perhaps not. We do well, here, to remember Lovecraft's third rule of ways in which sexuality can be introduced into a literary work: "Satirical glimpses of the erotic realities underlying non-erotic pretenses and exteriors." Given

Lovecraft's tongue-in-cheek puns on Wilde's surname in Upton's above declamations on Derby and the erotic connotations of the last quotation, it is not unreasonable to understand these passages as parodic tips of the hat to a playwright and poet whom Lovecraft admired, especially considering the ways in which Lovecraft's story and Wilde's *Importance of Being Earnest* function as critiques of high society and marriage, not to mention the parallels between Dorian Gray and Ephraim Waite. The decay of Derby in "The Thing on the Doorstep" represents Wilde's "decay" (and decadence) in Lovecraft's eyes and reveals the root of Lovecraft's views on Wilde. Max Nordau's *Degeneration* (1892) commented upon Wilde's aesthetic as leading to the devolution of society from human to beast.

The parallels between male characters in "Doorstep" and the men in Lovecraft's life as well as the authors whom he admired do not end with Frank Belknap Long and Oscar Wilde. There is the reference to Poe, who lurks somewhere hidden in the architecture of all Lovecraft stories. The relationship of the narrator to Edward Derby is of course similar to the relationship of the narrator to Roderick Usher in "The Fall of the House of Usher." Both narrators slowly watch the men closest to them in life slowly go insane. Derby is locked away in Arkham Sanitarium, which inevitably recalls Lovecraft's father, Winfield Scott Lovecraft, and his slow decline into death and insanity in the Providence "sanitarium," Butler Hospital. If Freud could have read Lovecraft's story, he would doubtless have theorized that if Derby represents Lovecraft's father, then the death of Derby is complex in an Oedipal way. Derby's own father dies, and prior to this Ephraim Waite "had died insane—under rather queer circumstances" (248). It has been quite rightly pointed out that Lovecraft's creation of the monstrous Cthulhu was a response to seeing his father's mental and physical decay during his final days in Butler Hospital. In keeping with this interpretation, the monstrous thing on Upton's doorstep also recalls his father.

If there is an Oedipal presence in "Doorstep," then where is the mother figure to complete the triangulation? Interestingly, the mother figure is hybridized with the father figure, insofar as Asenath and Ephraim are the same person. Asenath and Lovecraft's mother have more than a little in common, not the least of which is the strong control Sarah Susan Phillips Lovecraft exerted over her son and the fact that Asenath eyes Edward "almost continually with an almost predatory air" before she takes complete control over him. To complicate matters further, Edward's marriage to Asenath, as Peter Cannon notes, also has many parallels with Howard's marriage to Sonia: "With her strong will and designs on Derby, Asenath calls to mind Lovecraft's wife Sonia, who by all accounts (including her own) took the initiative in their relationship. See her memoir 'Lovecraft as I Knew Him'" (*More Annotated Lovecraft* 249). Cannon also points out the parallels between Edward's mother's death and that of Lovecraft's mother and the ways in which her death is, emotionally speaking, linked to his marriage with Sonia, as his wife helped him recover from it (246). Following his line of enquiry, Matolcsy links the death of Edward's mother to the details of Lovecraft's life:

> Daniel makes mention of Edward's 'habits of childish dependence,' resulting from his mother's early death—Lovecraft's mother dies when he is thirty-one—whereby for months the feminine Derby is "incapacitated by some odd psychological malady." Edward, first and foremost, projects his pathological love for the missing mother onto Asenath. Asenath-Ephraim's figure, however, is potentially perilous (the name Asenath actually draws upon the same etymology), for it is plainly patriarchal. (177)

Another excellent point made by Cannon is that the isolation of Derby's childhood as well his precocious literary talent is very (and more than likely purposely) similar to Lovecraft's early years. Considering all of Cannon's points we come to the crux of the matter, which I would argue is stated implicitly in the title: "The Thing on the Doorstep" is the story of an unwanted child, an abandoned child left on the doorstep, so to speak. Lovecraft's and the story's parentage and lineage are complex. To return to the tale's literary genealogy and to bring this discussion of it full circle, we must return to a consideration of Poe. Matolcsy makes a poignant comment that is never further discussed or developed in the essay: he states that, with regard to gender, the "Providence legacy of 'The Fall of the House of Usher' and 'The Yellow Wallpaper,' in Lovecraft's case, should not be underestimated" (171). Poe's and Perkins Gilman's stories use architecture to represent the walls that separate and confine men and women. This aspect of both stories does not go unnoticed by Lovecraft. Both Usher and Derby entomb (in the basement) the woman to whom each is closest, each woman returning to haunt the perpetrator of the attempted murder, just as Lovecraft and his story are haunted by their respective parents.

Lovecraft's characters exist at the doorsteps of many doorways that lead to various characters from his life and reading, and allow us to appreciate the fact that Lovecraft and his characters exist on the threshold. Interestingly, almost all Lovecraft's stories feature two males who discover a doorway to another state of mind or being, which is latent in everyone; one of the males in the story crosses beyond the liminal space and in doing so inevitably pulls the other character, usually the narrator, into the interstitial zone, trapping him between two worlds. In the words of Upton: "There are horrors beyond life's edge that we do not suspect, and once in a while man's evil prying calls them just within our range. Ephraim—Asenath—that devil called them in, and they engulfed Edward and are engulfing me." Matolcsy sees the border state almost solely with regard to gender: "in the shadows of the mind-exchange and gender-fusion motifs, the mythical figure of the androgyne takes shape" (176). The androgynous aspects of Ephraim-Asenath-Edward are indisputable; however, the hybridism of Lovecraft's character is not limited to gender, but extends to race and sexuality as well. The racial and gender otherness of Asenath is clear here, but the homoerotic link between Edward and Dan as well as Edward and Ephraim (through Asenath) is only implied. If Lovecraft's stories do not ever explicitly voyage into the realms of (hetero-, homo-, and bi-) sexuality, they implicitly explore the margin.

Another comment of Lovecraft's on gayness is equally positioned at the crossroads: "I don't know whether to kill it or kiss it!" (*SL* 1.280). Despite Lovecraft's self-proclaimed hatred of gays, there is conflicting evidence in his response to Gordon Hatfield, the first openly gay person he met: "I'm afraid he thought me a very crude, stupid, commonplace, masculine sort of person" (*SL* 1.281–82). According to Lovecraft's literary aspirations and concomitant view of himself and his talents, he would certainly disagree with the first three adjectives that describe his impression of Hatfield's perception of him, so considering the overall context and sentiment (that he appeared to Hatfield as what he is not) it is safe to assume that Lovecraft may have not considered it entirely accurate if Hatfield were to perceive him as a "masculine sort of person." Lovecraft and his characters, however, at certain times exist in a middle ground between society's hegemonic and dualistic constructs. A reconstruction of Lovecraft's identity as well as that of his characters (throughout stages of their transformations and the way they self-identify and are perceived by others) requires consideration of heteronormative aspects of "maleness" *as well as* gay, bisexual, and transgender elements in his life and works, which cannot be fully understood without a discussion of race as well.

Lovecraft occupied a state in between extremes: he had a wealthy lineage, but no considerable inheritance or formal education; his closest friends were gay or bisexual, but he became anti-L(esbian) G(ay) B(isexual) T(ransgender) in his later years. He grew up in Rhode Island, which Roger Williams purchased from the Narragansett tribe and which also contained the harbor, Bristol, where millions of slaves were brought into America. Built up with colonial structures, Providence was, much to Lovecraft's dismay, becoming the home of an increasing number of Cape Verdean, Italian, and Portuguese immigrants as well as African Americans. In the introduction to the Penguin edition of *The Call of Cthulhu and Other Weird Stories*, Joshi points out that Lovecraft, "who in his letters and essays expressed prejudice against African Americans, Jews, and other minorities throughout his life, was dismayed by the isolation amidst masses of 'foreigners' in the city" (xi). Joshi is exactly right in bringing our attention to the connection between Lovecraft's views on race and his personal sense of isolation.

The connection between Lovecraft's prejudices and his own circumstances is one of the paradoxes of Lovecraft's life and fiction. Untangling this paradox from his biography and written words leads us to the causes of Lovecraft's loneliness. His mother's and father's hospitalization for mental illness coupled with the decaying finances and status of his family name made Lovecraft a penniless and solitary anachronism in a very genteel Providence. Lovecraft dwelt on the cusp of two realms: the ivied walls of Brown University with its campus and surrounding neighborhood of Georgian and Victorian mansions and the pre-Revolutionary houses of Benefit Street, which had become the ramshackle dwellings of immigrants. Lovecraft could not afford to live in the whitest of neighborhoods, so racial otherness was located literally just outside his door, on his doorstep, so to speak. The juxtaposition of European immigrants living in the houses of English settlers is mirrored in "The Shadow over Innsmouth," and this story and others prove that architecture becomes one of the many constructs of race in Lovecraft's fiction. With neither money nor an Ivy-league education, Lovecraft could never court the company of those with whom he claimed the closest alliance, for (regardless of his family name) in terms of social status he was beneath their contempt. Lovecraft's creation of Arkham, then, is a coping-mechanism, a place in which his characters (his virtual selves) have access to the places in Providence that were off-limits to him: Miskatonic University (Brown) and the Miskatonic Club (a combination of the University, Hope, and Brown Faculty clubs and others). Lovecraft's Arkham is also a place in which non-whites are demonized, alien presences on the doorstep of the bastions of white privilege.

Although Lovecraft embarks on tirades tinged with prejudice against immigrants and gays, on one level he deeply identified with their state as outcasts. Like Lovecraft, they were barred from the upper echelons of society. This affinity with the marginalized citizens of Providence existed on a partially conscious and largely subconscious level, and its juxtaposition with Lovecraft's social striving to regain the aristocratic privileges he deemed his birthright created several f(r)ictions. Lovecraft's Providence of colonial architecture was under siege by diversity: Fox Point was becoming a largely Portuguese and Cape Verdean community; Sessions Street a Jewish community; Camp Street, a predominantly African American community; and Federal Hill, a community populated by immigrants from Sicily and mainland Italy. With these demographics in mind the plots of Lovecraft's stories can be seen to hinge on notions of race. In fact, his creation of the Cthulhu can be read in part as an attempt to create a civilization that predated the ancient ones of Egypt, Mesopotamia, China, and Rome.

In many ways this racial fiction is similar to the ones fabricated by the Nazi party (in which Lovecraft expressed a keen, sympathetic interest) to link the Aryans to the ancient people of Atlantis. Similarly, Lovecraft associates the Maine woods with American Indians by calling it "Chesuncook," the name of an actual town in Maine, but also by referencing

> terrible meetings in lonely places, . . . [and] Cyclopean ruins in the heart of the Maine woods beneath which vast staircases lead down to abysses of knighted secrets, of complex angles that lead through invisible walls to other regions of space and time, and of hideous exchanges of per-

sonality that permitted explorations in remote and forbidden places, on other worlds, and in different space-time continua.

By describing pre-American Indian cultural presences through these ruins, Lovecraft attempts to overwrite the New England wilderness and remove all traces, save the place name, of specific American Indian presence. Derby (temporarily possessed by Asenath) tries to allay Upton's suspicions about the trip into the wilderness by saying that this "trip was a bit queer, but it's really very simple. There are certain Indian relics in the north woods—standing stones, and all that—which mean a good deal in folklore, and Asenath and I are following that stuff up." The reader and Upton, however, know that the rites in the wilderness are cosmic, not American Indian, in their origin. In doing so, his story aligns itself with hundred-year old pseudo-cultural and physical anthropology and archeology—such as Josiah Priest's *American Antiquities* (1830)—that sought to attribute the ancient structures in New England and other parts of America to the Welsh, the Danes, and any other people that were not American Indian.[3] By making these ancient structures a gateway to the cosmic as well as the sites of pagan religious rites, Lovecraft attempts to give these theories a modern spin and authority by combining them with the astrophysics of his day to create a blend of ancient and cosmic otherness. The politics of the nineteenth-century pseudo-anthropological claims that Lovecraft draws on is clear: these "findings" represent an attempt to justify "Manifest Destiny" through a claim that a European presence predated a Native American one in America. Lovecraft aligns himself with earlier New England writers such as William Cullen Bryant, whose poem "The Prairies" claimed that the American Indians removed the earlier race through massacre, thereby attempting to justify westward expansion as a reclaiming of lands. By merely hinting at the presence of the early Republic's slaughter of American Indians to imbue the wilderness with a Gothic effect, Lovecraft is writing in the problematic tradition of Bryant, Hawthorne ("Young Goodman Brown" and *The Scarlet Letter*), and James Fenimore Cooper.

Lovecraft was troubled by the presence of not just African Americans and Native Americans, but also any non-Anglo immi-

3. More information can be found on nineteenth-century America's racist pseudo-science in *Documents of American Prejudice*, ed. S. T. Joshi.

grants to America. Take, for instance, "The Haunter in the Dark," in which the mysterious shadow of evil originates in a (Roman Catholic) church in the Italian neighborhood of Federal Hill and spreads over to Lovecraft's house on the edge of Brown University. Yet, interestingly enough, it is Robert Blake's obsession with the haunter in the dark that leads to his demise. The haunter so dominates his waking moments that he eventually occupies a space on the cusp of reality and the haunter's realm. Several of Lovecraft's characters are hybrids, existing halfway between races and genders. As discussed above, Edward Derby is a man of a very prominent New England family who ends up marrying and fusing his identity with Asenath Waite, a "dark" woman of a town where there was a "strange element 'not quite human'" mixed in the blood of its people. The thing that appears on the narrator's doorstep is also "not quite human," not quite man or woman, neither Anglo-American nor racially other.

In a recent article, David Simmons draws a connection between Lovecraft's ethnocentrism and the story "Facts Concerning the Late Arthur Jermyn and His Family":

> It is suggested that Arthur's untimely demise is due [to his] receiving an African artefact of horrific origins, a correlation that reflects Lovecraft's own anxieties concerning racial hybridisation. Talking of the immigrant population of New York's lower East Side Lovecraft suggests that "The organic things—Italo—Semitico—Mongoloid—inhabiting that awful cesspool could not by any stretch of the imagination be call'd human." (94)

Simmons and S. T. Joshi are two of few scholars who have considered the ways in which Lovecraft's personal identity as well as those of his characters are informed by his notion of England. Simmons delineates this construct by quoting Lovecraft's 1 April 1927 letter to James F. Morton: "If I could create an ideal world, it would be an England with the fire of the Elizabethans, the correct taste of the Georgians, and the refinement and pure ideals of the Victorians" (*SL* 1.123). We need not search very long to find Lovecraft's awareness of structural flaws in his assemblage of "Englands": for instance, Oscar Wilde's life and works in Lovecraft's estimation do not show forth the "pure ideals of the Victorians." His stories, then, are not the realization of this ideal world, but the exploration of the cracks and fissures in its foundation. As noted above, he creates a fictional "(New) England" as an escape from (1) the poverty that barred his access to wealthy Anglo-American society and (2) the multiculturalism of early twentieth-century Providence. In his works, Lovecraft seems to be telling his readers and himself, in the words of Salman Rushdie, that "we will not be capable of reclaiming precisely the thing that was lost; that we will, in short, create fictions, not actual cities or villages, but invisible ones, imaginary homelands" (10). Lovecraft's stories are filled with these invisible and imaginary cities, from Arkham to Sarnath

To account for the "Shadow of England" in Lovecraft's works, Simmons draws on Mikhail Bakhtin's theory of "the chronotope" as well as Hayden White's concept of "Metahistory." While these concepts are certainly a useful means of understanding the connections between the temporal and spatial dimensions as well as the historicity of the construct of Englishness in Lovecraft's work, they do not fully cover the fault lines of Lovecraft's "England." In addition to Bakhtin's "chronotope" and White's "Metahistory," Homi Bhabha's notions of "hybridity" and "interruption" as well as Edward Said's concept of "exile" offer a fuller picture of the centrality of race and gender to Lovecraft's fiction(al New "Englands"). In "DissemiNation," Bhabha notes that the lives and stories of diverse residents of, say, England interrupt the attempt of the white power structure to create and perpetuate myths of racial purity through works of literature, creating an imaginatively embellished past—such as that of Arthurian lore and legend. Lovecraft's Arkham is to a degree a New England that is a direct extension of the "Olde England" of the Elizabethans, Georgians, and Victorians. Lovecraft's main characters are often of English stock, such as Edward Pickman Derby. Just as the diversity of Providence "interrupts" Lovecraft's notion of New England, multicultural Arkham manifests in Lovecraft's narratives, haunting them with fears of miscegenation and racial "otherness." The result is characters and worlds that can best be understood by Bhabha's notion of "hybridity" and Lovecraft's struggle to accept the fact that New England is (and was) not (ever) consanguineous and culturally contiguous with "Olde England," but since the arrival of colonizers has been a transnational site of cultural contact, contestation, and combination.

Edward Said's notion of exile is equally important to an understanding of Lovecraft's fiction, especially Said's concept that the idea of a homeland is inextricably linked to an author's sense of exile.

Thus, the writer who perceives himself or herself to be in exile occupies a hybrid mental state, one neither fully within the borders of the parent country or the country of exile. As Simmons points out, Lovecraft's love of the United Kingdom resulted in his cultivating an "Englishness" that informed everything from the style of his dress to the style of his writing (epistles, fiction, and poetry). "'England' comes to function [. . .]," notes Simmons, "as a utopian location encompassing Lovecraft's conservative, elitist, and almost proto-Leavisite desire for a greater level of gentility, refinement, and high-culture" (90). "Of his more immediate contemporaries," continues Simmons,

> Lovecraft regarded the British fantasy writers Lord Dunsany, Arthur Machen, and Montague Rhode James highly. Lovecraft called James "a literary weird fictionist of the very first rank", favoured Dunsany's integration of a poetical style in prose, and was greatly enamoured of Machen's construction of a natural landscape imbued with the fantastical. [. . .] As Lovecraft stated in a letter to Frank Belknap Long dated June 3, 1923: "Dunsany is *myself*, plus an art and cultivation infinitely greater." (90–91)

Just as Lovecraft would trace his ancestors by blood back to the United Kingdom, he traced his ancestors by ink there as well, imagining himself and certain writers of England, Scotland, Wales, and Ireland as one literary family. As with his constructs of ethnic identity, this one is not without its paradoxes. As Simmons notes, Lovecraft stylistically distanced himself from most contemporary American writers, such as Ernest Hemingway and F. Scott Fitzgerald, but identified with earlier American writers such as Poe. What Simmons does not note is that the high culture of old and New England did not hold Lovecraft's genre of choice in very high esteem. The Gothic and romance were viewed with great suspicion by cultural elitists, but these genres' most recent offshoot, the "weird tale," was held by them to be in a class of speciousness all its own. Thus, Lovecraft's personal, familial, and authorial connection to England was a quest for legitimacy in response to the British and Anglo-Americans who looked down upon his means and means of employment.

II

Dream's Architecture and the Genealogy of the Weird Tale:
Sexuality and Race in 18th- and 19th-Century Gothic

This next section moves quickly through Lovecraft's predecessors identifying pieces that Lovecraft reassembles in his mosaic of short stories.
The essay ends with a final look at "The Thing on the Doorstep," and
after devoting necessary space to the elements of Lovecraft's life and
reading that influenced his writing, this essay concludes with a brief
glance at some of the works Lovecraft influenced. In his creation of a
racial Gothic sublime that has cultural legitimacy, Lovecraft traces his
fictional roots back to the nineteenth century. Bram Stoker's *Dracula*
(1897) can be read as a xenophobic novel concerned with the mixing
of Dracula's Transylvanian blood with that of the people of England.
Stoker's Lucy Westenra, like Lovecraft's Edward Derby, becomes a hybrid human/vampire who is possessed by racial otherness. Ephraim
Waite is a reworking of Count Dracula, a new-age vampire, who uses a
cosmic mesmerism rather than bloody fangs to gain eternal life: "On,
on, on, on—body to body to body—he means never to die. The life-
glow—he knows how to break the link. . . . It can flicker on a while
even when the body is dead." "Ephraim-Asenath is a subtle Lovecraftian mixture of the female vamp and the male vampire," notes Matolcsy; "since Asenath is a parasite of the body—she is contagious in her
disintegrating state—while Ephraim trains his abnormally strong will
by preying on the consciousness of others—he is twentieth century
American version of Bram Stoker's undead" (176).

For Stoker and Lovecraft, the Gothic becomes a means of discussing not only racial taboos but also sexual ones, as the vampire comes
to represent repressed erotic dreams (as he also does nearly a century
later in Francis Ford Coppola's film version and in Anne Rice's Les-
tat) most notably in *Dracula*'s early scenes: when Jonathan Harker
falls asleep in Castle Dracula and has an erotic dream of an encounter
with three undead women, and in later scenes in which the sleeping
Lucy Westenra is sexually and supernaturally preyed upon by the
Count. Chapter seven of the novel is peppered with language connot-
ing same-sex attraction. Dracula is xenophobia (re)incarnate, as his
Transylvanian teeth adulterate the blood of the British belles, Lucy
and Mina. Harker is also at risk of becoming contaminated when he is

visited in his nightmare by "three young women," two of whom
"were dark, and had high aquiline noses, like the Count, and great
dark, piercing eyes that seemed to be almost red when contrasted
with the pale yellow moon. The other was fair, as fair as can be"
(Stoker 39). The two women, like Dracula, are racially "other" to
Jonathan Harker, and are portrayed as demonic. In Lovecraft's tales,
dream is viewed as a border state between waking and death and sun-
sets and sunrises are, of course, border states between night and day
(as in Stoker's *Dracula*). As this comparison illustrates, another crucial aspect of understanding sexuality in Lovecraft's works is understanding that it is inextricably linked with notions of race,
architecture, and dreaming.

The ways in which sexuality is bound up with architecture,
dreams, and race in Lovecraft's works is not a combination that he
creates *ex nihilo*, but rather takes the forms of tropes and plotlines
that he incorporates from earlier writers, appearing in his tales in
transformed, albeit recognizable, configurations. In addition, then, to
considering Lovecraft's life, we must also survey Lovecraft's predecessors in Gothic, horror, and supernatural writing and how they use
tropes of dreaming to examine race and sexuality and how these literary conventions influence Lovecraft. Placing Lovecraft's writing on
a continuum with earlier writers allows us to see how he modifies,
adopts, subverts, and supersedes these existing tropes in his fiction.
Lovecraft often builds citations to other texts into his tales through
tropes of haunting and possession. The earlier writers are figured as
spectral or buried presences. Ironically enough, Lovecraft's utilization
of tropes or metaphors of haunting and possession to indicate the influence of earlier (often deceased) authors is itself a borrowed trope,
their convention of "haunting" haunting the architecture of his stories.

Just as Lovecraft's association of same-sex attraction with dreams
has a precedent in Stoker, so too does his use of architecture as representative of the mind as well as race and sexuality anticipated by
Stoker and many others. The parallel between architecture (or geology) of haunted structures and the haunted rooms (caverns) of the
mind that house nightmares and dreams is a trope with foundations
in Walpole's *The Castle of Otranto* (1764), Coleridge's "Kubla Khan"
([1803] 1816) and *Christabel* ([1800] 1816), Keats's *Eve of St. Agnes*
(1820), Thomas Love Peacock's *Nightmare Abbey* (1818), Jane Austen's *Northanger Abbey* (1818), Poe's "Ligeia," Hawthorne's *The House*

of Seven Gables (1851), Charlotte Brontë's *Jane Eyre* (1847), Emily Brontë's *Wuthering Heights* (1847), Lewis Carroll's *Alice's Adventures in Wonderland* (1865) and *Through the Looking Glass, and What Alice Found There* (1871), Stoker's *Dracula.* As Matolcsy has pointed out, "The Thing on the Doorstep" reverses the Gothic convention of a helpless and distressed damsel's being trapped in a ruined architectural structure: "we do not see a young woman pursued by a man and incarcerated in a ruin, but a young man, pursued by and incarcerated within the body of a woman, or, more precisely, the ruins of a female body" (173).

The use of dreams and nightmares in early Gothic and proto-horror writing anticipates an aspect of the Freudian subconscious—the id. Writers such as M. G. "Monk" Lewis used the dream as a means of expressing taboo sexuality, especially in *The Monk*'s (1796) depiction of Ambrosio's magically lulling the fifteen-year-old Antonia to sleep in order to rape what he eventually assumes is her dead body, combining the taboos of both pedophilia and necrophilia. Samuel Taylor Coleridge used the dream as a means to suggest another form of taboo sexuality—lesbian desire; his poem *Christabel* contains a scene in which the heroine for whom the poem is named awakes after sleeping in the arms of the vampirelike Geraldine and says," Sure, I have sinned" (l. 381). John Keats's *The Eve of St. Agnes* unfolds a Gothic verse narrative of star-crossed lovers, of Porphyro who sneaks into Madeline's room and attempts to seduce her while she is dreaming. A similar scene of sleep and seduction occurs in *Goblin Market* (1862), a poem in which Christina Rossetti grapples with mid-Victorian, Anglo-Catholic constructs of sexuality, a poem that associates same-sex attraction with the demonic influence of the goblins, especially as illustrated by Dante Gabriel Rossetti's frontispiece for the 1862 edition, an engraving depicting Laura and Lizzy sleeping in each other's arms and dreaming of the evil goblins; after Laura partakes of the goblins' fruits, she sleeps with Lizzie—"Golden head by golden head. . . . / Cheek to cheek and breast to breast / Locked together in one nest" (ll. 184–98)—and spends the next day "in an absent dream" and "longing for the night" (ll. 184–214).

Where we find expressions of taboo sexuality we also find expressions of racial otherness. For example, when Coleridge describes heightened states of imagination, the Orientalism in his writing comes into play, especially in "Kubla Khan; or, A Vision in a Dream" when he locates the dreamlike primary imagination in Xanadu and equates Xanadu with opium. De Quincey's *Confessions of an English Opium-Eater* sets opium-induced Gothic nightmares in Asia and equates opium use with the Malay. According to Coleridge's prose introduction to "Kubla Khan," he awoke from an "anodyne"-induced dream (of a "woman wailing for her demon lover" and an "Abyssinian maid"), thus writing a poem rife with the language of drug addiction and withdrawal, as well as sex. The "anodyne" is opium, a drug with imperial implications and often associated with dreamlike states of mind. It is no coincidence that Edgar Allan Poe also uses a Coleridgean narrator in "Ligeia" (1838), the story of a man who, while watching over his slumbering wife, Rowena, the second love he is about to lose to death, experiences "wild visions, opium-engendered," of Rowena taking on the features of his first bride, Ligeia, who had eyes "far larger than the eyes of our own race . . .[,] even fuller than the fullest of the gazelle eyes of the tribe of the valley of Nourjahad" (1459, 1452). Ligeia is reanimated yet again by Lovecraft, who was believed by many to have dreamed all his stories.

In "The Thing on the Doorstep," Edward Pickman Derby begins to take on the characteristics of the wife, Asenath, whom he murdered with his own hand. Asenath is able to possess her husband from beyond the grave through her dreamlike power of mesmerism. Crucial here to understanding the connection between dreamlike states of mind and racial as well as gender otherness is realizing that Asenath's power is what transforms Derby from an Anglo-American man to a (wo)man of color. According to Derby, "[Ephraim, her father] changed forms with her when he felt death coming—she was the only one he could find with the right kind of brain and weak enough will—he got her body permanently [. . .] and then poisoned the old body he put her into." If this passage were not included in the story, it would be difficult to know exactly when Ephraim's possession of Asenath occurs.

If we accept Derby's explanation of when the possession occurred, we must consider that Ephraim (or rather, Ephraim's body) died "just before his daughter entered the Hall School." It becomes clear, then, that when Asenath "displayed snatches of knowledge and language very singular—and very shocking—for a young girl; when she would frighten her schoolmates with leers and winks of an inexplicable kind," this was really Ephraim acting through his daughter. A close consideration of the story's chronology reveals that Asenath herself is really a very minor character. Her sad fate is only alluded to by Lovecraft, and it is exactly that of Derby: sealed in a dying corpse. It appears, at first glance, that this defeminization of the female means that this story is not about a woman at all. Ephraim is in full possession of Asenath for nearly the entire story. It is certainly significant that "The Thing on the Doorstep" is the only story Lovecraft wrote that features a female main character. (Once again, we find a paranormal state of mind—not dream in this instance, but possession—being utilized by Lovecraft to signal a border state between the Anglo-American and racial otherness.) As Ephraim possesses the body of Asenath and then of Derby, he becomes a symbol of gender and racial hybridity. Lovecraft describes Asenath as "dark . . . [with] over-proturberant eyes." As Cannon notes, "Asenath calls to mind Lovecraft's wife Sonia," and perhaps Lovecraft's own anti-Semitic sentiments toward his Jewish wife (*More Annotated Lovecraft* 247–49). Despite Lovecraft's marriage to Sonia and his friendship with Loveman, his anti-Semitism, homophobia, and racism are a recurring theme in his tales; the dreams and paranormal states of consciousness he describes serve as a conduit of racial otherness and cosmic horror into the Anglo-Saxon psyche of his protagonists.

III

The Possessive Case of Howard Phillips Lovecraft:
Sexuality, (Inter)Textuality, Reading, Writing, and Literary Influence
as Haunting and Possession

Lovecraft's border figures represent not only the liminal spaces between Anglo-Americans and racial "others," but also between man and women as well as straightness and gayness. With the constraints of propriety during Lovecraft's time, the marriage between Asenath/Ephraim and Edward is about as close as he could come to depicting a same-sex affair. Lovecraft once paid a visit to Robert Barlow, who was to become his literary executor, in St. Augustine. The fact that gay or bisexual men later came to edit and present Lovecraft to the literary world raises a number of interesting questions: What was it about Lovecraft and his writing that drew these particular men to it and to him? Were they performing some of the earliest "queer readings" of Lovecraft's works when they first read them and later edited them? As they rescue the decaying corpus of Lovecraft's work and revive it through editing it, even as it captivated them the first time they read it, does it go through a similar process as that of Asenath and Derby? Does the trope of possession and haunted structures (narrative, fictional, architectural, mental, and corporeal) in "The Thing on the Doorstep" and other Lovecraft tales function as a metaphor for reading and literary influence? Interestingly, Harold Bloom's theory of "anxiety of influence" contains a phase called *apophrades* (or return of the dead) in which an author who is long dead takes control over the mind and compositions of a younger author or reader. This theory aptly describes Poe's influence on Lovecraft and, in turn, Lovecraft's influence on Derleth.

It would not be entirely unprecedented if Lovecraft were, in "The Thing on the Doorstep," presenting a fictionalized interpretation of one of his predecessor's texts. Witness "The Rats in the Walls," Lovecraft's tipping of his hat to Poe. As has been pointed out by S. T. Joshi and other critics, the name of the main character in "Rats," de la *Poe*r contains Poe's first and middle initials as well as last name. And just as the beating heart under the floorboards in Poe's "Tell-Tale Heart" reveals a hidden male presence, so too do the bones under the foundation of de la Poer's abbey and the foundation of Lovecraft's plot structures (which reveal Poe's presence whose works Lovecraft has cannibalized). Lovecraft notes that "Ephraim lived in a half-decayed mansion" that represents his mind living in his half-decayed body. Always looking for a more suitable structure in which to live, characters are just as often trapped in houses as they are in bodies, and the two are metaphorically connected:

> Oddly, the metamorphosis did not seem altogether pleasing. People said he looked too much like his wife, or like old Ephraim Waite himself. . . . He now wished to move back into the old Derby mansion, but Asenath insisted on staying in the Crowninshield house, to which she had become well adjusted.
>
> Not long afterward my wife heard a curious thing from a friend—one of the few who had not dropped the Derbys. She had been out to the end of High St. to call on the couple, and had seen a car shoot briskly out of the drive with Edward's oddly confident and almost sneering face above the wheel. Ringing the bell, she had been told by

the repulsive wench that Asenath was also out; but had chanced to look up at the house in leaving. There, at one of Edward's library windows, she had glimpsed a hastily withdrawn face—a face whose expression of pain, defeat, and wistful hopelessness was poignant beyond description. It was—incredibly enough in view of its usual domineering cast—Asenath's; yet the caller had vowed that in that instant the sad, muddled eyes of poor Edward were gazing out from it.

Lovecraft's stories, such as "The Shunned House" and others, are about (1) exhuming male presences, whether spectral or physical, underneath structures or (2) about characters' being possessed by others.

All these scenarios are easily read as metaphors for a predecessor influencing a later author, the influence taking the form of possession or of a presence buried or lurking underneath a (plot) structure. The presence of male authors, such as Poe and Wilde, lurking in the subtexts of Lovecraft's story has already been demonstrated. However, literary predecessors are not the only ones who can possess and haunt an author; contemporary authors can haunt each other as well. Lovecraft's "Haunter in the Dark" is a response to a story by his contemporary Robert Bloch. Not only is the story dedicated to Bloch, but he appears in the story as the character Robert Blake. Blake is identifiable not only as Bloch, but also as Lovecraft. Interestingly, Blake is housed in a fictional version of the house Lovecraft actually lived in "on the crest of the great eastward hill near the Brown University campus and behind the marble John Hay Library" (DH 93–94). We do well to recall Lovecraft's comments about the British writer Lord Dunsany (1878–1957): "Dunsany is *myself*, plus an art and cultivation infinitely greater." Lovecraft's exchanging souls, identities, and literary homes with British and American predecessors and contemporaries is a convention in his stories, a trapdoor in their architecture that is discernible upon careful examination. His stories contain "in-jokes," so to speak, self-reflexive moments, literary allusions, and references that were recognizable to friends (such as Bloch) as well as those familiar with earlier and contemporary weird and gothic tales.

It should not come as a surprise that Derby's being possessed by Ephraim and Asenath Waite and taking on recognizable characteristics of his possessors takes place within a story that is itself possessed by pre-existing stories of possession, notably those by British authors Barry Pain (1864–1928) and H. B. Drake (1894–1963). In Pain's *An Ex-*

change of Souls (1911), for instance, the scientist Daniel Myas dies during an experimental attempt to exchange souls with his wife and assistant Alice Lade. As Joshi notes in the introduction to his edition of Pain's novella, Lovecraft's story contains recognizable characteristics of *An Exchange of Souls:* "One final detail that may clinch the hypothesis that Lovecraft did indeed read Pain's book and learn from it is in the strikingly similar use of the telephone at the conclusion of both tales" (Pain 8). In *Exchange*, the narrator is up late reading when he receives two phone calls from the departed, one in which the speaker on the other end of the line says matter-of-factly, "I am Daniel Myas and I am Alice Lade" (99). The next phone call contains unintelligible words, save the word "Cannot" repeated twice (100). Similarly, the narrator of "Doorstep" receives a call from Edward who is trapped in the decaying corpse of Asenath and is thus only able to repeat *"glub"* on the other end of the line. Pain's plotline is imprisoned in the architecture of Lovecraft's tale, and the phone call it is allowed is, well, a phone call. In one of the most clever, and self-reflexive literary allusions, Lovecraft employs a telephone to convey proof of (literary) possession and a cryptic message from beyond the grave (a communication from a past author), as Pain had passed away in 1928, five years before the writing of "Doorstep."

Lovecraft's alluding to other authors and their works implies that fiction is a medium through which one can switch or share personalities with other authors. This ability is not limited to the authors of weird tales, but also extends to readers (those who interpret literature and the text of one's own "story"). The subtext of Pain's novella and Lovecraft's tale is that the exchange of personalities or souls is a metaphor for the change that can potentially be brought about through experience and interpretation of texts (of memory), and for Pain this change of perspective is not unrelated to issues of gender. To demonstrate the power of reading, Lovecraft's stories as well as Pain's novella contain scenes that depict characters' reading and interpreting a variety of texts from literature to newspapers to performances to the actions of other characters. These scenes mirror the actions of the stories' actual readers who are interpreting Lovecraft and Pain's works.

It is noteworthy that within a novella that portrays transgender characters (and thus pushes the envelope of what is acceptable to the heteronormative propriety of its time) there should be a discussion of the propriety of the portrayal of gender switching:

I have occasionally seen, when for my sins I have been taken to a music-hall, a performance which is, I believe, intended to be amusing and funny—the impersonation of a woman by a man. It is a thing which always disgusts me. The more cleverly it is done, the more loathsome it is. If I happen to see that item on ahead in the programme, I take care to be out of sight and sound of it. I do not know if this is a special peculiarity or weakness of my own, but it helped to add to the difficulty of what I had to do. I had been the friend of Myas, and I had been the friend of Alice Lade. Whatever was waiting for me behind the door of the laboratory had a claim upon me. I, a plain, conventional, and unimaginative man, as Myas had described me, had by sheer force of circumstances been drawn into a very whirlpool of horror and morbidity. I had to go through the mud. (76)

It is also implied that what is waiting behind the door of the laboratory (and in Lovecraft's story, the doorstep) has a claim on the reader, who has unwittingly entered into an examination of a topic deemed taboo: transgender and transsexuality. By the end of the story, the narrator (and perhaps the reader) accepts the revelation that Myas and Lade have in fact become the same soul in the afterlife, thus revealing the gender to be an earthly and to a degree cultural construct. This epiphany is in sharp contradistinction to Lade/Myas' moral interpretation of the result of the experiment, for when the narrator speaks to the soul of Myas in the body of Lade, he tells them, "you have done something which is against Nature." "That is exactly it. And Nature punishes," replies Lade/Myas (83). Thus Pain leaves the morality of gender as ambiguous as the gender of Lade/Myas. "Neither Pain nor Lovecraft addresses the potentially bizarre possibilities of gender-switching," writes Joshi; "if anything, Pain is a bit more forthright on the subject than the sexually repressed Lovecraft could allow himself to be" (Pain 8). Indeed, Pain's description of Myas's hands as "rather too white and well shaped" (11) is a more direct transgendering of his character than Lovecraft's noting that Derby was unable grow a moustache. Pain portrays Myas's effeminacy through references to his diet, dress, and physical features. Pain's more forthright portrayal of transgender characters does lead to more of a moral examination of gender than is undertaken by Lovecraft.

Lovecraft's being influenced by reading the works of his predecessors is mirrored in "The Thing on the Doorstep" by Derby's delving "deep into the actual runes and riddles left by a fabulous past for the guidance and puzzlement of posterity. He read things like . . . the forbidden *Necronomicon* of the mad Arab Abdul Alhazred, though he did not tell his parents he had seen them." Derby's reading represents his dalliance with the forbidden, with racial and religious "otherness" outside of the scope of his Anglo and Anglican upbringing. It also reveals another racially "other "male whose ideas come to possess Derby, as it is the *Necronomicon* that contains the formula that allows Ephraim to possess Asenath and Derby. Lovecraft's anxiety of the soporific effects of tracing the characters of his predecessors' writing too closely is evident in his explanation of the way Derby's writing was too much under the spell of the texts he had been reading, which "had slowed down his literary growth by making his products derivative and overbookish."

As one male author begets the next, there is a *homotextuality* and hybridity present in the intertextuality of these works. However, the literary and spiritual possession is also one that overwrites the presence of women authors and characters. If Ephraim does replace Asenath, then this is in line with a number of sexist male texts in which women are replaced. Mary Shelley's *Frankenstein* is a protest against this very aspect of literature as Victor, the typical Romantic male author who wants to save the world, creates another male, thereby (as Anne Mellor has pointed out) replacing women's role in pregnancy and childbirth. Authors during Shelley's time, such as Monk Lewis and Ann Radcliffe, for instance, had stitched together bits of earlier plots by other male writers such as Horace Walpole. The intertextuality of *Frankenstein*, with its allusions to the works of Mary Shelley's father, William Godwin, and her husband, P. B. Shelley, not to mention their editing and introducing the text, make it a women's text that is possessed by male presences. Interestingly, Mary Shelley's novel reverses this process by reworking of another tale by a male: Coleridge's *The Rime of the Ancient Mariner* (1798). Like Shelley's novel, this poem contains the framing device of a story within a story, and the moral of each tale is contingent upon the correct interpretation of the listener: just as the wedding guest rises a sadder and wiser man after listening to the mariner's tale, Walton heeds the wishes of his crew and abandons his wild ambitions after hearing Victor's tale. Equally, the MS to whom Walton's letters are addressed reads and interprets the tale and we as the readers of her letters are their last recipients. So, the monstrous qualities of Coleridge's mariner, Shelley's creature, and Lovecraft's animated corpse of Asenath are meant to function as a warning, an admonishment (as the root word of "monster" implies). Matolcsy's interpretation of Asenath-Edward's warning is as follows:

> The Asenath body, the empty feminine shell is an animated monster in its own right, too. The monstrous mind and the monstrous body are incapable of total unification, since within the self's boundaries their heavily gendered identities, instead of exulting in each other's presence, thrust each other toward disintegration. [. . .] Lovecraft's tale is one such horrific representation [. . . of] the androgyne's disruption, both physiological and psychic, fits perfectly well his early twentieth-century view of cosmic indifference and belief in the ultimate failure of any harmony, totality, and unity of being. (177–78)

IV

"On, on, on, on—[story] to [story]—he means never to die": Lovecraft's Literary Afterlives

As is demonstrated above, Lovecraft's stories are influenced by numerous Gothic authors, this influence being a literary from of possession. Lovecraft also goes on to possess more than a few authors whose works are possessed not only by his works, but also by the works that possessed him; Anne Rice's *The Tale of the Body Thief* (1992) is influenced by Stoker and, as S. T. Joshi has pointed out, "The Thing on the Doorstep" (*Modern Weird Tale* 239). Additionally, the homoeroticism between an older man and a young man that is only implicit in "Doorstep" is explicit in Rice's *The Vampire Armand* (1998), in which sexuality and race are linked to architecture and predatory vampirism. The notion featuring two male characters among whom there is homoerotic attraction, which pushes one over the edge to commit a heinous crime is repeated, as is Lovecraft's demonization of gayness, in the recent films *The Talented Mr. Ripley* (1999) and *Hannibal* (2001). The cross-dressed male who has a problematic relationship with his deceased mother is repeated most famously in Alfred Hitchcock's *Psycho* (1960). Lovecraft's depiction of a fear of powerful women is not unique, and is a part of many stories and films, such as *The Attack of the 50 Foot Woman* (1958).

With a little consideration, even a partial list of Lovecraft spinoffs becomes unwieldy, especially with regard to tropes of architecture and dreaming that reference race and sexuality. Dreams and nightmares figure prominently in many of Stephen King's works (*The Dead Zone* [1979], *The Dark Half* [1989], *Nightmares & Dreamscapes* [1993], and, ironically enough, *Insomnia* [1994]); in *'Salem's Lot* (1975), King also makes use of another longstanding convention of dreams in supernatural literature: Shirley Jackson's *The Haunting of Hill House* (1959), William Peter Blatty's *The Exorcist* (1971), Jay Anson's *The Amityville Horror* (1978), Stephen Mark Rainey and Elizabeth Massie's *Dreams of the Park* (1999), and many more. Stephen King's "Jerusalem's Lot" (1978) carefully weaves many of Lovecraft's tales together, especially "The Haunter of the Dark" (1935) and "The Rats in the Walls" (1924). The tales portray storylines and bloodlines of families inextricably and atavistically linked to Gothic structures. These tales also blend architecture and dreams together by leading the reader down "the nightmare corridors of delirium" ("Jerusalem's Lot"; *Tales of the Cthulhu Mythos* 433).

In "Concerning Dreams and Nightmares," an introductory essay to a volume of Lovecraft, Neil Gaiman lays out the architecture and geography of Lovecraft's fiction according to border states, or more precisely, bordering cities—the topography of Minneapolis and St. Paul, Minnesota; the Mississippi River that divides them; and Interstate Highway 94, the corridor that connects the Twin Cities of dream and nightmare: "If literature is the world, then Fantasy and Horror are twin cities, divided by a river of black water. . . . And if Horror and Fantasy are cities, then H. P. Lovecraft is the kind of long street that runs from the outskirts of the first city to the end of the other. It began as a minor thoroughfare, and is now a six-lane highway, built up on every side" (*Dreams of Terror and Death* vii). If Lovecraft has created such a long sextuple carriageway between the Cities of Fantasy and Horror, then Gaiman has extended that inner-state highway "into the darkness beyond" (xii) and into a neighboring state of mind: the Dreaming, itself a vast and ever-changing architectural structure in its own worlds. In Stephen King's introduction to Gaiman's *World's End* (1994), he points out the reference to *Dracula* in the volume, and that the stories in *The Sandman* series take the reader "away to worlds that never existed." Gaiman also notes while introducing Lovecraft that "A Tale of Two Cities," the first story in *World's End*, is one of his most Lovecraftian stories (x).

In this story of the twin cities of reality and dream, Gaiman works Lovecraft's city of dream, Kadath, into the dream of a city. The story also critiques the dream of a nation, the American dream, as it shows the disillusionment of a man who has achieved the job in the big city, but wanders the streets by night and day in search of solace. One evening, after working long hours, he takes the sub(conscious)way home and ends up traveling magically into the city's dream, where he remains trapped for years. Just as Poe lurks in the architecture beneath Lovecraft's architectural and literary structures, Lovecraft haunts the nether-realms beneath Gaiman's city. The postmodern parable ends with man's warning of the day the city ever wakes. Originally published serially as individual comic books, the Sandman's sojourns have been collected into a ten-volume set of graphic novels, which presents the fragmented narratives as one story arc. Collected in this way, the story seems to have all the segmentation, disjointedness, and surreal qualities of a dream; its form matches its content. Like Lovecraft's stories, Gaiman's tales deal with issues pertaining to turn of century advances in science that threaten to rupture human identity as it is known. Gaiman's storyline also accurately represents the fragmentation and simultaneity of reality, a postmodern reality in which people can move in and out of several realms of representation, some more dreamlike than others: film, television, telephone, internet, and virtual reality. Dreaming in Lovecraft is linked to science and the cosmic, replacing the religious beliefs of Christianity, and Gaiman brings this brief tour through the realms of dream full circle by presenting the death of Dream. In a Nietzsche-like (as well as Lovecraftian) twist at the end of the series, Dream, not God, is dead, and the Devil has retired, leaving Dream with a nightmare on (and the key to Hell in) his hands. Dream, of course, does not remain dead long, but is reincarnated in a way that makes him a postmodern Christ, and a remaking of Ephraim, just as Ephraim is a reworking of Dracula. With Morpheus alive and well once again, the future of dreams and nightmares in supernatural literature remains secure; however, "what dreams may come," to appropriate Hamlet's line, in twenty-first-century literature the Sandman surely knows, but only his brother, Time, will tell.

A discussion of Lovecraft's haunting presence in graphic novels would not be complete without a discussion of Hans Rodionoff, Enrique Breccia, and Keith Griffen's *Lovecraft* (2003), who seek to haunt readers with Lovecraft in the way that he was haunted by his reading:

The blurb on the dust-jacket queries: "Were these visions of horror only in his mind, or could he see into a world that couldn't be seen? . . . Either way the story of America's greatest horror writer is a tale as haunting as the demons that plagued him." It is also essential to end with a discussion of *Lovecraft* because it forges a link between Lovecraft and (homo)sexuality in the popular imaginary, especially among his past and present devotees. John Carpenter, who introduces *Lovecraft*, is quick to note Lovecraft's presence in his works:

> Evil can come from many places. . . . The evil is the dreaded other, the Outsider, the Alien. This kind of evil is something that I find myself continually exploring. During many of these explorations I've looked down and seen the footprint of someone who had passed the same way before me—the footprints of Howard Phillips Lovecraft. Most people who have watched my movies will notice my recognition of those footprints. From Innsmouth references in *The Fog*, to the general premise of *In the Mouth of Madness*, I have used the tools of the cinema to put my own unique spin on the Lovecraftian mythos. Few authors can claim the distinction of becoming an adjective. Lovecraftian. As much as *Frankenstein* and *Dracula* are considered classics, people don't often claim a story to be "Shellian" or "Stokeresque." . . . Which brings me to the book that you hold in your hands, the love sonnet of another Lovecraft aficionado. It's something of a rite of passage among those of us who work in the horror trade. Almost everyone who writes in this genre, from Stephen King to Clive Barker, has written at least one Lovecraftian tale.

Carpenter's introduction is quoted at such length because it is, in many ways, the perfect conclusion to this study. He not only talks about the realms of nightmare as being inextricably linked to otherness, but places Lovecraft's travels through these realms on a continuum with his predecessors. He also constructs an all-male line from Lovecraft's work through his own and those of Barker and King as well as the author of the graphic novel, Hans Rodionoff, whose story he refers to as a "Love Sonnet." The homoerotic overtones do not end there, as the story depicts Lovecraft dressed as a girl and declaring his gender as such. The story literally demonizes sexuality: the opening scene depicts *coitus interruptus* between Lovecraft's parents, as midway through the sexual act Winfield begins to grow fangs and Sarah becomes Cthulhu-like from the waist down. Racial otherness enters the plotline in the form of Lovecraft's dressing up as the "mad Arab" Abdul Alhazred, whose *Necronomicon* he has been reading much to chagrin of his mother and in accordance with his father's prophetic fears. So to escape his mother who wishes to burn the book, Lovecraft creeps to a remote place to read the *Necronomicon*, but is discovered by a gang of kids: "What are you doing down here, Lovey? This isn't the place for queers," the leader of the little rascals says to him. The bully then grabs the *Necronomicon* and pronounces it a "queer book," only to be punished by being devoured by a beast conjured from its pages. Young Howard then wanders from the realms of Providence into Arkham where he is told by one of its denizens that there is "No home, here, Lovey. No home for Sissy-Boy." Holding his book all the while, Lovecraft walks into a deserted church (that recalls the one from "The Haunter in the Dark") where he hides the book among its run-down architecture, the architecture of nightmare.

When Howard finally makes it back to Providence's Angell St. safely, his running away is blamed upon his grandfather, who is upbraided with the following words: "do you see the damage that your horrible stories do?" Just as Derby's reading has a profound effect on him, Lovecraft's reading is a form of possession that affects his behavior, which is blamed on his grandfather's reading as well: "Too much of his grandfather's influence, I think. All those ghost stories he reads. Edgar Allan Poe, Ambrose Bierce." Howard and his family exist on a border state between the horrors of his grandfather's stories and their dysfunctional Providence household. Eventually, a shoggoth kills Lovecraft's grandfather and Lovecraft learns the truth: imagined worlds are as real as the one in which he lives. Immediately after his grandfather's funeral, Lovecraft returns home and begins writing. This graphic novel depicts the world of Lovecraft's emotional life in which he lived through his reading and writing, and in which their spectral presences continue to haunt his life.

The author would like to thank S. T. Joshi, Tim Evans, Chris Koenig-Woodyard, Gregg Nelson, and John Rykhus for their excellent suggestions and feedback on earlier versions of this article. My research was funded by a fellowship from Brown University's John Nicholas Brown Center for the Study of American Civilization. Additional thanks are owed to Henry L. P. Beckwith, Jr., Alice Beckwith, Joyce Botelho, David Shih, and John Stanley.

Works Cited

Barlow, R. H. *On Lovecraft and Life.* Ed. S. T. Joshi. West Warwick, RI: Necronomicon Press, 1992.

Beckwith, Henry L. P., Jr. *Lovecraft's Providence and Adjacent Parts.* West Kingston, RI: Donald M. Grant, 1979 (rev. ed. 1986).

Bhabha, Homi K. "DissemiNation: Time, Narrative, and the Margins, of the Modern Nation." In *Nation and Narration.* 1990. New York: Routledge, 2004. 291–322.

Bloom, Harold. *The Anxiety of Influence.* Oxford: Oxford University Press, 1973.

Davis. Sonia H. *The Private Life of H. P. Lovecraft.* Ed. S. T. Joshi. West Warwick, RI: Necronomicon Press, 1985 (rev. ed. 1992).

Derleth, August. August Derleth Papers, State Historical Society of Wisconsin, Madison, WI.

Derleth, August, ed. *Tales of the Cthulhu Mythos.* New York: Ballantine, 1998.

Eberle-Sinatra, Michael. "Science, Gender and Otherness in Shelley's Frankenstein and Kenneth Branagh's Film Adaptation." *European Romantic Review* 9 (Spring 1998): 253–70.

Ellman, Richard. *Oscar Wilde.* New York: Knopf, 1988.

Gaiman, Neil. *The Sandman: World's End.* Vol. 8. New York: DC Comics, 1994. 10 vols.

Goddu, Teresa. *Gothic America: Narrative, History, and Nation.* New York: Columbia University Press, 1997.

Joshi, S. T. *Lovecraft: A Life.* West Warwick, RI: Necronomicon Press, 1996.

———. *The Modern Weird Tale.* Jefferson, NC: McFarland, 2001.

———, ed. *Documents of American Prejudice: An Anthology of Writings on Race from Thomas Jefferson to David Duke.* New York: Basic Books, 1999.

Matolcsy, Kálmán. "The Innsmouth 'Thing': Monstrous Androgyny in H. P. Lovecraft's 'The Thing on the Doorstep.'" *Gender Studies* 1:3 (2004): 171–79.

Lauter Paul, et al., ed. *The Heath Anthology of American Literature.* 3rd ed. Volume 1. New York: Houghton Mifflin, 1999.

Lévy, Maurice. *Lovecraft: A Study in the Fantastic.* Tr. S. T. Joshi. Detroit: Wayne State University Press, 1988.

Lovecraft, H. P. *The Call of Cthulhu and Other Weird Stories.* Ed. S. T. Joshi. New York: Penguin, 1999.

————. *The Dream Cycle of H.P. Lovecraft.* Introduced by Neil Gaiman. New York: Del Ray, 1995.

————. *Essential Solitude: The Letters of H. P. Lovecraft and August Derleth.* Ed. David E. Schultz and S. T. Joshi. New York: Hippocampus Press, 2008. 2 vols.

————. H. P. Lovecraft Papers, John Hay Library, Brown University, Providence, RI.

————. *More Annotated Lovecraft.* Ed. S. T. Joshi and Peter Cannon. New York: Dell, 1999.

McCloud, Scott. *Understanding Comics: The Invisible Art.* New York: HarperCollins, 1993.

Nelson, Gregg. "Architecture in the Fiction of H. P. Lovecraft." M.A. thesis. University of Wisconsin–Eau Claire, 2002.

Nordau, Max. *Degeneration.* Introduction George L. Mosse. Lincoln: University of Nebraska Press, 1968.

Pain, Barry. *An Exchange of Souls.* Ed. S. T. Joshi. New York: Hippocampus Press, 2007.

Poe, Edgar Allan. "Ligeia." In *Heath Anthology of American Literature.* Ed. Paul Lauter, Richard Yarborough, et al. Vol. 1. Boston: Houghton Mifflin, 1998. 1450–61.

Priest, Josiah. *American Antiquities and Discoveries in the West: Being an Exhibition of the Evidence That an Ancient Population of Partially Civilized Natons, Differing Entirely from Those of the Present Indians, Peopled America, Many Centuries before its Discovery by Columbus.* Albany: Hoffman & White, 1838.

Rodionoff, Hans, Keith Giffen, and Enrique Breccia. *Lovecraft.* New York: Vertigo, 2003. n. p.

Rushdie, Salman. "Imaginary Homelands." In *Imaginary Homelands: Essays and Criticism 1981–1991.* London: Granta, 1991. 9–21.

Said, Edward. *Reflections on Exile and Other Essays.* Cambridge, MA: Harvard University Press, 2002.

Simmons, David. "H. P. Lovecraft and the Shadow of England." *Symbiosis* 11 (2007): 89–104.

Stanley, John H., ed. *Books at Brown.* 38–39 (1991–92). Providence, RI: The Friends of the Library of Brown University, 1992.

Stoker, Bram. *Dracula.* Introduction George Stade. New York: Bantam Books, 1981.

West, Cornel. *Race Matters.* Boston: Beacon Press, 1993.

Young, Iris Marion. "The Scaling of Bodies and the Politics of Identity." In *From Modernism to Postmodernism.* Ed. Lawrence Cahoone. Oxford: Blackwell, 2003. 370–82.

Briefly Noted

S. T. Joshi's extensively revised and updated bibliography of H. P. Lovecraft has been completed and is scheduled to appear later this year from the University of Tampa Press. The date of its appearance has not been set, but it will probably be issued in the fall or early winter. It includes exhaustive information on all publications by Lovecraft (including translations in at least twenty-five languages) and, most significantly, a comprehensive listing of Lovecraft criticism. Joshi's original bibliography (Kent State University Press, 1981) appeared just as the scholarly revolution on Lovecraft was commencing, and therefore it did not include much of the work by such scholars as Donald R. Burleson, David E. Schultz, and others. One article, however, that escaped Joshi's purview is David Simmons's "H. P. Lovecraft and the Shadow of England," *Symbiosis* 11, no. 1 (April 2007): 89–104. This article studies Lovecraft's Anglophilia and its influence upon his fiction and thought. *Symbiosis* is a "Journal of Anglo-American Literary Relations."

"Clever Lines": Some Thoughts on Lovecraft's *Ad Criticos*

Phillip A. Ellis

Perusal of *The Ancient Track* reminds us of, and partly obscures, a fact about *Ad Criticos*, namely that, although it is not the first poem or poems by Lovecraft, the four books are nonetheless the first genuine examples of his ability with poetry. Some of his earlier satiric verse has some merit. "Providence in 2000 A.D." (*AT* 191–92) is, like *Ad Criticos*, of a reasonable length, so as to develop more fully the satire implicit in the verse's subject matter, unlike the intervening and thinner "Fragment on Whitman" (*AT* 192–93) and "[On Robert Browning]" (*AT* 193). Yet, on the whole, the four poems of *Ad Criticos* combine to create a piece that lessens the impact of these other poems individually, or else in tandem. Although "Providence in 2000 A.D." had been published in the Providence *Evening Bulletin* of March 4, 1912 (*AT* 491), it was the combined publication of the first two books of *Ad Criticos* in January 1914 and February 1914 respectively (*AT* 492), and the later publication of the other two, initially in *Saturnalia and Other Poems* (Joshi & Schultz 2) with later publications in both the Necronomicon Press edition of *H. P. Lovecraft in the Argosy* (Joshi, *Argosy* 38) and *The Ancient Track* (*AT* 196–98) that included all four books, that combined to emphasise the achievement of *Ad Criticos* itself. What, then, given this status as the first properly meritorious poem or poems by Lovecraft, is the critical legacy of the four books?

Unfortunately, *Ad Criticos* has received scant attention from critics; namely, S. T. Joshi himself has been almost the only critic to discuss them. Apart from *H. P. Lovecraft in the Argosy*, the bulk of Joshi's comments are in his biography of Lovecraft, which emphasises the importance of the first two books on Lovecraft's later career and, indeed, life (Joshi, *Life* 95–96). With *H. P. Lovecraft in the Argosy*, we receive a general overview of the controversy over John Russell's use of satiric

verse, and its importance for Lovecraft as a whole, but we also have
the various letters and poems collected that are germinal to that issue.
It is a sourcebook, rather than a study of *Ad Criticos*. It would be useful to help create something of a critical dialogue about the four poems. In doing so we can begin to approach Lovecraft as he once saw
himself, as a poet, and this approach is important. It would also be useful to gain an introduction to *Ad Criticos*, looking at its place in Lovecraft's work, then at one common aspect of the four constituent
poems, an emphasis on language and literacy, before coming to a tenta-
tive conclusion about them. Before doing so, however, it would be
wise to give brief consideration to a couple of points about them.

Which brings us to an integral question: is *Ad Criticos* one poem
or four? Certainly, they are treated as one poem in *The Ancient
Track*, albeit in four separate books. Keeping in mind that only the
first two books were individually published in Lovecraft's lifetime,
and the fact that, although they concern the same subjects, they are
nonetheless disjointed, it is possible to argue that they are not one
poem, but four. So, are they four individual poems, not one? In light
of their unity of subject and title, it should be preferable to consider
them a tight sequence of four separate pieces. Though we may expect, from the use of "Liber Primus," "Liber Secundus," and so on,
that they are parts of a single, united work, such an expectation is
misleading at best. For the purposes, then, of this essay, the work will
be considered a sequence of four poems. *Ad Criticos* will be used to
refer to all four, the separate titles "Liber Primus," "Liber Secundus,"
and so on, to each individually. Which brings us to gloss over the ba-
sics of the wider controversy encompassing the poems.

As the controversy has been covered elsewhere, by Joshi, there is
no real reason to restate the details. Those interested can easily read
about the controversy in both *H. P. Lovecraft: A Life* (93–97) and the
introduction to *H. P. Lovecraft in the Argosy* (5–7); the latter, as
noted, is really a sourcebook of the various letters and poems, so
those interested in perusing the primary documents should consider
that first. It is also covered in the notes to *Ad Criticos* in *The Ancient
Track* (*AT* 492). So it is fruitless to cover, essentially, the same ground
already excellently covered in these readily accessible volumes. What
we need is not so much a recapitulation of the controversy, unless
doing so will uncover new and germane material previously ne-
glected, but, rather, the accumulation of material about the poems

themselves. We need analysis, criticism, not scholarly details. Having said this, then, it is important to start the process with some general remarks about the place of *Ad Criticos* in Lovecraft's poetry.

Of course, the place of *Ad Criticos* within the poetry is important for a fuller reading of it, given that it has repercussions for the reading of his poetic oeuvre as a whole. As noted, it stands at the opening phases of his career as a poet. It was responsible, in a sense, for that career, since, by enabling him to encounter amateur journalism, and to develop into a primary figure in that sphere, the poems of *Ad Criticos* develop an importance far beyond their immediate circumstances allow us to see. We must also consider, overall, aspects of Lovecraft's mature poetry. We can clearly divide it into two main phases, based upon the diction developed and language used. The first phase is marked by a more archaic diction, and by the use of more archaic models, such as the epistolatory verse and the pastorals of the Georgian poets. This period largely coincides with the classicist period of Lovecraft's aesthetic thought, although it does merge into the decadent phase. The second phase of Lovecraft's poetic oeuvre is one characterised in large part by a simplicity and contemporaneousness of diction. Lovecraft, simply, is speaking in the language of his times, in accordance with the various dicta he promulgates to, in particular, Elizabeth Toldridge (for which see the various volumes of *Selected Letters;* the collected correspondence with Ms. Toldridge has yet to be published in a separate volume). *Ad Criticos* belongs to that first phase, the archaic phase, of Lovecraft's poetic practice. It also displays a number of aspects that help tie the poems together into a unity.

As can be expected for any poems within a sequence such as *Ad Criticos,* the four poems are clearly marked by common aspects, aspects that help tie the poems together into a tighter unity. The diction is one. They demonstrate one based clearly and openly upon Georgian models. Joshi argues that Dryden's *Mac Flecknoe* was probably a stronger model than Pope's *Dunciad* (Joshi, *Life* 122) for the poems. This influence is evident by a comparison of the diction and other stylistic features of the poems, something that is outside the scope of this present study. There is also a unity created by a shared prosody. All four poems are constructed on a metrical base of iambic pentameters, of heroic couplets. There is also a very strong emphasis on end-stopped lines in the four. We find, for example, enjambement in only twelve of 175 lines (that is less than 7% of all lines in the four pieces). There is also a very notable unity of subject. Very rarely does Lovecraft digress from his attacks upon his opponents. One notable example is in "Liber Secundus," where he writes

> Here once a nobler JACKSON wag'd his wars,
> And died a hero in a glorious cause.
> Lost is the cause, but deathless STONEWALL'S fame.
> Alas, that lesser men should bear his name!

(AT 195, ll. 31–44)

Here we find that while there is a digression from the immediate aim of the attacks upon his opponents, it is to refer once again to the prime cause of the controversy itself: Fred Jackson. The unity of subject, the poems as replies to criticisms of Jackson's fiction, and the other aspects that help unify the four poems help lead to the misleading treatment of the four as a unified poem in *The Ancient Track*.

What we will do, in the bulk of this essay's remainder, is to look more closely at one primary aspect of note: the emphasis upon language and literacy in the four poems. This is primarily thematic, related to the words and images of the poems, yet it helps clearly demonstrate that the poems are unified by more than primarily formal characteristics.

The emphasis upon language and literacy occurs in all four poems. One occasion, in "Liber Primus," is of interest. Lovecraft, in lines 23–26, writes:

> In truth, my words are not beyond the reach
> Of him who understands the English speech;
> But Crean, I fear, by reading Jackson long,
> Hath lost the pow'r to read his mother tongue.

(AT 194)

Here we find a contrast between Lovecraft's letters and the fiction of Jackson. Lovecraft's letters are written in English, and are comprehensible to those who speak English. Left implicit are their effects. The language of Jackson's fiction is left implicit, yet their effects are explicit: they corrupt the reader's ability to understand English. So that Crean, by reading Jackson to some extent, is no longer capable of understanding English; he has been corrupted, made lesser, and made a figure of fun. This is one example of the use of language and literacy to score a point against the poet's detractors. There is a related point made elsewhere in this poem. We read, for example, the line "Pure fiction wanes, and baser writings rise—" (*AT* 194, l. 45). What is interesting is that Lovecraft glosses over the definition of what he considers pure fiction. In contrast, he points to Jackson, and, additionally, Jackson's supporters, as examples of the "baser writings" (the term "writings," of course, encompasses both fiction and letters). This allows us to see Lovecraft constructing a hierarchy of excellence. "Pure fiction" is to be considered better and "higher" than the "baser" material. This is echoed in an earlier couplet; Lovecraft writes:

> Scrawl on, sweet Jackson, raise the lover's leer;
> 'Tis plain, you please the fallen public ear.

> (*AT* 194, ll. 39–40)

Note the "fallen," which has an analogous and implicit correlation with the "baser" of line 45. These are examples of Lovecraft's rhetoric, and his use of a language that reinforces through similarity of connotation and implicit meaning. This brings me to consider, briefly, an interesting piece of self-revelation by Lovecraft in the same poem.

In line 30 of "Liber Primus," Lovecraft writes: "No line of fiction e'er was writ by me!" (*AT* 194). Of course, Lovecraft is being disingenuous here. He had written fiction, albeit fiction as a child, that he had repudiated. We even have some of his juvenilia: "The Little Glass Bottle," "The Secret Cave," and "The Mystery of the Grave-yard" are examples (all published recently in *MW* 7–16). And yet, given this, it is also ingenuous. It plays on a common meaning of fiction, as something that is invented, or is imagined (Macquarie). That is, it refers to fiction as a falsehood. With this sense in mind, Lovecraft is also claiming that he has only spoken the truth in the debate, and this multiplicity of meanings helps remind us of the uses of ambiguity, and of double senses (such as we find in irony and sarcasm) by Lovecraft to help convey his meaning. We see further aspects in the second poem of the sequence, some of which refer to the genre of satire.

In "Liber Secundus," Lovecraft refers to the genre of satire in two passages. He does this self-referentially: he writes satire, that mentions satire, and this helps create a sense of distance and artificiality to the poem. We read, and are made aware that we read, a poem. This is skillfully done. In the first passage, we read the following couplet:

> Help'd on by books, both sacred and profane,
> He seeks to shine in the satiric strain. (*AT* 195, ll. 9–10)

Here the self-referentiality is not as evident as in the second passage. Lovecraft glosses over, that is, the fact that this poem is a satire, at the same time as he diminishes his opponent's abilities; Saunders "seeks" but does not succeed. He tries, and that is all. The second passage occurs shortly after the first. Again referring to Saunders, and to his over-reliance upon a dictionary in criticising Lovecraft, we read:

> "Jacksonian", "Jacksonine", "Josh Billings-gate"
> Claim no existence but as satire's tools;
> Owe no allegiance to linguistic rules. (*AT* 195, ll. 12–14)

The first line in this extract bears some small scrutiny. The first word listed, "Jacksonian," can be considered a legitimate word formed by a standard affix ("-ian") to a proper name (in the same way that we derive Lovecraftian from Lovecraft). It has a legitimate linguistic existence outside of the immediate satire, yet remains one of "satire's tools." "Jacksonine," however, is quite a delicious pun on "asinine." It is one of the satire's tools, and remains a neologism (though one worth promulgating further). "Josh Billings-gate" plays on a satiric pseudonym; it is another invention like Jacksonine, again a neologism. In repeating them here, though, Lovecraft more than refers to the earlier letter (Joshi, *Argosy* 9–10). He resurrects their purpose and states, in essence, that Saunders is incapable of detecting satiric intent through language. Saunders, as he earlier said, "seeks to shine" at satire, but here he fails at the effective use of language. The "no allegiance" in line 14 is disingenuous—all perform the tasks of adjectives, and adhere to the linguistic "rules" of such, but what is objected to is book-learning, not wits. This leads to the next extract, which once again refers to language.

The later reference to Elizabeth E. Loop contains the following couplet:

> Whoe'er this lady's firm esteem would seek,
> In monosyllables must ever speak. (*AT* 195, ll. 27–28)

This is one of the more celebrated couplets in the sequence, and rightly so. Note, though, that the attack is upon the language, and the inability of Ms. Loop to handle more than "simple" English. In her letter to the Log-Book, she points out specific examples of Lovecraft's

vocabulary that she objects to: "labyrinthine, laureled, luminary, lu-
cubrations, and many others" (Joshi, *Argosy* 12) The joke in this passage is simply delightful, in Lovecraft's presumption that Ms. Loop
would not understand the word "monosyllables" itself, and as a result
fail to feel the sting in the barb. Lovecraft relies, then, on perceptions
and examples of the various targets' abilities with the English language. This brings us to consider a later passage, similar in intent to
this one.

In reference to Ms. E. E. Blankenship, Lovecraft writes:

> Exactitude the fair one hardly heeds,
> Since she "erratic" for "erotic" reads,
> But unimportant 'tis, for by my troth,
> Jackson's erratic and erotic both! (*AT* 195–96, ll. 43–46)

Again he attacks the targets' problems with English: here her misreading, or assumption, of "erratic" for "erotic." In doing so, he makes fun
of her misreading, then uses this to launch another attack on Jackson.
S. T. Joshi has compared Lovecraft's attacks in these poems to shoot-
ing fish in a barrel. That may need to be amended to "large fish" and
"small barrel." The satire is so withering, so successful that there is little that the target could do but retreat, silenced; there is a distinct
lack of any further letters from Ms. Blankenship in regard to the Jackson issue.

This leads to one final passage in "Liber Secundus." This is a couplet that reads:

> Laconic Bonner takes the leader's place,
> And throws his modest "classic" in my face.

(*AT* 195, ll. 21–22)

Here we find an interesting use of language in regard to literature.
The term "classic" can be problematic. As with all questions relating
to the canons of literature, there is an assumption of what a classic
work is. Lovecraft plays on this. He takes Bonner's use of the word,
with its overtones of this application to literature, and mocks him.
He uses pungent irony, mocking Bonner's ability to understand his
words, his language, without recourse to further attacks. The satire is
telling and shows us Lovecraft's mastery of the form.

There is a sense of futility with the third, and fourth, poems of the sequence. Though we read them, and though they were meant to be read by their targets, it is unlikely that they were submitted for publication. Why this is remains an enigma; the circumstances have been lost to us and remain unknown. There is, once again, an emphasis upon language and literature. The latter aspect is notable in this poem in a couple of passages and deserves some attention.

Lovecraft echoes Russell in the following couplets:

> To aid his cause, he points with logic's art
> At Boz, and Cooper, Avon's bard, and Scott:
> "Behold," he cries, "thro' classic pages move
> The sweet delusions of idyllic love." (*AT* 196, ll. 13–16)

The familiar "Boz" relies upon the ideal reader identifying the name "Boz" with Dickens, just as Russell did with "Fenny" for James Fenimore Cooper (Joshi, *Argosy* 20). What Lovecraft does, in echoing the "classic" authors, is to make fun of the subject. They wrote about "delusions of idyllic love," rather than something real. He mocks, that is, the treatment of the phenomenon of love. Notable is the use of the allusion to Shakespeare, rather than the name itself: when Lovecraft writes

> He lights on me, and stings with careless courage,
> As if I were the Hudibras of our age. (*AT* 196, ll. 7–8)

he again relies for effect upon allusion to make his point. This reminds us of the earlier use of "classic": Lovecraft here relies upon having an ideal reader capable of comprehending the origin and nature of Butler's figure of Hudibras. He uses an allusion to an earlier work, that is, to point toward the literary and technical aspects of his target's verse. But that reference to the technical aspects, to the literary construction rather than its content, finds further echoes in this poem.

The reference to Hudibras is, of course, matched to an earlier mention of Samuel Butler:

> Russell, like Butler, seeks to school the times
> In four-foot verse bestrown with double rhymes.
>
> (*AT* 196, ll. 5–6)

There is, here, the beginnings of an emphasis on the technical aspects of his target's verse. This is made clear in the following passage about

F. W. Saunders's "Ruat Caelum" (Joshi, *Argosy* 21). The rather lengthy passage is worth rereading:

> To grave heroics does his taste incline;
> His verse is modell'd after Pope's (or mine).
> A worthy measure, worthily employ'd;
> By no false accent is the ear annoy'd.
> The wit is biting, and the language pure;
> The sense, like Browning's, is a bit obscure:
> The thoughts in most ingenious cloaks are wrapp'd;
> The metaphors, tho' somewhat mix'd, are apt.

(AT 196, ll. 21–28)

Lovecraft does go on further, admitting the skill and ability of Saunders. He admits defeat, in essence. And the passage reinforces the earlier mention of technical aspects and leads into the fourth poem.

"Liber Quartus," although the shortest of the four, resumes the focus upon the technical aspects of verse-writing with a rather lengthy passage:

> His learned lines the rules of metre scorn.
> In true trochaic rage the bard begins,
> When, lo! an odd iambus intervenes.
> Some eight lines down, he strikes the ballad form,
> But soon a dactyl swells the shapeless swarm:
> The fifteenth line assumes heroic length,
> And stands apart in solitary strength.
> As for the rest, what man among us knows
> If it be verse, or merely rhyming prose?

(AT 197, ll. 18–26)

Here the secure, confident Lovecraft returns. Unlike the earlier passage about Saunders, the target here is worth attacking: the poem itself, Richard Forster's effort (Joshi, *Argosy* 22), is manifestly flawed on technical grounds. Indeed, for the most part, this poem concerns itself with the various lines employed; here, and in the earlier "In well-turn'd lines, with sickly venom writ" (*AT* 196, l. 5), are there mentioned the technicalities of verse. The poems echo the shift of the debate into verse, and they lead in turn to further poems not covered in this essay. In these ways, then, have the aspect of language and literacy been addressed, in varying ways in the four poems. Tellingly, they are associated with the various attacks upon the targets of Lovecraft's satire. The heavy emphasis on this aspect is considered and reasonable: it reflects the poems' emphasis, and they reinforce our sense of them as essentially literary documents. They are poems about literature (or as Lovecraft might reasonably argue, the lack of it).

In a sense, this has not been an opening salvo in a critical debate upon the four poems of the *Ad Criticos* cycle. That has already been fired, by S. T. Joshi. Unlike his treatment, which has concentrated upon the biographical accident of their position and importance for Lovecraft's creative life, I have been content to look primarily at the poems as things in themselves. I have been content to look at the unity of the four poems, arguing that they display characteristics that combine the four individual poems into a narrow cycle of verse. One such characteristic, one such aspect, has been the emphasis placed upon both writing and literacy in the four poems. This emphasis upon the poems as themselves has not been Joshi's. And it may not be others'. But it stands as a challenge to my fellow scholars: it is time to look at these and other poems and to help create somewhat of a critical dialogue about them. They, and other poems, deserve critical attention in their own right, even as they remain overshadowed by more attractive, more influential fiction and thought. We cannot fully understand Lovecraft without looking at these works, and what they represent for his creativity, given his early self-image as a poet. It is a step toward seeing him as he saw himself, not how we see him as we wish him to have been.

Works Cited

Joshi, S. T., *H. P. Lovecraft: A Life.* West Warwick, RI: Necronomicon Press, 1996.

———, ed. *H. P. Lovecraft in the Argosy: Collected Correspondence from the Munsey Magazines.* West Warwick, RI: Necronomicon Press, 1994.

———, and David E. Schultz. *An H. P. Lovecraft Encyclopedia.* 2001. New York: Hippocampus Press, 2005.

Macquarie University. *The Macquarie Dictionary on CD-Rom.* CD-ROM. Revised 3rd ed. Sydney: Macquarie Library, 2001.

"The Rats in the Walls," the Rats in the Trenches

Robert H. Waugh

> [. . .] Generations of toppled heads
> have come to roost in my priory. (Ashbery 50)

H. P. Lovecraft wrote only a few stories that take place outside New England, and most of them do not wear very well; a few of them are concerned with the Great War, but only in a rather peripheral way. "Dagon" and "The Temple" take as their settings the German submarine warfare; and part five of "Herbert West—Reanimator," taking place behind the Allied lines in France, was written to prove that even an American, Lovecraft in this case, for a bit of money could succeed in the Grand Guignol tradition. In none of these can we say that the story is very successful. The exception is "The Rats in the Walls," although the reasons for its success are more difficult to fathom than may be at first apparent. It seems to comprise two plots that do not fit very well together, one the story of the cannibalistic family and the other the story of the rats, stories that do not exist on the same level of reality. Surprising as the story of the family is, Lovecraft's loving historical details and his fascination with the relation of England and its ancient Roman and atavistic past assure its realism. The story of the rats is a very different sort of tale. Based upon old fables, it remains undecidable and fantastic. The stories are connected only through the perception of the narrator, the last, insane, cannibalistic member of the family, who may or may not hear the rats in the walls, or, to put it another way, who hears what is most probably not there. We might attempt to say that the family cult through the ages is an attempt to propitiate the instinctual rats of human aggression; but such a formulation is not very satisfying since it does not account for the different natures of the two stories.[1]

I propose another reading of this hybrid. Although it takes place in 1923, I believe it is Lovecraft's World War I story, centering upon the narrator's cry, "The war ate my boy, damn them all" (*DH* 44). But to understand it in this way we need to recall the life of the trenches.

"Do you remember the rats; and the stench / Of corpses rotting in front of the front-line trench[?]" Siegfried Sassoon asked (267). We have many testimonies to the life of the trenches and the part the rats played in it, distinguished by "their hunger, vigor, intelligence, and courage" (Fussell 49). Richard Aldington wrote they were "huge" (52). But a soldier could think of them as his brothers. Consider these lines from Wilfrid Owen's "A Terre":

> Not worse than ours the existences rats lead—
> Nosing along at night down some safe rut,
> They find a shell-proof home before they rot. (65)

Something of the same perception occurs in David Jones's work, *In Parenthesis*, as the platoon prepares to go over the top:

> Long side by side lie like friends lie
> on daisy-down on warm days
> cuddled close down kindly close with the mole
> in down and silky rodent [. . .] (157)

With more of an edge Rosenberg makes the same point in his poem "Break of Day in the Trenches":

> Only a live thing leaps my hand,
> A queer sardonic rat,
> As I pull the parapet's poppy
> To stick behind my ear.
> Droll rat, they would shoot you if they knew
> Your cosmopolitan sympathies.

---

1. This dual nature of the story may arise from the two legends HPL made use of in Baring-Gould's *Curious Myths of the Middle Ages*, which Steven J. Mariconda has traced in detail. One chapter recounts the legend of St. Patrick's Purgatory, the other the legend of the rats that devour Bishop Hatto. The two legends are different in kind, the one a mythic geography associated with a real place in Ireland, the other a narrative of a judgment executed upon a cruel prelate by an army of rats.

Now you have touched this English hand
You will do the same to a German. (103)

The passages are intimate because at a certain point in the trench experience anything creaturely alive becomes a soldier's brother. This is
not Delapore's feeling at first, but we should keep it in mind. Shortly
before the catastrophe he does consider "the hapless rats that stum-
bled into such traps [as the pits] amidst the blackness of their quest in
this grisly Tartarus" (*DH* 44). By this point in the story he has become
as hapless and as trapped as they. Rather different are the internal
rhymes of E. W. Tennant:

I can see them all asleep, three men deep,
And they're nowhere near a fire—but our wire
Has 'em fast as can be. Can't you see
When the flare goes up? Ssh! boys; what's that noise?
Do you know what these rats eat? Body-meat!
(cited in Gilbert 287)

Our brothers are our enemies. At the conclusion of his poem "Trench
Poets" Edgell Rickword writes of a corpse lying in no-man's-land, "He
stank so badly, though we were great chums / I had to leave him; then
rats ate his thumbs" (98). Here, in no-man's-land, the place that was
especially ill-fitted, both hunger and dissolution were satisfied. Considering this place that did not belong to humanity, David Jones wrote:

You can hear the rat of no-man's-land
rut-out intricacies,
weasel out his patient workings,
scrut, scrut, sscrut. (54)

No-man's-land was the special home of the rat. One of the voices in
The Waste Land has this in mind when he says: "I think we are in
rats' alley / Where the dead men lost their bones" (40). Eliot of
course was not in the war; he was merely picking up the language of
the trenches that had become a part of the patois of the day, and the
lines well express the difficulty of Delapore's position after the death
of his son. We should keep in mind that Lovecraft read *The Waste
Land* shortly before writing "The Rats in the Walls" (Joshi 314–16).

After we have read these testimonies, it is no wonder that Paul
Fussell says that they were the "famous" rats of the war (49). Not

only were they a part of the normal life in the trenches; they became one of the icons of the peculiarly bestial nature of the war upon which poets and others, such as Lovecraft, could draw.

Besides the Great War and the War Between the States, about which I will say more later, one other political event occurs in the story, so muted that we are liable not to notice it. This is the death of President Harding, which the narrator announces in solemn tones as he and his cohort of archeologists and scientists return to Exham Priory: "I felt myself poised on the brink of frightful revelations, a sensation symbolized by the air of mourning among the many Americans at the unexpected death of the President on the other side of the world" (*DH* 40). Harding, of course, had died in the middle of various investigations into the corruption of his administration, so after the initial shock his death came rather as a sense of relief to the nation. Lovecraft, both a Republican and a realist, dismisses the man in a letter as a "handsome bimbo" but adds, "I'm sure sorry he had the good luck to get clear of this beastly planet" (*SL* 1.253); cosmic indifferentism conflicts with human sympathy. In contrast, Lovecraft had no truck with Woodrow Wilson, whose project of the League of Nations he described in 1931 as "Woody Wilson's monumental asininity" (*SL* 3.272). Lovecraft had written an article against the League and argued against it in several letters. The good thing about Harding, in his view, was that he had, albeit with some qualms, successfully opposed the entrance of the United States into the League. America was to have nothing to do with old Europe—unlike the narrator of "The Rats in the Walls" who cannot help himself from plunging into the truth of Europe and into the truth of his own material, genealogical, and psychic inheritance. One theme of the story would seem to be that whatever the consequences may be it is not so easy to dismiss Europe.

Harding represents a complex of themes for Lovecraft. He could not have been ignorant of the charge, much bandied about during the campaign for the White House, that Harding's ancestry had black blood in it; that, as Harding, put it his people had perhaps "jumped the fence" (Russell 40). With that detail in mind the function of Nigger-Man in the story becomes all the more significant. Only someone or something connected with the fearful other, be it the cult of death in Egypt or the voodoo cult in Mexico, could for this narrator further suggest hidden meaning, place him "on the brink" of revelation. The death of Harding and the mourning for him makes him a psychopompos like Nigger-Man, guiding the mind of the narrator downward to hidden meanings.

Needless to say, Lovecraft like many other people of his generation had fierce feelings about the war that had brought them to the confusing world of the 1920s, which seemed to have so little in common with the world before the war. At first he felt that England and Germany were committing racial suicide, since both shared an Aryan heritage; as he put it in his 1915 article, "The Crime of the Century," they were "blood brothers" (CE 5.14). As the war continued, however, and his Anglophilia took hold, he reacted to the German strategies violently. The German blood brother becomes the Hun, whose "savage lust of combat" is something the politer nations have need of if they are to win the war (SL 1.53). In the poem "Germania—1918" he is a "rav'ning beast" (AT 418); when America enters the war "The Goth, unheeding, plans continued wrong, / And ruthless drags his brutish horde along" (AT 420). What has happened to our brother? In galloping anapests Lovecraft answers that question in the slightly earlier poem, "Ad Britannos—1918: "'Tis the blood of the past that is raging within him, / The hot blood of pillagers ruthless and bold" (AT 414). The German nation has experienced a mass regression; that is to say, it is destroyed in the same way as Delapore is destroyed. As much as any other man Lovecraft suffered the effects of Allied propaganda, which he was later to condemn; but the propaganda has fruitful consequences in the story.

The problem with this language is its abstraction. In his letters, essays, and poems Lovecraft shows little awareness of the actual nature of trench warfare, of barbed wire and machine guns, to say nothing of rats. The Somme and Gallipoli do not move him. What does move him is the submarine warfare that sinks the Lusitania, an event that lies behind "Dagon" and "The Temple," stories, however, that do not finally appeal to the details of such warfare but to the element of the ocean in which something more monstrous than the submarine resides. Herbert West, a monster in his own right, stays far behind the lines when he volunteers as a doctor during the war for the sake of the fresh body parts it provides. None of these characters understands the experience of the men in the trenches that Valentine Fleming describes, who are "unable to reply to the everlasting run of shells hurled at them from three, four, five or more miles away and positively welcoming an infantry attack [. . .] as a chance of meeting and matching themselves against human assailants and not against invisible, irresistible machines" (cited in Gilbert 112). The war remains for Lovecraft what he called it early on, "this stupendous fray" (*CE* 5.14); on the one hand it is gratifyingly large, an expression of sublimity, but on the other hand it is a mere brawl. Though "fray" is cognate to fear as Doctor Johnson noted, who also mentioned its archaic significance of "a battle; a fight" ("Fray"), it now signifies little more than "a noisy quarrel; a brawl" (*OED* "Fray"). Some contradictory feelings about the Great War hamper Lovecraft's comprehension of it, but we should admit that it was difficult for many people to comprehend.

Now we return to that cry, "The war ate my boy." But it is not the war that ate the narrator's son. He did, he and his forbears. The violence of the family regresses to prehistoric times, as though Darwin and Freud had opened up the door on the animalistic instincts of the race, absolving humans of their violence; but evidence of violence in America lies much closer to hand in the Revolution and in the War between the States,[2] a violence institutionalized in West Point, and rampant up and down the frontier as the new Americans removed the Native Americans from their lands. The narrator describes the burning of the Delapore plantation as though the family had nothing to do with the acts of the Confederacy; yet the father of the narrator was at the time "in the army, defending Richmond" (*DH* 27). More specifically, however, it became a commonplace among the Lost Generation after the War to End All Wars that the older generation through acts of fatuous arrogance were guilty of initiating the war, of sending their sons off to the war, and of bullheadedly continuing the war when the nature of life in the trenches, brothers to the rats, had become evident. Wilfrid Owen expresses this in the last two lines of his poem, "The Parable of the Old Man and the Young," in which he retells the story of Abraham and Isaac. Once more an angel offers the old man a ram to sacrifice instead of his son: "But the old man would not so, but slew his son, / And half the seed of Europe, one by one" (42). One of Kipling's "Epi-

---

2. The narrator, incidentally, never says "The War between the States" or "The War of Northern Aggression," though he was born in the South of a proud Southern heritage. Instead he uses the Northern phrase, the "Civil War" (*DH* 27); he has purposefully turned his back on the South, just as his ancestor had turned his back on England. For reasons that shall be clear later, I believe that for his personality, being of both the South and the North, the more contumacious "War between the States" would better express his true feelings.

taphs of the War" says bluntly, "If any question why we died, / Tell them, because our fathers lied" (443). Delapore is as guilty of these acts as are the other fathers. Because of these lies the sons were happy to deploy for the war.

There is another aspect to this story of a father eating his son that we cannot ignore. It is the story of old Saturn, to which Lovecraft was to allude in 1926 in "Pickman's Model," when Pickman paints a Goya subject to life: "The monster was there—it glared and gnawed and gnawed and glared" (*DH* 23). The two stories must have some knot in common, the one from the father's point of view and the other from the son's—let us recall that Pickman is most likely a changeling who meets an ill end. The family that eats together is dead meat together and defeated together. The two stories record Oedipal aggressions from the oral stage. Chronological time, that is to say adult, senile time, devours the eternity of the child; and the story of the rats, like so many of Lovecraft's stories, records a span of very specific years that conclude in the apocalypse of the Great War.

But should we accuse Delapore, the narrator of the story, of such acts as incestuous cannibalism? In making such an accusation we need to look at his words more carefully. His narrative is double-layered. On the one hand it presents a story in the past tense that nevertheless presents events that surprise him in a lived now; on the other hand, as a true past tense, this is a story told by a madman, whose words are not to be taken as raw evidence of factual events. For instance, early in his account the narrator describes Norrys as "a plump, amiable young man" (*DH* 28). Later he comments that Norrys was "stouter" (*DH* 38); and later, immediately before the climax, he again marks Norrys as "plump" (*DH* 44). The swinish creatures that he sees in his dreams have "flabby features" (*DH* 37); and he denies too intensely in his final madness that "it was not Edward Norrys' fat face on that flabby, fungous thing!" (*DH* 44). Now whether Norrys was plump and stout, fat and flabby or not is beside the point when we discover that the narrator, who is oppressed by visions of hunger, has attempted to eat him in his madness. Quite simply, then, since his narration is colored by his madness, we must read it carefully.

For instance, when he and Norrys first investigate the sub-cellar, he finds on its walls the word *Atys* and comments, "The reference [. . .] made me shiver, for I had read Catullus and knew something of the hideous rites of the Eastern god" (*DH* 37). Leaving aside the question why this allusion to castration should make an elderly man who has lost his only son shiver, the construction "and knew" is less than precise, for it either means "and therefore knew" or "and also knew." If as a child learning Latin this businessman read the Catullus poem in which Atys is a character, he would not necessarily have learned anything further about the god Atys—but why should the businessman have learned such information unless led to it by the propensities of the family? Is not his "shiver" akin to the "tickle" (*DH* 122) the old man in "The Picture in the House" feels when he pores over the cannibals' abattoir? The phrase, then, makes us ask more questions than we had expected about the old man who narrates the story.[3]

Another sign of the problems in this man's narrative is his use of the word "doubtless" and "must." He is extremely insistent that the reader read the text as he intends it should be read and see the things that he believes he has seen. His first use of this language is so low-key we are liable to miss it: "What I afterward remembered is merely this—that my old black cat, whose moods I know so well, was undoubtedly alert and anxious to an extent wholly out of keeping with his natural character" (*DH* 33). The next morning, to explain to a servant Nigger-Man's scratching at the new panels, "I told the man that there must be some singular odour or emanation from the old stonework" (33), though he believes no rats or mice "could hardly be found" there for some three hundred years (33). The climax of the story brings this language to a crescendo. When Nigger-Man seems to leap into the gulf, "I was not far behind, for there was no doubt after another second. It was the eldritch scurrying of those fiend-born rats" (44). When he bumps into "something soft and plump," presumably Norrys, he argues in retrospect, "It must have been the rats" (44). In the last paragraph, speaking of his guards, he says, "They must know that I did not do it. They must know it was the rats" (45). The final effect of this language is double. On the one hand we are convinced that he is insane and that we must doubt very much that any substantial rats infest the Priory; but on the other hand we are convinced

---

3. Given the prudery of the English-speaking world that Byron excoriates in *Don Juan* 1.41–45, we may wonder how the narrator, a simple businessman, learned of this poem. For what it is worth, my fourth-year Latin text from high school, dating from 1933, does not have the poem in its selections from Catullus (Carlisle and Richardson 373–89).

that the rats represent some kind of inner reality that we must accept for the sake of our own sanity. If we deny the rats we deny something compulsively real in ourselves.

What do we actually know about this narrator? First, let us be careful about his age. Seven years old when the plantation was burned, apparently during the siege of Richmond in 1865, he apparently was born in 1858. After the war the family came North, where he became over the years "a stolid Yankee" (*DH* 27), so stolid a Yankee that he exhibits Republican sympathies at the death of Harding. When his son was ten years old in 1904, he was forty-six. He was fifty-nine when his son went to war and sixty at the war's conclusion, when his son returned "a maimed invalid" (*DH* 28), at the same time that he bought Exham Priory. He began the rebuilding of the Priory when he was sixty-three years old and sixty-five at its completion when he moved in and the events of the story overwhelmed him. Since it is possible that he was born earlier than we have supposed, we can be certain, considering the normal life spans of the time, that this is indeed the narration of an old man who may soon die, believing himself the last of his line. Is there not, then, already a touch of dementia in his stubborn determination to rebuild and refurbish the Priory, bypassing the injuries of the War between the States, the American Revolution, and the English Civil War? He says that it was the "legendry" of the Priory, recounted in his son's letters, "which definitely turned my attention to my transatlantic heritage, and made me resolve to purchase and restore the family seat" (*DH* 28), a resolve for which Norrys bears some of the blame since it was he who recounted that "peasant superstition" to the young Delapore in the first place.

How did the father regard this "legendry"?

In a variety of ways. Once he arrives he finds himself "ostracised" and "disliked" by most of the villagers, for little reason he thinks except that he is a member of this ancient, "abhorrent" family, though he is well received by Norrys (*DH* 29). This dislike he believes comes from the legendry; English tradition has a long memory, although memory may be distorted. The architecture of the Priory, what remains of it, indicates a Roman, druidic, and predruidic past, associated with the worship of the Magna Mater. The antiquary aspects of these remains disinfect them of any terror. More charged for the narrator are the tales and ballads that surround his family in the medieval period, especially those from the Welsh border: "These myths and ballads, typical as they were of crude superstition, repelled me greatly," he writes, perhaps because they were "unpleasantly reminiscent" of his cousin "who went among the negroes and became a voodoo priest after he returned from the Mexican War" (*DH* 30–31). Clearly there is more to this family that has nobly upheld the traditions of the antebellum South than he would allow. His disgust for a cousin who "went among the negroes" is palpable.

The narrator is less disturbed, he assures us, by "tales of wails and howlings" or of "graveyard stenches after the spring rains" or of "the squealing white thing"—all these tales are "hackneyed spectral lore" that a man of taste, a confirmed skeptic, cannot be moved by (*DH* 31), although these are just the kind of thing that prove factual later. He admits that "accounts of vanished peasants" might have some truth, "though not especially significant" given medieval habits, for after all "prying curiosity meant death" (*DH* 31)—which is to say that he condones any murder that his ancestors committed in the past. As Paul Montelone suggests, "If anything took place at the site it would be for him conventionally evil, uncivilized surely, offensive, ungentlemanly, decadent, a stain on his family tree, but not innately or absolutely evil. His moral reading of the legendry would be [. . .] wholly commonsensical. He is after all a businessman" (19)—an American businessman, I would add, so determined to be an Englishman that he is willing to accept the ethics of an aristocracy that would display the heads of their murdered peasants on the battlements of the Priory, heads that give some point to his later dream of "a Roman feast like that of Trimalchio, with a horror in a covered platter" (*DH* 40). Is it any wonder that he finds himself disliked by the villagers?

Finally there are those "extremely picturesque" tales of witches' sabbaths and "most vivid of all" the story of the rats, "that unforgettable rodent army," pouring out of the Priory to devour everything in its path, "for it scattered among the village homes and brought curses and horrors in its train" (*DH* 31). This is a demonic version of Browning's "The Pied Piper of Hamelin," in which the rats, to a jolly patter of anapests and recherché rhymes, live side-by-side with the townspeople. The rats, according to his account at this moment, are a spectacle, distanced by the observing eye; but when he experiences them in the Priory he only hears them, and the ear delivers a much more immediate experience.

What, then, are we to say of the narrator according to his account of the "legendry"? He is a racist American who has assumed, rather easily, a benign view of the values practiced by his aristocratic ancestors. A head on the bastion does not disturb him. In addition, unmoved by the story of the rats, he does not accept the possibility of instinctual motivations. Though he is attracted and repelled by the legendry, he does not admit that the sins of old England have anything to do with him; he is another version of the American Adam, returning to England in all innocence to recapitulate a story by Henry James. The villagers therefore may have personal reasons to dislike him, not simply, as he assumes, because he is a member of an ancient family of bad barons. A victim of the typical American discontinuity, dramatized by the letter burned by the Federal troops, he attempts to overcome it; but it cannot be overcome through mere imitation and a rationalized modernity, his aesthetic gothicism and electric lights.

He needs his Nigger-Man. As much as Longrifle needs Chinkachook, Ishmael needs Queequeg, and Huckleberry Finn needs Jim, this white-as-white narrator needs the dispossessed and the other; and if Leslie Fiedler's analysis in *Love and Death in the American Novel* is persuasive, then Lovecraft is as American an author as Cooper, Melville, and Clemens. Delapore could know nothing if it were not for his familiar and intimate connection to American racism.

Three elements combine here. One is his love of the cat, his only connection now with his former life in America when he was an innocent businessman. The next is the racism implied in the cat's name, a detail prepared earlier in his account of the negroes "howling and praying" as the plantation of the family burned to the earth, as though those slaves were that concerned with the destruction of the plantation house that emblemized their oppression (*DH* 27); this element is connected with the cousin who "went among the negroes" (*DH* 31). The third is the cat as cat, a symbol of intuitive knowledge that Lovecraft had inherited from Baudelaire's poems in *Les Fleurs du mal*. His cat, the beloved pet and symbol of the oppressed that return possessed with dark knowledge, allows him to hear what the cat hears, the rustling of the rats in the draperies, the sense that although he had rebuilt the Priory as a modern, gothic imitation of the Priory as it had been, this Priory now, a symbol of his own will and a substitute for his family and for his son, was now infested with creatures of animalistic instinct that shall lead him to the truth of himself and of his family.

The other cats, cats as cats, also attest to the existence of the rats, but for the narrator and for his Nigger-Man they exist fearfully. And Nigger-Man and the other cats agree that the direction the rats are taking is downward. Their going down, a word repeated several times in the father's narration, brings him and the men with him, including Norrys, to the twilit grotto of the climax.

At the same time, however, as Nigger-Man and the other cats are disturbed, the narrator has begun to have the dreams that attest to the grotto. He knows of it before Sir Arthur Brinton, an authority on the Troad and presumably on Atys and Cybele, opens the door of the altar. A number of elements are at work here. First is Lovecraft's insistence that dreams connect with a reality that otherwise the dreamer would not know (Burleson 140). Second is the major Lovecraftian theme, in which several scientific thoughts intersect: that humanity has evolved from earlier life forms to which an individual might once more devolve, usually with most unpleasant consequences. Third, however, in my reading of the story is the devolution implied in the trench experience. The soldier either goes mad, or he learns to turn off the sensory impact of the bombs, machine-guns, mortars, and screams of the wounded. It may be objected that every protagonist in a Lovecraft story suffers from such traits as alienation and a living death; my point is that in this story these traits and others find their accurate historical context in the war. According to Eric Leed's analysis of the character of a man in combat during World War I, the soldier finds himself alienated from civilian experience but possessed of a secret no one in civilian life could discover, buried in the trenches and invisible, a person who lives only when dead and buried, polluted and sacred, dead but reborn into a new comradeship that cuts across class lines and national affiliations, imprisoned by the new impersonal technology, no longer human, living a life that only a mythological language could account for, homeless and compelled to relive his homelessness. He becomes a brother to the rat. Everyone, German and American and Englishman, is a brother to the rat. That is to say, the father dons the character of the son, his son who had become a rat, because he has already suffered these traits from the time he was driven out of Carfax and took on the invisibility of the Yankee businessman. Then, having lived with his maimed son for two years after the war, he suffers from the same liminality that his son the soldier had internalized, and attempts to find his home in the Priory to which his son had pointed him. By coming to the Priory he attempts to be prior to every father and every son in his family's history; despite his cultured pretense, he must acknowledge that he is the archetypal swineherd in the grotto, who is prior to all this except the rats that in his dream overwhelm the scene.

But though the cats and the dreams attest to the presence of the rats, neither the narrator nor the reader ever see one, not the barest tip of a tail. According to the narrator's account of the legendry, the "epic of the rats" is the "most vivid of all" (*DH* 31), yet he sees nothing. Nevertheless, they are a "scampering army of obscene vermin," a "lean, filthy, ravenous army" (*DH* 31). The first night he hears the rats it is a mere "low, distinct scurrying" (*DH* 34), but the next night "the walls were alive with a nauseous sound—the verminous slithering of ravenous, gigantic rats," which make the tapestry perform "a singular dance of death" (*DH* 35). These rats, "in numbers apparently inexhaustible, were engaged in one stupendous migration from inconceivable heights to some depth conceivably, or inconceivably, below" (*DH* 36). These rats have something of the lemming about them, devoted to Thanatos. The next night he hears "the same babel of scurrying rats" and becomes convinced, given their downward plunge, that the entire cliff on which the Priory rests is "riddled with questing rats" (*DH* 38). Now he associates the rats with pride and the confusion of tongues and with tunnels that, punningly, challenge him with a puzzle—and the reader too. At the climax in the grotto he is beset by "the eldritch scurrying of those fiend-born rats, always questing for new horrors and determined to lead me on" to the realms of Nyarlathotep, "the mad faceless god" (*DH* 44). At this point we realize that Nigger-Man has a double nature; he is a mythic manifestation of Nyarlathotep, and he is simply one of the several naturalistic cats that attest that something wrong riddles the Priory, while in a remarkable transformation the rats also become a mass psychopompos that leads the narrator to the realm of a meaningless death that he feels compelled to explore despite his fear and repulsion. Cat and rat are conflated; but at this point neither cat nor rats need guide him any further, for it is not "the viscous, gelatinous, ravenous army that feast on the dead and the living" (*DH* 44), specifically on Norrys, but he that feasts. He is the rat. That is the significance of the degeneration of tongues he experiences, his personal babel, that concludes "chchch . . ." (*DH* 45). He becomes the rat that he always was; and thus his task force finds Nigger-Man, no longer plunging downward into "the illimitable gulf of the unknown" but "leaping and tearing" at the throat of the narrator who is "crouching in the blackness over the plump, half-eaten body of Capt. Norrys" (*DH* 45). Note that word "half-eaten." Only a very large rat or a swarm of rats could have devoured that amount.

But why should the narrator want to eat Capt. Norrys? First, it was the Norryses that received the Priory after Walter de la Poer slaughtered his family and fled to the banks of the James River, probably late in the reign of James if a plantation on the banks of the James seems a plausible option. A small mystery surrounds this matter, whether it was the Stuarts or the Protectorate that gave the Norryses the land. I think there can be little doubt that the de la Poers would have been loyalists during the English Civil War. Some time passed before the land was allotted to the Norrys family, so it is quite possible that their fortunes rose with that of the Parliament and Cromwell. The de la Poers were Barons, whereas the Norryses were never anything more than gentlemen. "Shall a Norrys hold the lands of a de la Poer?" the narrator pointedly asks (*DH* 44).[4] And if all this is true, then by a pun it makes an insane sense that *Norrys* plays an evil part in the War of *Northern* Aggression. In addition, Capt. Norrys symbolically takes the place of the maimed Alfred, and the narrator may unconsciously hold that easy-going young man responsible for Alfred's death; he can certainly hold him responsible for the narrator's purchase of the fatal Priory. Shortly before he attacks Norrys the young man's posture in the abattoir, "used as he was to the trenches" (*DH* 43), reminds him of Norrys's part in the war. In any case, in an act of unconscious filicide he may be killing his own son Alfred when he kills Norrys, his son's good friend; and thus we are reminded of the older generation's responsibility for that war.

Lovecraft achieves a remarkable transformation of the rats through the course of the story. At first associated with the "rav'ning" German army, the war that killed the narrator's son, the rats become something more, a "gigantic" creature that performs a "dance of death," a medieval emblem of death's ubiquity. He cannot answer the riddling "babel" because he is the thing itself; he cannot answer himself because the letter has been lost, but also because no one can answer the riddle that he

---

4. John Hitz goes so far as to argue, I think with some exaggeration, that the Norrys family were usurpers of the de la Poers' land (32).

himself is without dire results. Oedipus comes to mind, who answers the riddle of the sphinx, man, and the riddle of himself, the man that kills his father and marries his mother, at the cost of stabbing his eyes out. It is important that the founder of the Delapores in Virginia commits patricide, that the narrator regains his heritage through the death of his maimed son, and that the narrator feels fear at the death of the highly questionable father of the nation, President Harding. At the conclusion, however, the rats transcend personal psychology; they represent a mass psychology in which every war is inevitable and devouring. Not only did the war eat the narrator's son, the War Between the States ate Carfax "and burnt Grandsire Delapore and the secret" (*DH* 44). Thus human discontinuity is not simply a fact of the migration that every American suffers; it arises from the human participation in an animal aggression that always seems greater than the individual, sweeping the individual along because aggression is built into the human psyche, which then insists upon building it into its institutions, even if they are institutions of peace like the League of Nations. This "wave of hunger" (Montelone 21) is actuated by every priority; and thus the rats plunge downward in the walls of a Priory.

The psychosis of the narrator, then, is not personal. When he eats his son, we eat ours.

Epilogue

It is gratifying to recognize that "The Rats in the Walls" found one of its first posthumous publications in *The Dunwich Horror and Other Weird Tales*, which appeared in the Editions for the Armed Services that S. T. Joshi writes "introduced Lovecraft to large numbers of servicemen still stationed in Europe after the war" (637–38). One can only speculate that this story appealed to them for the very reasons outlined in this essay.

Works Cited

Aldington, Richard. "In the Trenches." In *The Penguin Book of First World War Poetry*.

Ashbery, John. "Fuckin' Sarcophagi." In *Can You Hear, Bird?* New York: Farrar, Straus & Giroux, 1995.

Burleson, Donald. "On Lovecraft's Themes: Touching the Glass." In David E. Schultz and S. T. Joshi, ed. *An Epicure in the Terrible: A*

Centennial Anthology of Essays in Honor of H. P. Lovecraft. Ruth- erford, NJ: Fairleigh Dickinson University Press, 1991.

Byron, George Gordon, Lord. *Don Juan and Other Satirical Poems.* Ed. Louis I. Bredvold. New York: Odyssey Press, 1935.

Carlisle, Lois, and Davida Richardson, ed. *Fourth Year Latin: Selections from Virgil, Ovid, Catullus, Martial, and Horace.* 1st ed. 1933. Bos- ton: Allyn and Bacon, 1948.

Eliot, T. S. *The Complete Poems and Plays 1909–1950.* New York: Harcourt, Brace, 1952.

Fiedler, Leslie. *Love and Death in the American Novel.* 1960. New York: Stein & Day, 1966.

Fussell, Paul. *The Great War and Modern Memory.* London: Oxford University Press, 1977.

Gilbert, Martin. *The First World War: A Complete History.* New York: Henry Holt, 1994.

Hitz, John Kipling. "Some Notes on 'The Rats in the Walls.'" *Lovecraft Studies* No. 40 (Fall 1998): 29–33.

Johnson, Samuel. *A Dictionary of the English Language.* 4th ed. Lon- don: W. Strahan, 1773. 2 vols.

Jones, David. *In Parenthesis.* London: Faber & Faber, 1963.

Joshi, S. T. *H. P. Lovecraft: A Life.* West Warwick, RI: Necronomi- con Press, 1996.

Kipling, Rudyard. *Verse 1885–1918.* Garden City, NY: Doubleday, 1921.

Leed, Eric J. *No Man's Land: Combat and Identity in World War I.* Cambridge: Cambridge University Press, 1979.

Mariconda, Steven J. *On the Emergence of "Cthulhu" and Other Ob- servations.* West Warwick, RI: Necronomicon Press, 1995.

Montelone, Paul. "'The Rats in the Walls': A Study in Pessimism." *Lovecraft Studies* No. 32 (Spring 1995): 18–26.

Owen, Wilfred. *The Collected Poems.* Ed. C. Day Lewis. New York: New Directions, 1964.

Rickword, Edgell. "Trench Poets." In *The Penguin Book of First World War Poetry.*

Rosenberg, Isaac. *The Collected Works.* Ed. Ian Parsons. Foreword by Siegfried Sassoon. New York: Oxford University Press, 1979.

Russell, Francis. *The Shadow of Blooming Grove: Warren G. Harding in His Times.* New York: McGraw-Hill, 1968.

Sassoon, Siegfried. "Aftermath." In *The Penguin Book of First World War Poetry.*

Walter, George, ed. *The Penguin Book of First World War Poetry.* London: Penguin, 2006.

Knowledge in the Void: Anomaly, Observation, and the Incomplete Paradigm Shift in H. P. Lovecraft's Fiction

Kálmán Matolcsy

Pseudo-Science and the Supramundane

The Lovecraftian weird tale is an intergeneric form, capable of retaining the major elements now regarded as the distinctive features of such literary genres or modes as the Gothic, horror, and the fantastic. Thus it is far from surprising that a great number of H. P. Lovecraft's stories, primarily "The Whisperer in Darkness," *At the Mountains of Madness*, and "The Colour out of Space," seem somewhat science-fictional. As J. Vernon Shea maintains, "surely the basic themes of science-fiction, the reachings out into time and space, had very much to do with the body of [Lovecraft's] work" (138). S. T. Joshi's *Weird Tale*, however, disconnects Lovecraft's "quasi science fiction stories" from science fiction proper and defines them simply as a subgenre of the weird tale, based on the Lovecraftian realist method of handling the central element of alternative reality: "*Quasi science fiction* is a development of supernatural horror in that the real world is again presupposed as the norm, but the impossible intrusions are rationalized in some way. . . . [M]ost of the later Lovecraft fall into this category" (*The Weird Tale* 7).[1]

One of the reasons for the abundance of "quasi–science fiction" in his work may be that Lovecraft himself was an amateur scientist

---

1. Elsewhere Joshi maintains that HPL, "virtually singlehandedly, created an amalgam of horror fiction and what we would now term science fiction" (*Decline of the West* 54).

from an early age. As he writes, "In 1899 . . . [m]y predilection for
natural science, fostered by my Aunt Lillian, took form in a love of
chemistry. . . . [B]efore many months had elapsed, I was deep in experimental research, having a well-equipped laboratory in the cellar"
(*Lord of a Visible World* 13). Nonetheless, in spite of his functional
acquaintance with chemistry, physics, and astronomy, the tales contain mostly elements that may be termed merely pseudo-scientific. It
is easy to list such normative features of Lovecraft's quasi science-
fiction stories, as Fritz Leiber, indeed, has done in his celebrated
"Through Hyperspace with Brown Jenkin." Similarly, Robert
Weinberg in "H. P. Lovecraft and Pseudomathematics" identifies in
"The Dreams in the Witch House" references to non-existent science
such as non-Euclidean calculus and a space-warp, points of "made-up
science which had very little or no relation to the real work of the
period" (113). Weinberg contends,

> [u]nfortunately, while [Lovecraft's] grasp of science and mathematics
> might have been greater than the average layman [*sic*], it was not
> strong enough to present a convincing picture to the careful reader.
> Further, Lovecraft made the cardinal mistake of speculation of the
> impossible. While to the non-scientist, this may not sound like much
> of a sin, it is the cardinal mistake of the uninformed. (Weinberg 117)

Lovecraft certainly was knowledgeable enough to use the pseudo-
scientific concepts as mere tongue-in-cheek references to science fiction proper rather than seriously intended references to natural science, and therefore reproaching Lovecraft for not having used the
right terminology with their proper denotations misses the mark. Not
primarily because in fiction the status of the extratextual referent is
itself rather problematic, but because the axis of scientific thought in
Lovecraft's fiction is not the casual, slightly erroneous integration of
Einsteinian physics or other theories but an inclination to rationalize
the supernatural.[2] Although Lovecraft—far from making a "mistake"—deals with "a speculation of the impossible" (Weinberg 117),
his "impossible intrusions are rationalized in some way," as Joshi puts

---

2. In spite of this, specific references to Einstein and the theories of relativity
are easy to find in several of the stories, such as "The Shunned House" (106),
"The Whisperer in Darkness" (213), *Mountains of Madness* (31), or "Witch
House" (307).

it (*Weird Tale* 7). As he argues, Lovecraft's quasi science fiction "is a more advanced form because it implies that the 'supernatural' is not *ontological* but *epistemological:* it is only our ignorance of certain 'natural laws' that creates the illusion of supernaturalism" (7). This refinement of the supernatural element comprises a crucial method in Lovecraft's stories, especially with regard to its rendition of the problems of human knowledge.

In his 1998 dissertation, Bradley Alan Will identifies the distinctive feature of Lovecraft's work as "the supramundane": it is that phenomenon "which exceeds human understanding but is not supernatural" (19). "The presence of the supramundane," Will maintains, "indicates the inadequacy of the human faculty of understanding rather than, as with the supernatural, the intrusion of elements from outside the natural world" (19). Even though Will does not pay a tribute to Matthew H. Onderdonk's "The Lord of R'lyeh," the notion of the supramundane in Lovecraft is clearly as old as Onderdonk's essay, published in 1945. Onderdonk calls the effect the "supernormal," and his view is not far from Lovecraft's, who interpreted such phenomena in his fiction as "*supplements* rather than *contradictions* of the visible and mensurable universe" (*SL* 3. 295–96). Supramundane phenomena in Lovecraft are *rationalized* variations of the supernatural, which provides the gist of the dichotomized Lovecraftian fantastic, the major problematic of confrontation between the searching intellect and the cosmos.

In "Whisperer," the pseudo-Akeley's paean about the Outer Ones highlights the scientific streak in the story, identifying the extraterrestrial beings as supramundane, their existence and affiliated phenomena as "*supplements* rather than *contradictions*" to our knowledge:

> Do you know that Einstein is wrong, and that certain objects and forces *can* move with a velocity greater than that of light? With proper aid I expect to go backward and forward in time . . . You can't imagine the degree to which those beings have carried science. There is nothing they can't do with the mind and body of living organisms. (*DH* 253)

Through the supramundane, the schema of fantastic confrontation is rationalized[3] and not in any way realistically modeled. This is not to say

---

3. Although Todorov in his seminal work provides ample explication of the fantastic turning into the fantastic-uncanny or the uncanny, I find that HPL's

that Lovecraft regarded his work as completely unrealistic. As he emphasizes in "Notes on Writing Weird Fiction," "Inconceivable events and conditions have a special handicap to overcome, and this can be accomplished only through the maintenance of a careful realism in every phase of the story *except* that touching on the given marvel" (*CE* 5.177). It is fairly commonplace that writers of the weird need a basic external reality for their forays into the fantastic. Nonetheless, instead of merely presupposing reality as a basis for its subversion by the fantastic, Lovecraft uses his setting and characters to establish a scientific basis for the supramundane. Even Edmund Wilson, one of Lovecraft's earliest and most vitriolic critics, commends Lovecraft's scientific thought while condemning the majority of his work as "tales of the marvellous and the ridiculous" (47): "He had a scientific imagination rather similar, though much inferior, to that of the early Wells" (49). The flaws in Wilson's overall approach, however, permeate his view of Lovecraft's scientific side, since he is convinced that, for example, "The story called 'The Colour out of Space' more or less predicts the effects of the atomic bomb" (49). Wilson, followed by Weinberg and many others, simply gets it wrong, since it is not the representation of certain achievements of science that makes Lovecraft's fiction scientific—that would only vindicate claims for Lovecraft's pseudo-science. Although the Lovecraftian text does not always promise or deliver the precise representation of extratextual science, which critics like Weinberg demand of it, on the metaphorical level it more often contributes to the knowledge about twentieth-century science. The Lovecraftian text does not indulge in the actual science of Einsteinian physics, molecular chemistry, or early-twentieth-century astronomy—however cleverly and accurately these may be woven into the fabric of many tales[4]—but

---

tales do not fit his schema entirely. In HPL we usually find an anomaly that first seems fantastic and later is explained, but not simply explained away. HPL's special method resembles a mixture of the uncanny and the marvellous, to use Todorov's terms. The unearthly phenomena, the texts suggest, should be representable and explicable by an altered, elevated, or more sophisticated version of human science, and is, theoretically, far from totally unattainable—hence uncanny. However, it remains alien to our world and explained only by that hypothetical future science—hence marvellous.

4. For instance, in "Whisperer," the then recently discovered Pluto is the origin of malignant alien entities, and most of the stunningly realistic setting of *Mountains of Madness* (1931) rests on actual accounts of Antarctic explora-

in general philosophical notions about the growth, scope, and aim of natural science. On a most general level, Lovecraft's fiction contributes to our knowledge of human scientific inquiry and the major problems of epistemology.

The Insurmountable Anomaly and the Incompatibility of Paradigms

When attempting to delineate such a scientific dimension in the Lovecraftian text, we encounter an apparent problem at the outset; that is, the Lovecraftian text seems not to concentrate exclusively on natural science as such. Many of the narrator-protagonists, for instance, are artists, dreamers, and the like; and, although the plot frequently discloses scientific research, rarely do we encounter a *detailed* description of such research or experiment comprising the greater part of the tales (with the possible exception of "The Colour" and *Mountains of Madness*). Peter Medawar in *The Limits of Science* provides the following definition:

> [T]he word "science" itself is used as a general name for, on the one hand, the procedures of science—adventures of thought and stratagems of inquiry that go into the advancement of learning—and on the other hand, the substantive body of knowledge that is the outcome of this complex endeavor . . . (3)

Based on Medawar's rendition, almost all Lovecraftian texts can be designated as belonging to the realm of the scientific. The Lovecraftian text, most significantly, deals with the modes and results of acquiring knowledge and the problems encountered during the process. Lovecraftian tales, therefore, are all topical of science. There appear four distinctive groups: (1) *tales about science and scientists*—*Mountains of Madness*, "Witch House," or "Herbert West—Reanimator";[5] (2) *tales about a general inquiry*, for example, genealogical or antiquarian—"The Shadow over Innsmouth," *Charles Dexter Ward*; (3) *stories of detection*

---

tion, including, for instance, Admiral Byrd's (1928–30).

5. In the Medawarian sense, it is of course unnecessary to discriminate between the natural sciences and life sciences as such (*Mountains of Madness* and "Herbert West" fluctuating between the two, as it were), or even Walter Gilman's mathematics in "Witch House" (which could also be seen as a framework for scientific work proper).

and investigation—"The Call of Cthulhu," "The Horror at Red Hook";[6] and (4) *stories of scholars outside the field of natural science*—"The Dunwich Horror." Nevertheless, to be able to outline clearly what dimension of science the Lovecraftian text enters, we should rely on certain Lovecraftian ground rules.

The Lovecraftian text views natural science as, first and foremost, materialistic. Even the anomalous entities in Lovecraft are basically of a material nature.[7] This premise, which the Lovecraftian story never fails to generate, ultimately serves the purpose of establishing the supramundane facet of the cosmic effect. To be supramundane, however, these entities or phenomena have to be "composed of"—as the narrator of *Mountains of Madness* speculates—"matter more widely different from that which we know" (*MM* 68). Similarly, Akeley in "Whisperer" writes in one of his early letters: "I tried to photograph [the monster] . . ., but when I developed the film *there wasn't anything visible except the woodshed*. What can the thing have been made of? I saw it and felt it, and they all leave footprints. It was surely made of matter—but what kind of matter?" (*DH* 236). Similarly, Joshi asserts, "the quasi-materiality of [Lovecraft's] entities was for him a philosophical necessity, and he in fact had some admirable success in depicting monsters which, while harmonising with a modified materialism, nevertheless expand it to its very limits" (*Decline of the West* 85). It is precisely this contradiction between classical materialism and the nature of alien matter in the Lovecraftian text that supports an interpretation of the monsters as scientific anomalies.

Thomas S. Kuhn, one of the first and major theorists of scientific anomalies, in his groundbreaking work *The Structure of Scientific Revo-*

---

6. The connection between detection and science, as in the case of detection and the Gothic novel, is a prevalent one, commencing with Poe's Dupin and culminating in Arthur Conan Doyle's Sherlock Holmes.

7. These may be "forces" or "gods," according to what stance we assume, the reader-critic's or that of some of the lower-order characters. Robert M. Price asserts, "[T]here is a direct continuity between Lovecraft's scientism and his mythology . . . Lovecraft's Great Old Ones, on the narrative level, appear to be gods and/or extraterrestrials, neither of which Lovecraft accepted as real. But on a deeper level it is fairly clear that Lovecraft uses his titans Yog-Sothoth, Cthulhu, and others to symbolize the indifferent, inexorable forces of the cosmos which blindly produced *Homo sapiens* and will finally unknowingly destroy them again" (27).

lutions, integrates the thought of anomalies into his theory of paradigm shifts: "Discovery commences with the awareness of anomaly,
i.e., with the recognition that nature has somehow violated the para-
digm-induced expectations that govern normal science" (52–53). In the
Lovecraftian text, the anomaly, as a rule, conforms to the characters'
confrontation with the supramundane. Will interprets the supramundane as "a depiction of an anomaly of the highest order—an anomaly
which cannot be resolved" (42). In "Cthulhu" the alien entity is hit and
is halved by the steamboat *Alert* but its body does not become dysfunctional, rather its remnants are gathered together again:

> There was a bursting as of an exploding bladder, a slushy nastiness as
> of a cloven sunfish, a stench as of a thousand opened graves . . . For an
> instant the ship was befouled by an acrid and blinding green cloud,
> and there was only a venomous seething astern; where—God in
> Heaven—the scattered plasticity of that nameless sky-spawn was
> nebulously recombining in its hateful original form . . . (*DH* 153)

In "Cthulhu" there are other instances of anomaly, and the unnatural
behavior of Cthulhu's "body" appears rather belated in the sequence of
events. In other tales, such as "Dunwich" or, especially, "Colour," there
appears a gradual build-up of anomalous events that ultimately provides a heightened sense of the total contradiction of natural law. The
meteor that ruins the lives of a backwoods farmer and his family in
"Colour" is the origin of the anomaly series. First, the meteor's texture
is wholly unknown, the rock emits a certain glow, it refuses to cool, it
is peculiarly soft—can only be "gouged rather than chipped" (*DH* 57),
and the specimen little by little shrinks and finally disappears from the
laboratory desk, the glass beaker with it.[8] Then, the scientists at Miskatonic University discover a small globe of nebulous substance in the
meteor, which, after bursting like a bubble, disappears as well. Meanwhile the strange color permeates all around it, animate or inanimate:
the farmhouse faintly glows by night, the animals mutate in a certain
unnerving fashion, the vegetation acquires a disturbing radiance, and

---

8. The idea of the anomalous meteor appears to originate in "Cthulhu," written in 1926. There the material of the curious statuette is similarly wholly
alien: "Totally separate and apart, its very material was a mystery; for the
soapy, greenish-black stone with its golden or iridescent flecks and striations
resembled nothing familiar to geology or mineralogy" (*DH* 148–49).

the trees sway even when there is no wind. Finally the Gardner family slowly diminishes; they go mad one by one, and those who do not disappear disintegrate bodily—they crumble and turn into gray powder. Soon the farm itself falls apart, but the bleak, gray "blasted heath" area in its place continues to grow in diameter each day, adhering to the story's cosmic quality. These comprise only the major anomalous points in the story, and there are countless others. For instance, inexplicable thunderbolts crashing into the farm, long descriptions of mutated animals and vegetables, and a constant subliminal noise that the family falls into the habit of listening to.

In the Lovecraftian text the central anomaly is not concentrated. It is scattered around the text, and, most importantly, the various elements are built up gradually toward a climax, establishing what Will calls a feeling of "unfathomable anomaly" (7). The anomalous phenomena—facets of the central anomaly—ultimately reach the stage where some fundamental natural law or scientific theory is contradicted to the point of intolerance (usually earlier for the reader than for the narrator-protagonist). Such fundamental natural laws and theories contribute to what Kuhn calls "normal science" (10). Normal science is mainly distinguished by a ruling paradigm and the regular appearance of minor puzzles that scientists can solve. The notion of "paradigm" is crucial to Kuhn's theory and I will greatly expand on it later. At the moment, however, suffice it to say that a paradigm is partly understood as a set of scientific theories, methods, modes—or even a *Weltanschauung*—that dominates the scientific field and governs scientific inquiry at any given time (Kuhn 175). Examples are easy to find: Ptolemaic cosmology, Newtonian mechanics, or Einstein's physics each was a quasi-exclusive paradigm of its age.[9] As Kuhn asserts, "Normal science consists in . . . extending the knowledge of those facts that the paradigm displays as particularly revealing, by increasing the extent of the match between those facts and the paradigm's predictions, and by further articulation of the paradigm itself" (24).

Yet there remain puzzles, a definitive feature of normal science, as

---

9. Quasi-exclusive, since there occurred transitive periods—occasionally literally hundreds of years—when the various paradigms and worldviews co-existed and a constant struggle was taking place. For instance, parts of the latter two—Newton's and Einstein's physics—still dominate much of natural science, and do it simultaneously.

John Watkins contends: "There will always be apparent discrepancies or anomalies. Normal research largely consists of resolving these anomalies by making suitable adjustments which leave the paradigm intact" (27). In Kuhn's view there is, once in a while, a radical leap from normal science to "extraordinary science,"[10] and it occurs in the field of puzzles. At one point the overwhelming number of anomalies presented to any paradigm tilts the balance toward another bundle of scientific explanations and an alternative vision: "the emergence of new theories is generally preceded by a period of pronounced professional insecurity. As one might expect, that insecurity is generated by the persistent failure of the puzzles of normal science to come out as they should" (67–68). When a number of anomalies or a major anomaly necessitates a leap from normal science, there commences a state of crisis:

> . . . if an anomaly is to evoke crisis, it must usually be more than just an anomaly . . . Sometimes an anomaly will clearly call into question explicit and fundamental generalizations of the paradigm . . . Or . . . the development of normal science may transform an anomaly that has previously been only a vexation into a source of crisis . . . When, for these reasons or others like them, an anomaly comes to seem more than just another puzzle of normal science, the transition to crisis and to extraordinary science has begun. (Kuhn 82)

In Lovecraft there are countless examples for both normal and extraordinary science, and the tension between the two brings about the supramundane effect. In "Dunwich" the strange rumbling and other noises appearing in the hills "still form a puzzle to geologists and physiographers" (*DH* 158), a puzzle that, to Professor Armitage, looms as an anomaly. In "Colour" the scientists from Miskatonic University "fumble away" in the field of normal science, devoting their time to smaller puzzles. They regard the meteor and its behavior, therefore, as a pressing anomaly, one that would radically change their normal science. Curiously, but not without an explanation, when the shrinking rock specimen finally disappears, they abandon further investigation of the abnormally altered farm and its inhabitants, denying even having ob-

---

10. On the relationship of the two levels, there remain differing views. Karl Popper, for instance inserts "many gradations" between Kuhn's normal scientists and extraordinary scientists ("Normal Science" 54).

served anything anomalous in the first place.

Kuhn provides an example for this kind of evasive behavior: "Though they may begin to lose faith and then to consider alternatives, [scientists] do not renounce the paradigm that has led them into crisis. They do not, that is, treat anomalies as counter-instances, though in the vocabulary of philosophy of science that is what they are" (77).[11] He also provides an explanation: "These hint what our later examination of paradigm rejection will disclose more fully: once it has achieved the status of a paradigm, a scientific theory is declared invalid only if an alternate candidate is available to take its place" (77). Important as normal science may be,[12] the high-energy state of extraordinary science, however, is what accounts for the emergence of new theories: "crisis loosens the rules of normal puzzle-solving in ways that ultimately permit a new paradigm to emerge" (Kuhn 80). The novel paradigm will normally be able to explain the anomalies on their own grounds, while also explaining most of the earlier, non-anomalous, phenomena.

A major crisis, where rigid paradigms open up to multiple questionings, leads the way to a "scientific revolution" as Kuhn understands it: "the successive transition from one paradigm to another via revolution is the usual developmental pattern of mature science" (12). In the revolution—the analogy taken from the social sciences—the whole of the preceding paradigm is "burned up." Even though an exceptionally thoroughgoing student of scientific revolutions, Kuhn seems uniformly unspecific about the sense of "paradigm": "In its established usage, a paradigm is an accepted model or pattern, and that aspect of its meaning has enabled me, lacking a better word, to appropriate 'paradigm' here" (23). Kuhn himself observes his failure at a definition in the 1962 book and provides a double definition in his 1969 postscript (a paradigm, in the latter, is a worldview or a more-

---

11. This effect is oftentimes called "tenacity." See Paul Feyerabend's "Consolations for the Specialist," especially 205.

12. Critics of Kuhn either see him as praising or reproaching normal science. See Lakatos and Musgrave, ed., *Criticism and the Growth of Knowledge.* The representative of still another view, Popper, believes that science is and should be a state of constant struggle between opposing worldviews. He concludes, "Kuhn is mistaken when he suggests that what he calls 'normal' science is normal" ("Normal Science" 53).

or-less material element of that [175]). In reality, while having in mind a "model or pattern," Kuhn uses paradigm, as Margaret Masterman demonstrates, in as many as twenty-one different senses in *Scientific Revolutions* ("The Nature of a Paradigm" 61–65). These twenty-one Masterman subsumes under three classes: (1) *metaphysical paradigm* or *metaparadigm*—"a metaphysical notion or entity, rather than a scientific one"; (2) *sociological paradigm*—"a universally recognized scientific achievement"; and (3) *artefact paradigm* or *construct paradigm*—"an actual textbook or classic work," "supplying tools," "an analogy," or "a grammatical paradigm" (65). Masterman argues that *metaparadigms* are the only kind of paradigm to which "Kuhn's philosophical critics have referred," taking the sense of the expression for granted and overlooking the other two components (65). In the present study of the Lovecraftian text, I am going to utilize not only the *metaparadigm* but also the *sociological paradigm.*

Lovecraft was an ardent mechanistic materialist. He also inclined to call himself, somewhat erroneously, a pessimistic materialist, as Joshi in his *Decline of the West* powerfully demonstrates. The stance of Lovecraft's fictional characters is, in the greater part of the stories, analogous to that of their creator. As Maurice Lévy asserts, "it is manifest that many of [the protagonists] are projections of the author [Lovecraft] himself, who through the illusion of literature thus enters his own imaginary world" (42). Not solely because Lovecraft must have found it fascinating to let his characters enter his life or vice versa (Joshi, Donald R. Burleson, Timo Airaksinen, and many others are skeptic about this view),[13] but also because Lovecraft, as R. Boerem contends, was consciously working in the tradition of the "gentleman narrator," invented by Poe, Sheridan Le Fanu, Arthur Machen, and several others—writers whose work Lovecraft both admired and theorized upon in his "Supernatural Horror in Literature." As Boerem

---

13. Joshi contends, "In terms of the fiction, I am very aware that the attribution of a given statement or sentiment to Lovecraft is at times highly problematical: no creative artist is so naive as to make any of his characters simple mouthpieces for his views" (*Decline* v). A similar sentiment leads Burleson to abstain from traditional criticism and attempt a deconstructive study of HPL and Airaksinen to assert that all of HPL's writing can be subsumed under the category of fiction, even his letters. See Burleson's *Disturbing the Universe* and Airaksinen, *The Philosophy of H. P. Lovecraft.*

stresses, some of a gentleman's major characteristics around the *fin de siècle* were education, occupation, and income (258). Out of these "virtues," as they were then observed, Lovecraft crafted his protagonists (many of whom are the narrators of the stories as well), partly in conformity with his own image. "By far, the great number of Lovecraftian narrators are scholars," Boerem observes. "Most of these are scholars by temperament and inclination. . . . In later stories, the students become teachers or professors" (266–67). As gentlemanly students, professors, and scholars, the mindsets of Lovecraftian protagonists involve the materialistic, the logical, the rational, and the empirical. For example, Thurston, the narrator of "Cthulhu," keeps referring to his "callous rationalism" (*DH* 132), "the ingrained scepticism then forming my philosophy" (*DH* 130), or his attitude of "absolute materialism" (*DH* 144). Professor Nathaniel Wingate Peaslee also introduces himself in "The Shadow out of Time" thus:

> After my graduation I studied economics at Harvard, and came back to Miskatonic as instructor of Political Economy in 1895. For thirteen years more my life ran smoothly and happily. I married Alice Keezar of Haverhill in 1896, and my three children, Robert K., Wingate, and Hannah, were born in 1898, 1900, and 1903, respectively. In 1898 I became an associate professor, and in 1902 a full professor. At no time had I the least interest in either occultism or abnormal psychology. (*Dreams in the Witch House* 336–37)

The supposed sanity of the character is hence fully established with the help of a scholarly bent—and a rather prosaic kind at that—and a happy family life. The narrator of "The Shunned House," despite being a sort of shady lover of the macabre, describes his method as inherently scientific: "I was disposed to take the whole subject with profound seriousness, and began at once not only to review the evidence, but to accumulate as much more as I could" (*MM* 246). Even "dreamers"—Randolph Carter from *The Dream-Quest of Unknown Kadath*, Kuranes from "Celephaïs," the narrator of "Polaris," and many others—usually discourse on such a worldview, even if they do not completely adhere to it (although when the horror arrives, they react similarly to other rational characters). Against this materialistic-rationalistic metaparadigm, the Lovecraftian failure of cognition, the disintegration of the intelligent human being, is set.

The Lovecraftian paradigm is not only a metaparadigm—a set of theories or a worldview that provides working methods for any one scientist—it is also a *sociological paradigm*. Although I mostly concur with Will's contention that "Lovecraft, Clarke, Gibson and other authors of the supramundane do not share Kuhn's confidence in the human capacity for understanding" (42), I see the Lovecraftian protagonist's failure as a result not only of a lack of cognitive prowess, but also of a lack of a sympathetic community of scientific minds. Although many paradigms bear the name of one scientist-thinker-philosopher, in Kuhn's view the route to and the establishment of the new scientific paradigm is a social process, not the work of an extreme genius:

> The anomaly itself now comes to be more generally recognized as such by the profession. More and more attention is devoted to it and more and more of the field's eminent men. If it still continues to resist, as it usually does not, many of them come to view its resolution as *the* subject matter of their discipline. (83)

The Kuhnian paradigm, provided it ultimately arises out of an acute scientific debate, is, therefore, a sociological paradigm.

The Lovecraftian protagonist, the gentleman narrator, is as a rule secluded from the greater part of humanity. In "Dunwich," Professor Armitage and his two fellow-academics are able to defeat the Whateley monster due only to their concerted efforts. Similarly, in *Charles Dexter Ward* it takes a lynch mob to wipe out the danger lurking in the Pawtuxet woods. Carroll defines what he calls the "complex discovery plot" as the distinctive pattern for horror plots. He asserts, "After the hesitations of confirmation, the complex discovery plot culminates in confrontation. Humanity marches out to meet the monster" (102). There appear tellingly few stories in the Lovecraftian text that correspond to Carroll's "complex discovery plot" pattern. In Lovecraft the "marching out," apart from a few exceptions, does not take place. His narrator-protagonists surrender their human form ("Innsmouth," "The Thing on the Doorstep," "The Shadow out of Time"), go raving mad ("The Rats in the Walls"—although madness is usually a "privilege" merely of the lesser, atavistic characters), or simply die before they can ultimately confront the monster and defeat it ("Witch House," "Doorstep," *Charles Dexter Ward*). Their anti-hero status necessarily stems from their hopeless solitude. Moreover, the horrors—although confirming the "unfathomable," hereafter "insurmountable," anomaly—usually remain hidden from the rest of humanity. Lovecraftian horror emphasizes a constant menace, not just an all-shattering revelation: it paradoxically insists on the severity of the peril through delineating its marginality. In *Mountains of Madness*, for instance, both the seclusion of the research site (the near-farthest, unexplored regions of the Antarctic) and that of two members of the scientific society (only Danforth and Dyer fly beyond the "mountains of madness" to explore the Cyclopean city) are emphasized. As Stefan Dziemianowicz contends, Lovecraft "acknowledged one of the unwritten rules of supernatural fiction: horror is most effective when it comes to a solitary character in a solitary place" (159). The hidden menace and the decentralized role of the Lovecraftian anti-hero are both causes and entailments of the fact that the sociological paradigm remains incomplete in the Lovecraftian text. If there exists a scientific community, it soon disintegrates, as seen in "The Colour," and the solitary protagonist is not capable of establishing a new paradigm on his own. The perilous anomaly will not be fully discovered, fully comprehended or fathomed, let alone incorporated into a new paradigm. As Joshi reminds us, these anomalies are "events which, although 'supplements' to natural law and science, can nevertheless not be integrated into science as currently understood" (*Decline* 83).

This insurmountable anomaly, as such, appears as a radical disturbance in the order of things as they are observed and interpreted by the solitary scholar in the given science. Still, as Masterman epitomizes, the anomaly, has also to be seen as a product of the paradigm itself:

> [Kuhn's] essential point is that an anomaly is an untruth, or a should-be-soluble-but-is-insoluble problem, or a germane but unwelcome result, or a contradiction, or an absurdity, *which is thrown up by the paradigm itself being pushed too far* . . . The anomaly, to be a true anomaly, has got to be produced from within the paradigm. (82–83)

In Kuhn's words, "Anomaly appears only against the background provided by the paradigm. The more precise and far-reaching that paradigm is, the more sensitive an indicator it provides of anomaly and hence of an occasion for paradigm change" (65).

The Lovecraftian central anomaly, similarly, has to arise from within the Lovecraftian materialistic paradigm itself in order to comply with the requirements of the supramundane phenomenon. As I have

demonstrated, there prevails a necessary contrast between the materialist paradigm and the "supra-materialistic" anomaly; yet—and the Lovecraftian text is precise on this point—the anomaly had existed before
its having moved into scientific view. Cthulhu, for instance, is an entity
that had set foot on the Earth before the time of man, and has been
lurking ever since in his "nightmare corpse-city of R'lyeh, that was built
in measureless aeons behind history by the vast, loathsome shapes that
seeped down from the dark stars" (*DH* 150). Also, in *Mountains of
Madness* the strange, extraterrestrial, barrel-shaped creatures landed on
Earth "not long after the matter forming the moon was wrenched from
the neighbouring South Pacific" (*MM* 66). Thus, Cthulhu and the Old
Ones do not appear unknown because they are novel to the human
world at the time of confrontation, but rather since they are phenomena that had existed but were ignored by, and became marginal to,
human science. It is the human race's ignorance that rendered them invisible. These phenomena have only been recognized by such counter-
cultural and non-scientific trends as represented by Abdul Alhazred's
Necronomicon and the ghastly couplet:

> That is not dead which can eternal lie,
> And with strange aeons even death may die. (*DH* 141)

The concern here with the barrier between death and life may also be
interpreted in terms of the marginalized anomalous: the text speaks
about the different reality of the extraterrestrials (things "which can
eternal lie") as having been effaced ("dead") but finally unveiled ("not
dead"). The final paradox "death may die" attempts to describe the relationship of this revelatory knowledge to the unknowable, since it is
impossible for humans to imagine death dying. The degree of "unknowability" inscribed in the couplet corroborates the supramundane
effect, since, strangely out of range of its genre—the grimoire should be
not only descriptive but prescriptive concerning magical techniques—
it is not the least certain about what Cthulhu is and how we may
know and represent his properties. Left to future inquiry to investigate
into the matter, Cthulhu and the Old Ones seem purely supernatural
for readers of the *Necronomicon.*

Moreover, the anomalous phenomena, such as Cthulhu, R'lyeh, or
the color out of space, are concealed from human inquiry not only
because they are cryptic in their own way—unseen, incomprehensi-
ble, or mostly imperceptible—but because in Lovecraft human sci-

ence basically operates imperfectly. Although constructed as a major guideline for scientific inquiry, the existence of any dominant paradigm inexorably entails the imperfection of science through the imperfection of that same paradigm. As Masterman emphasizes, "since the effect of these paradigms is drastically to restrict their fields, [they] collapse, when extended too far, by their own make-up; without any necessary accentuating irritation from nature at all" (84). Similarly, Watkins hypothesizes that "a scientific crisis may have theoretical rather than empirical causes" and provides a different explanation from Masterman's: "a dominant theory may come to be replaced, not because of growing empirical pressure . . ., but because a new and incompatible theory has been freely elaborated" (31). Although Lovecraftian tales establish the empirical nature of Cthulhu and other monsters as representatives of matter, in the wake of Watkins the constant fluctuation of various incompatible paradigms, as one of the major flaws of natural science, hugely influences the Lovecraftian shift between paradigms.

Observation and the Lovecraftian Paradigm Shift

The incompatibility of any two paradigms, in Kuhn's rendition, is a necessary condition for a scientific revolution.[14] The idea of a scientific revolution is today deeply engraved in the public mind: we talk about the Copernican revolution or the revolutionary breakthrough in genetics. As Alexander Bird summarizes, "Kuhn draws a political parallel with institutions which generate political problems for which those institutions are unable to find an agreed resolution" (277). According to Kuhn, in revolutions, or "paradigm shifts," "[p]aradigms gain their status because they are more successful than their competitors in solving a few problems that the group of practitioners has come to recognize as acute" (23). Being more successful, however, is not equivalent to having greater prowess in finding "truths." As Bird observes, "[t]hat theories from different paradigms are incommensurable is the reason why Kuhn's picture of science is often called *relativist*, as standards of rationality are relative to a paradigm, not absolute" (277).

---

14. That is the reason why the Lovecraftian text cannot envision the evolution of paradigms, only a revolution of them. On evolutionary epistemology (interpreted mainly through Popper's work) see Peter Munz's *Our Knowledge of the Growth of Knowledge*.

"For positivists the natural sciences have a prerogative as vehicles of positive knowledge, by virtue of their special relationship to the experiential foundations of knowledge," as Nicholas Jardine points out (11). He goes on to assert, "[f]or scientific realists the natural sciences have a prerogative as potential bearers of objective truth by virtue of their having as their manifest subject-matter 'the world,' the ultimate arbiter of truth" (11). What is cast as the cross-section of the positivist and realist worldviews is where the Lovecraftian protagonist roughly stands at the outset of the story. If we call the Lovecraftian protagonist's initial paradigm the "outset paradigm," then the new one becomes the "superparadigm" (named after its conjunction with the supramundane). Truth for the Lovecraftian protagonist, then, according to the outset paradigm, consists in the belief that the world comprises matter (materialism), and that knowledge is gained through a mixture of experiential contact with the world and the use of human reason (empiricism), as in the already quoted "absolute materialism" and "callous rationalism" of the narrator of "Cthulhu" (144, 132). Still, it is almost a commonplace by now that the protagonist at the end of the story turns towards another kind of worldview—not a paradigm yet, for obvious reasons—than the one he embraced in the outset paradigm. David Ashby Oakes notes, "[t]he evolution of the character's beliefs allows Lovecraft to present the devastating emotional and psychological consequences of the discoveries the narrators make in their search for knowledge, and helps to make the revelations uncovered serve as sources of destabilization" (63). Thurston, when recounting the vastly anomalous story of Cthulhu, admits toward the end that "[m]y attitude was still one of absolute materialism, *as I wish it still were*" (*DH* 144). The narrator's attitude toward the new superparadigm is highly informative. His wish that "it still were" as before is ultimately misplaced. Given that the superparadigm takes account of the cosmic interstice between the outset paradigm and the insurmountable anomaly, it foreshadows its own paradoxical incompleteness. It never will be as before, since the previous stage of knowledge has crumbled in face of the anomaly and the cosmic spaces eventually prove infinite, immeasurable, and unknowable. It further exacerbates the problem that a scientific situation is plausible in which more than two paradigms struggle for their own recognition. Masterman, in fact, distinguishes three "states of affairs": "dual-paradigm science," "multiple-paradigm science," and even "non-paradigm science"—the last especially observable at the commencement of a scientific development (71). Nevertheless, if we take a state of dual-paradigm science in the Lovecraftian text for granted, how do we account for the apparent incommensurability? The shift proves to be a result of the tension revealed in the apparent incommensurability of paradigms. Kuhn characterizes the turn occurring in a paradigm shift using the analogy of a Gestalt switch (111–14), a kind of double vision that has bearings on the problem of observation. The narrator of "Cthulhu" attests to the sudden change in perspective. When he has read Johansen's manuscript about the discovery of Cthulhu, he "places it in the tin box beside the bas-relief and the papers of Professor Angell":

> With [the document] shall go this record of mine—this test of my own sanity, wherein is pieced together that which I hope may never be pieced together again. I have looked upon all that the universe has to hold of horror, and even the skies of spring and the flowers of summer must ever afterward be poison to me. (*DH* 154)

The Gestalt switch makes the narrator of "Cthulhu" see the world in dull colors; every flower is a frightening reminder of the cosmic interstice that poisons potential human interaction with the cosmos. Those Lovecraft stories that do not involve such a dramatic description of the Gestalt switch are all the more problematic for it, delivering the Lovecraftian cosmic sensation rather imperfectly. "The Shunned House," for instance, contains references to science and materialism, such as the equipment installed by the intrepid "night guards" in the moldy cellar where the anomaly is supposedly observable (*MM* 253). It is, however, not the scientific mood that evaporates successful Lovecraftian horror here, but a kind of knowing anticipation of the narrator and his uncle with which they wait on the thing, at a time where their meager evidence only consists of strange descriptions and unexplained deaths. This in itself ruins the characteristic *mood* of the weird (idealized by Lovecraft in "Supernatural Horror in Literature"), which the constant reference to the anomalous, interestingly, further exacerbates:

> What baffled us was our utter ignorance of the aspect in which we might encounter the thing. No sane person had ever seen it and few had ever felt it definitely. It might be pure energy—a form ethereal and outside the realm of substance—or it might be partly material;

some unknown and equivocal mass of plasticity, capable of changing at will to nebulous approximations of the solid, liquid, gaseous, or tenuously unparticled states. (*MM* 252)

Here the outset paradigm has long dissolved, and the narrator's stance has taken a fantastic bend toward the superparadigm, with a full acceptance of the supramundane: "Such a thing was surely not a physical or biochemical impossibility in light of a newer science which includes the theories of relativity and intra-atomic action" (*MM* 252). This is also the reason why the "ending is in a sense a little weak; there is nothing left to dread, but only a horrible memory," as Burleson argues, "[i]n comparison with some of Lovecraft's later work in which the horror lingers at the story's closing" (*H. P. Lovecraft: A Critical Study* 100). What a huge difference the description in "The Shunned House" makes from, say, the carefully constructed, gradually disclosed, and shocking anomaly series in *Mountains of Madness*.[15]

However startling the evolving new vision of the Gestalt switch, it also projects the necessary unknowability of what it observes. Bird, in the propositional tradition of logical positivism, argues that for a scientific statement to be truth-evaluable "it must be such that its truth can be determined by observation" (126). He implies that the truth condition of scientific propositions, the warp and woof of theories, depends upon a proper method of observation (126). Bird draws a distinction between such statements ("O-statements") and statements that cannot be corroborated by factual data deriving from observation ("T-statements" 126). Both the observable and the unobservable play a considerable role in the Lovecraftian text. As K. Setiya contends, "Lovecraft's philosophy and fiction were deeply enmeshed . . . in his speculations on the human perceptual apparatus" ("Empiricism" 21). In "Dunwich," for instance, the power of the two major anomalies, the Whateley twins, resides in the principles of perceiving and not perceiving, of hiding and showing: the monstrous parts of Wilbur are, essentially, hidden under his clothes, revealed only by the watchdog that manages to tear him apart. The other twin is itself the ultimate unob-

---

15. I would also add that in "The Shunned House" we have the least successful integration of "the new physics" of Einstein and Planck into the Lovecraftian universe, compared to, for instance, "Witch House," where Gilman's studies are initially seen as a curious academic interest.

servable: it is an invisible monstrosity, first in its total isolation on the boarded upper story of the Whateley building, later in the revelation that human eyes cannot indeed see it. The unobservable can appear, however, in less extreme examples than "Dunwich": for instance, as a phenomenon that is unknowable or cannot be accounted for, not even with the help of various instruments. Such are the mysterious color from the meteor in "Colour" or the anomalous means of transport of the Outer Ones, or Mi-Go (using their membranous wings, propelled by solar winds) in "Whisperer."

As Bird summarizes Kuhn's and Feyerabend's concession of the incommensurability thesis, "[i]n their view there is no theory-independent observation language that can be used to express the observational consequences of competing theories in a way that is neutral between the theories" (278). He also calls our attention to the fact that observation itself is relative and non-absolute: "there is nothing objective about observation" (132). Even the positivist A. J. Ayer concedes in his 1940 *The Foundations of Empirical Knowledge* that "material things may present different appearances to different observers, or to the same observer in different conditions" (3). Observation with the help of instruments precipitates further problems, chiefly the fact that being a part of the observable world, instruments distort the supposed objectivity of observation. "All observations are made by means which are themselves an integral part of what is to be observed" (Munz 9). What is more, interpreting human reason as a special instrument, the argument from "theory-ladenness" argues for something along the same lines. Thus, if the Lovecraftian superparadigm (the would-be, all-inclusive paradigm) seems to incorporate different standards of observation from the outset paradigm, the two cannot be leveled. Still, the inherent materiality of the anomaly should provide a link between the two paradigms. Bird distinguishes between "observation" and "detection" (134). In this manner, it may be possible for the outset paradigm to detect the anomaly, while it cannot actually observe it. For example, the unseen Whateley "brother" thrashes through farms and woods in "Dunwich," and while the tracks and devastation are clearly observable, the cause of it is only detectable. Even so, Bird concludes: "Whatever the difference between the concepts detection and observation, they are clearly linked, and one of the features that links them is the fact that they are both success words" (134). Whereas the Lovecraftian text claims the radical novelty of the anomaly, that anomaly's structure or nature is somehow already accounted for in the outset paradigm (and not only in the form of a lack, a premonition): the outset paradigm seems capable of observing and, thus, defining the anomaly. This remains markedly in consonance with the fundamental paradoxical nature of Lovecraftian epistemology. The observable slides into the unobservable; in "Dunwich" the pursuing professors manage to make the invisible monster visible, only for a moment. Even here, however, in spite of the telescope, the local Curtis Whateley's attempts to relate what he has seen seem a far cry from observational precision: "Bigger'n a barn . . . all made o' squirmin' ropes . . . hull thing sort o' shaped like a hen's egg bigger'n anything, with dozens o' legs . . . all like jelly, an' made o' sep'rit wrigglin' ropes pushed clost together . . . great bulgin' eyes all over it . . ." (*DH* 194).

Thus, it appears, the Lovecraftian text appropriates a radical paradox concerning empiricism itself, and the paradox lies at the heart of the supramundane. The protagonist—endowed with the methods of, and usually working as a practicing scholar in, the outset paradigm—is able to observe the anomaly. Nevertheless, when hypotheses and conjectures start to form about that anomaly, the outset paradigm fails, and it is time to replace it with another one, the superparadigm. Bird asserts that one of the major methods of empiricism is induction; that is, inference from the observed to the unobserved (169). The problems of induction are numerous: from Hume to Popper, many thinkers strove to demonstrate that induction can never be the basis of a reliable scientific method, in spite of the fact that natural science seems quite successful in employing it.[16] It is indeed impossible to gain *a priori* knowledge (to draw inferences from past experiences to future ones), since (1) it is unfeasible to believe that the observer accounted for every natural phenomena concerning the scientific problem and, what is more, (2) there is absolutely no guarantee that the phenomena of the past will continue to appear and behave in the same way in the future as well. In Lovecraft, besides the obvious lack of social support to complete the superparadigm, other problems prevail, touching upon or resembling the fallacy of induction: In the cases where the anomaly is in reality unobservable, there is no initial

16. See David Hume's *An Enquiry concerning Human Understanding*, especially sections four and five, and Popper's *The Logic of Scientific Discovery*.

knowledge on which to build later knowledge; the couplets of the *Necronomicon* are too vague and cultist's beliefs too obscure to account for the epistemic weirdness. The disappearance of evidence is another well-known Lovecraftian effect, as, for example, the sublimation of rock and beaker in "Colour." Similarly, in the finale to "Whisperer," there are the objects in the chair "which the investigators did not find when they came later on" (*DH* 271). In "Cthulhu," the fate of the sealed tin box with the Cthulhu statuette and vital documents is foreshadowed, together with the probable assassination of the narrator: "Let me pray that, if I do not survive this manuscript, my executors may put caution before audacity and see that it meets no other eye" (*DH* 154). In "The Music of Erich Zann" the pages where the mad violist Zann "had begun to write out his horrible secret" are sucked out through the window (*DH* 90), while in "Dunwich" and *Mountains of Madness* even Wilbur's body and the ice specimens themselves vanish. Where the evidence disappears, the process of observation is incomplete and experiments are not repeatable; therefore, the possibility of scientific confirmation and testing of hypotheses vanishes. With similar flaws in mind, Kuhn notes "the immense difficulties often encountered in developing points of contact between a theory and nature" (30). Popper also articulates the problem:

> The empirical basis of objective science has thus nothing "absolute" in it. Science does not rest upon solid bedrock. The bold structure of its theories rises, as it were, above a swamp. It is like a building erected on piles. The piles are driven down from above into the swamp, but not to any natural or "given" base; and if we stop driving the piles deeper, it is not because we have reached firm ground. We simply stop when we are satisfied that the piles are firm enough to carry the structure, at least for the time being. (*The Logic of Scientific Discovery* 111)[17]

Although most comfortable with materialism, Lovecraft writes about his strongest wish to provide in his stories "the illusion of some strange suspension or violation of the galling limitations of time, space, and natural law which forever imprison us and frustrate our

---

17. It is for similar reasons that Paul Feyerabend argues against the reality of a unified scientific method in his celebrated study *Against Method: Outline of an Anarchistic Theory of Knowledge* (London: Humanities, 1975).

curiosity about the infinite cosmic spaces beyond the radius of our sight and analysis" ("Notes on Writing Weird Fiction" [*CE* 5.176]). Since Lovecraft himself embraced the outset paradigm of his protagonists, he envisioned the greatest cause for fear in the unreliability of science in representing and explaining novel natural phenomena. Lovecraftian epistemology is one of brooding peril, since his protagonist disintegrates on the verge of the impending superparadigm. Nevertheless, it is not only the void between one science and the other that engenders the sublime, but also a potentially successful match between the superparadigm and the anomaly. As Joshi asserts, "Lovecraft expressed serious reservations on the ability of the human mind to endure certain kinds of knowledge" (*Decline* 107). The source of danger in science, then, seems to have turned here from the unreliability argument to the hypothetical success of a superparadigm. As Burleson argues, Lovecraft's macro-theme is *"the ruinous nature of self-understanding, . . .* the crisis of coming to knowledge of one's place on the cosmic canvas" ("Lovecraft and Interstitiality" 33). Similarly, Oakes asserts that "[Lovecraft's] fiction focuses on the possibility that the search for knowledge will lead to revelations that will forever change humanity's view of the universe and its place in it" (55). This is perhaps best explicated in the opening passage of "Cthulhu":

> The most merciful thing in the world, I think, is the inability of the human mind to correlate all its contents. We live on a placid island of ignorance in the midst of black seas of infinity, and it was not meant that we should voyage far. The sciences, each straining in its own direction, have hitherto harmed us little; but some day the piecing together of dissociated knowledge will open up such terrifying vistas of reality, and of our frightful position therein, that we shall either go mad from the revelation or flee from the deadly light into the peace and safety of a new dark age. (*DH* 125)

Setiya in "Lovecraft on Human Knowledge: An Exchange" interprets the above quotation as an example of "Lovecraft's ambivalence to knowledge" (23). In a discussion with Joshi on the connections and contradictions between "Cthulhu" and the biographical data about Lovecraft, he quotes Lovecraft's letters to find the two major ingredients of the apparent ambivalence: "'the joy of pursuing truth' and 'the depressing revelations of truth' (as materialism may in a certain sense be interpreted as a pessimistic philosophy—despite Lovecraft's Epicureanism)"

(Setiya and Joshi, "Lovecraft on Human Knowledge" 23). In contrast to (or, rather, in addition to) Setiya, I believe that in Lovecraft we may highlight something more than the simple ambivalence of the author. The paradoxical nature of the Lovecraftian text has been pointed out by many critics. Setiya bases his argument on the framed structure of "Cthulhu." The story closes with the narrator's chiasmus that "What has risen may sink, and what has sunk may rise" (169). Burleson in "Lovecraft and Chiasmus/Chiasmus and Lovecraft" maintains that "as a habit of mind in Lovecraft the pattern seems to range from the phonemic level through the level of syntax all the way up to the most global level that a story may encompass" (80). Thus, perhaps not only the syntax of "Cthulhu" is plagued with the chiasmic structure, but its thematic level also presents us with "Lovecraft's conscious or unconscious inclination toward the ABBA pattern" (75). The plunge into the investigation of Cthulhu—symbolized in the story-structure by the opening up of ever deeper layers of narration—earns Thurston the need to renounce his materialism, his outset paradigm. Therefore, the outset structure of *AB* (investigator entering the area of the investigated—"the piecing together of dissociated knowledge" [*DH* 125]) turns into *BA* (the area investigated assailing or infecting the investigator—"terrifying vistas of reality, and of our frightful position therein," "the deadly light" [*DH* 125]). The *ABBA* pattern can be interpreted as the magical formula of science in Lovecraft. When science is limited, knowledge fails. When science—effected by a plunge into the unknown—develops, it entails horror through the crossing and the investigation of the cosmic interstice, a region not meant to be traversed, but still, a condition necessarily stirred (hence Lovecraft's forbidden texts that lure the reader into studying them).

What the opening and closing passages from "Cthulhu" tell us is that the central Lovecraftian paradox appears to prevail in suspension between the limitations of science and the success of science. Should the superparadigm be accepted, humanity would perish from the knowledge. Otherwise, the blind, gaping maw of the unknown universe will most certainly swallow us—science in its limitation detecting but not explaining the peril. As Burleson argues, Lovecraft's "supertheme" is stresses that "[h]umans, alone among earth's acknowledged tenants, are just sufficiently well developed mentally and emotionally to ponder the tragedy of their own vanishingly small dash of color on the universal canvas" (*Disturbing* 158).

Lovecraft himself could not envision the paradigm shift taking place. A conservative most of his life, he went on defending "strong" materialism against the theories of Einstein and Planck. Yet he could see the inevitability of one such route out of a worn-out science, as his fiction displays. He himself was a paradigm shifter in his literary field after all, drawing attention to the importance and relevance of the cosmic—the absurdity of "a notion of purpose in the utter absence of evidence" ("In Defence of Dagon" [*CE* 5.52]). He was, after all, to use Fritz Leiber's term, a "Literary Copernicus" (50).

Works Cited

Airaksinen, Timo. *The Philosophy of H. P. Lovecraft: The Route to Horror*. New York: Peter Lang, 1999.

Ayer, A. J. *The Foundations of Empirical Knowledge*. 1940. London: Macmillan, 1964.

Bird, Alexander. *Philosophy of Science*. London: UCL, 2000.

Boerem, R. "Lovecraft and the Tradition of the Gentleman Narrator." In Schultz and Joshi. 257–72.

Burleson, Donald R. *Lovecraft: Disturbing the Universe*. Lexington: University Press of Kentucky, 1990.

———. "Lovecraft and Chiasmus/Chiasmus and Lovecraft." *Lovecraft Studies* No. 13 (Fall 1986): 72–75, 80.

———. "Lovecraft and Interstitiality." *Lovecraft Studies* No. 37 (Fall 1997): 25–34.

Carroll, Noël. *The Philosophy of Horror; or, Paradoxes of the Heart*. New York: Routledge, 1990.

Dziemianowicz, Stefan. "Outsiders and Aliens: The Uses of Isolation in Lovecraft's Fiction." In Schultz and Joshi. 159–88.

Feyerabend, Paul. *Against Method: Outline of an Anarchistic Theory of Knowledge*. London: Humanities, 1975.

———. "Consolations of the Specialist." In Lakatos and Musgrave. 197–230.

Hume, David. An Enquiry concerning Human Understanding. 1748. Ed. Tom L. Beauchamp. Oxford: Oxford University Press, 1999.

Joshi, S. T. *H. P. Lovecraft: The Decline of the West*. Mercer Island, WA: Starmont House, 1990.

———. *The Weird Tale*. Austin: University of Texas Press, 1990.

———, ed. *H. P. Lovecraft: Four Decades of Criticism*. Athens: Ohio University Press, 1980.

Kuhn, Thomas S. *The Structure of Scientific Revolutions*. Chicago: University of Chicago Press, 1996.

Lakatos, Imre, and Alan Musgrave, ed. *Criticism and the Growth of Knowledge: Proceedings of the International Colloquium in the Philosophy of Science, London, 1965*. Vol. 4. Cambridge: Cambridge University Press, 1970.

Leiber, Fritz. "A Literary Copernicus." 1949. In Joshi, ed. *Four Decades*. 50–62.

———. "Through Hyperspace with Brown Jenkin: Lovecraft's Contribution to Speculative Fiction." 1966. In Joshi, ed. *Four Decades*. 140–52.

Lévy, Maurice. *Lovecraft: A Study in the Fantastic*. 1972. Tr. S. T. Joshi. Detroit: Wayne State University Press, 1988.

Lovecraft, H. P. *The Dreams in the Witch House and Other Weird Stories*. Ed. S. T. Joshi. New York: Penguin, 2004.

———. *Lord of a Visible World: An Autobiography in Letters*. Ed. S. T. Joshi and David E. Schultz. Athens: Ohio University Press, 2000.

Masterman, Margaret. "The Nature of a Paradigm." In Lakatos and Musgrave. 59–90.

Medawar, Peter. *The Limits of Science*. Oxford: Oxford University Press, 1989.

Munz, Peter. *Our Knowledge of the Growth of Knowledge: Popper or Wittgenstein?* London: Routledge, 1985.

Oakes, David Ashby. "Twentieth-Century American Gothic Literature as Cultural Artifact: Science and Technology as Sources of Destabilization in the Fiction of H. P. Lovecraft, Richard Matheson, and Stephen King." Ph.D. diss.: Texas Christian University, 1998. DAI 59:5 (1998): 1573.

Onderdonk, Matthew H. "The Lord of R'lyeh." 1945. *Lovecraft Studies* No. 7 (Fall 1982): 8–17.

Popper, Karl R. *The Logic of Scientific Discovery*. Rev. Ed. London: Hutchinson, 1968.

———. "Normal Science and Its Dangers." In Lakatos and Musgrave. 51–58.

Price, Robert M. "H. P. Lovecraft: Prophet of Humanism." *Humanist* 61:4 (July 2001): 26–29.

Schultz, David E., and S. T. Joshi, ed. *An Epicure in the Terrible: A Centennial Anthology of Essays in Honor of H. P. Lovecraft*. Rutherford, NJ: Fairleigh Dickinson University Press, 1991.

Setiya, K. "Empiricism and the Limits of Knowledge in Lovecraft." *Lovecraft Studies* No. 25 (Fall 1991): 18–22.

———, and S. T. Joshi. "Lovecraft on Human Knowledge: An Exchange." *Lovecraft Studies* No. 24 (Spring 1991): 22–23, 34.

Shea, Vernon J. "On the Literary Influences Which Shaped Lovecraft's Works." In Joshi, ed. *Four Decades*. 113–39.

Todorov, Tzvetan. *The Fantastic: A Structural Approach to a Literary Genre*. Tr. Richard Howard. Ithaca, NY: Cornell University Press, 1975.

Watkins, John. "Against 'Normal Science.'" In Lakatos and Musgrave. 25–38.

Weinberg, Robert. "H. P. Lovecraft and Pseudomathematics." 1971. In Darrell Schweitzer, ed. *Discovering H. P. Lovecraft*. San Bernardino, CA: Borgo Press, 1987. 113–17.

Will, Bradley Alan. "The 'Supramundane': The Kantian Sublime in Lovecraft, Clarke, and Gibson." Ph.D. diss.: University of Oklahoma, 1998. DAI 59:9 (1999): 3451.

Wilson, Edmund. "Tales of the Marvellous and the Ridiculous." 1945. In Joshi, ed. *Four Decades*. 46–49.

Briefly Noted

Italian Lovecraftian activity continues at a gratifyingly high level. At least two additional issues of *Studi Lovecraftiani* appeared in 2008, a Winter issue and a Spring issue. They contain original articles by such Italian scholars as Giacomo Bencistà, Raffaella Benvenuto, Luca Foffano, and Luigi Musolino, and translations of articles (several of which appeared in *Lovecraft Studies*) by Gilles Menegaldo, Will Murray, and Paul Montelone. In addition, each issue contains an extensive section of detailed and scholarly reviews. *Studi Lovecraftiani* is edited by Pietro Guarriello. Issues can be ordered by contacting studilovecraft@yahoo.it. Giacomo Bencistà and Andrea Becherini have written *Menzonga e Persecuzione nell'Orrore di Dunwich di H. P. Lovecraft* (*Deceit and Persecution in H. P. Lovecraft's "The Dunwich Horror"*) (Pineto: Edizioni Dagon Press, 2008), a substantial monograph on Lovecraft's novella.

H. P. Lovecraft and the Archaeology of "Roman" Arizona

Marc A. Beherec

In 1925, newspapers reported one of the most exciting archaeological discoveries of H. P. Lovecraft's lifetime: The records of a mediaeval Roman colony in the American Southwest, a land called Calalus by its inhabitants. Though the "find" led the Arizona State Museum to fund excavations outside of Tucson, the remains were early condemned by the majority of the academic community, and newspaper articles of the period quickly go from lauding the find to lumping the Calalus material together with other famous hoaxes. The remarkable news stories did not escape the eager antiquarian Lovecraft's notice. Love-craft briefly alludes to the incident in his novella "The Mound," apparently expecting his readers to be familiar with it. However, the reports were very similar to some of his dreams and early fictions, and the odd news items seem to have spurred him to rework his own ideas. These "Roman navigators in strange and distant parts" (*SL* 5.374–75) that had haunted Lovecraft were recast into dreams still greater, transforming his navigators first into a prehuman races and aliens on the strange and distant planet earth.

Lovecraft's own knowledge of the events in Arizona likely came from the *New York Times*, which saw fit to print extensively on the story in December 1925. Lovecraft lived in New York then, and it seems unlikely that he could have missed the headline at the top of the Sunday paper on December 13: "Puzzling 'Relics' Dug Up in Arizona Stir Scientists." Although subheadings warned that some authorities maintained serious doubts about the artifacts, mention of Latin inscriptions and Masonic emblems on artifacts which "Purport to Chronicle the Arrival of Roman Jews" in America could only have fired the imagination of a man like Lovecraft. The very next day another front-page article declared, "Arizona University Will Study

'Relics'" (*New York Times*, December 14). More skeptical articles were printed December 16 and 17, as the story moved to later pages in the paper. Indeed, from the 14th on, these articles often contained the statements of professors who either felt they were misrepresented by the article of December 13 or felt the need to qualify their statements in that article. The series of articles was capped with an article by Silas Bent in the following Sunday's paper, "Bogus Relics of Past Tempt Collectors" (*New York Times*, December 20), which did not overtly condemn the Arizona artifacts, but which did compare them to such hoaxes as the Cardiff Giant and the Ohio Decalogue.

Lovecraft alludes directly to the incident in "The Mound" (1929–30). The puzzled narrator of this novella, who cannot believe that he is really reading the narrative of a lost follower of Coronado, declares, "Surely this was the clever forgery of some learned cynic—something like the leaden crosses in New Mexico, which a jester once planted and pretended to discover as a relique of some forgotten Dark Age colony from Europe" (*HM* 155). Lovecraft is clearly working from memory here, as he misplaces the find from Arizona to New Mexico, but the facts are basically the same. Although Lovecraft did believe that the Phoenicians likely carried out transatlantic navigation, and possibly even attempted colonization of what is now the United States,[1] he did not believe that the Romans ever carried out such a feat.

Lovecraft's summary is a good condensation and evaluation of the first article's claims. The very first paragraph of the first *New York Times* article on the artifacts, datelined Tucson, Arizona, boldly stated:

> After investigation by a number of scientists, first announcement was made here today of the excavation near Tucson of cast lead swords, crosses and other objects bearing Latin and Hebrew inscriptions which, taken at their face value, are held to mean that Roman Jews

---

1. "One theory which I have suggested—as an unscientifick layman—is that the hook nose of the Atlantick coast Indian comes from the Phoenician mariners—typical Semites—whom it is natural to suppose must have been washed across the ocean alive during the long centuries of Tyrian and Cathaginian voyaging beyond the Pillars of Hercules. Or if such stray infusions be deemed insufficient to account for the prevalence of the beaked physiognomy, then it is by no means extravagant to presuppose to the existence of some abortive and forgotten attempt at Punic colonisation." *SL* 3.131.

crossed the Atlantic in the Dark Ages, penetrated to Arizona and founded a kingdom which lasted from about 700 A.D. to 900 A.D. (*New York Times*, December 13, p. 1)

This article printed extensive excerpts from a statement released by a group that claimed to be investigating the find, as well as photographs and translations of some of the key inscriptions and rebuttals from other experts. The issuer of the statement is unnamed, but one can imagine that the group included Charles E. Manier, Thomas Bent, and historian-schoolteacher Laura Coleman Ostrander.

According to the declaration, Tucson resident Manier discovered a curious lead object eroding from a cut bank in September 1924. Once cleaned, it was discovered to be two crosses riveted together, with Latin inscriptions and three rude profile portraits inscribed thereon. Several other artifacts were reportedly later found by Manier and his friend Bent, who joined him in a venture to excavate the site for fun and, if possible, profit. These included more leaden crosses with Latin inscribed alongside symbols and a few Hebrew words, a cross with a lead snake entwined about it, and an odd "cross-crescent"—a snake-entwined cross atop which several bulbs and projections stretch out from the central bar, one in the shape of a "Moslem" half-moon pointed upwards. This artifact bears several Hebrew words and "Masonic symbols," and the lead snake is reminiscent of the copper or bronze serpent of Numbers 21:9 and II Kings 18:4. Photographs and descriptions of these artifacts were printed on the 13th. Supposedly battle-scarred lead swords and spears, as well as what was purported to be a processional standard, were also described in this article, and photographs of these were printed on December 14th.

Lovecraft's protagonist's bewilderment in "The Mound" regarding the Tulu metal is similar to how intrigued the University of Arizona scientists were with their artifacts' metallic composition. The Arizona artifacts were tested to determine their precise chemical content, which prominent Arizona State Museum archaeologist Byron Cummings declared was "somewhat puzzling" (*New York Times*, December 14, p. 10). Some of the objects included small quantities of silver, gold, antimony, and tin, while others contained only lead and antimony, which suggested two different sources for the lead. Even more oddly, such objects have no parallels anywhere in the world. As early as 1927 Lovecraft may have been inspired by such archaeological anomalies when he made use of an out-of-place metal Roman object—in this case a silver Roman eagle standard found in the Spanish hills—as the sequel to the dream that Frank Belknap Long reworked into *The Horror from the Hills* (cf. *SL* 2.202, 216). Lovecraft's Tulu metal was unearthly rather than merely used oddly, but it is easy to see the newspaper's accounts of the one influencing Lovecraft's imaginative image of the other.

What is most interesting about the "Roman" artifacts is the narrative they purport to chronicle—"a story," the finders' statement states, "that covers a period of 125 years and is replete with hardships, wars and romance" (*New York Times*, December 13, p. 27). University of Arizona Classicist Frank Fowler determined that all the Latin inscriptions, once proper names and dates are removed, are direct quotations from classical authors such as Virgil, Horace, Caesar, and Cicero, or are common classical expressions. They are all phrases commonly used in Latin textbooks of the time to illustrate particular grammatical constructions, and were put together poorly on the artifacts with many misspellings (*New York Times*, December 16). The few words of Hebrew, which led to the claim that the inscriptions were made by Roman Jews, were common words like *shalom* (peace), which could also be easily gathered by a twentieth-century hoaxer. Nevertheless, the statement from which the earliest *New York Times* article drew quotes from a narrative Ostrander claimed to have constructed based on the disjointed inscriptions. According to Ostrander, in A.D. 775 the settlers were "carried forth over the sea to Calalus, an unknown land" (*New York Times*, December 13, p. 27). There they encountered "a people ruling widely," a group called Toltezus, with whom they would struggle for supremacy throughout the life of their colony. Ostrander decided the Toltezus must be the Toltecs, precursors to the Aztecs. However, despite the fact that Toltec history and archaeology was shadowy in 1925, even then it should have seemed strange to suggest that sizable numbers of Toltecs—whose capital was the city of Tula, in the Basin of Mexico—were so far north.[2] However, European-American legends of Mesoamerican peoples hiding treasure in the Southwest, Texas, and the lower Midwest abound, and the groups' names appear in local

2. Cf. Herbert J. Spinden's *Ancient Civilizations of Mexico and Central America*. This book was in HPL's library at the time of his death (*LL* #829).

place names such as that of Toltec, Arizona, a town near the site. It is easy to see why hoaxers may have wished to claim that this advanced civilization was in the area or not known that it was not.

Possibly one reason why Lovecraft took such note of the Calalus reports is that they were very similar to imaginings of his own. Discussing historical fiction with Robert E. Howard, Lovecraft wrote, "The thing which I would probably enjoy most in connexion with history would be bringing utterly separate culture-streams into anomalous contact—as in having a Roman washed across the ocean on a derelict galley and landed amidst the Mayas, or having a Greek cross the great deserts to China" (*SL* 4.297). "Just as you think of Vikings in the Hellenistic-Roman world," he wrote to Fritz Leiber, "so do I think of Roman navigators in strange and distant parts—washed across the Western Ocean to unknown shores, camping on the future site of Providence and fighting the coppery predecessors of the Narragansetts and Wampanoags, or captured by the soldiers of the Mayas and forced to escape from ornately carven dungeons in Guatemalan jungles" (*SL* 5.374–75).

Indeed, such stories made up a large amount of Lovecraft's destroyed juvenilia. The very month before Calalus made the *New York Times*, Lovecraft wrote to his aunt, "The idea of a Roman settlement in America is something which occurred to me years ago—in fact, I began a story with that theme (only it was about Central America & not U.S.) in 1906 or 1907, tho' I never finish'd it."[3] This was one of several stories Lovecraft wrote between the ages of fourteen and sixteen which "had to do with strange survivals of Roman civilization in Africa, Asia, the Antarctic, the Amazon Valley, and even pre-Columbian North America" (*SL* 4.336). Writing to Clark Ashton Smith, Lovecraft describes what may have been the most elaborate of these stories:

> They are all destroyed now, but I wish I had kept the one (based on an actual dream of 1904) about *Roman Providence*, with its familiar hills crowned with many-columned temples and its forum near the site of the Great Bridge (I had a marble bridge there—the Pons Æbutii, named from L. Æbutius, the founder of the colony of B.C. 45, which was tragically cut off from the mother respublica whence the colonising fleet of six quinquiremes had sailed.) I had Roman wars

---

3. HPL to Lillian D. Clark, 14–19 November 1925; quoted in Joshi, *H. P. Lovecraft: A Life* (75). This material is omitted from the letter as it is printed in *Letters from New York* (246–50).

with the Narragansetts, Wampanoags, and Pequots, a gradual blood mixture which gave the whole mass of Eastern Indians their still-unexplained (in view of the known Mongoloid basis of the whole race) aquiline features, and a final destruction of MOTIATICUM (2nd *Moshassuck*) by an earthquake. I had the story begin with the exhumation of a Roman column on the ancient hill during the digging of a sewer-main—the universal perplexity it aroused, and the dreams it inspired in one lone student. My native highway Angell Street (*actually* the Wampanoag Trail, older than English colonisation, and *naturally* determined as the shortest line between the ford at the head of the bay and the narrow ferrying-place in the Seekonk River) was a Roman road, lined with tombs as it stretched beyond the marble temples and brick-and-plaster houses of urban Motiaticum. (*SL* 4.336)

By the late 1920s, years after the Calalus reports, Lovecraft was actively contemplating resurrecting his ideas of Roman America. In a September 16, 1929, letter to Elizabeth Toldridge, he writes:

The cuttings you enclosed are all interesting. That Roman coin in the Indian grave could be used fictionally to sustain a notion on which I have been ruminating for years—a forgotten colony of Rome on American soil, including a city of Roman architecture with temple-crowned citadel, columned forum, & marble arenas & baths. I would have it come in conflict with the representatives of some native civilization—Maya, Aztec, &c.—& perhaps suffer extirpation in a desperate battle, or sink amidst an earthquake. (*SL* 3.27)

By Ostrander's and her colleagues' accounts, something very much like what Lovecraft describes is recounted on the Arizonan lead crosses. No city was found in association with the crosses, but the Ostrander's translations do mention a city over which the people's rulers reigned, a walled city named Rhoda which was at first encompassed by hills and later extended to a plain (*New York Times*, December 13, p. 27). But as strong as these images were for Lovecraft, it is also easy to imagine that old enemy of anachronisms abandoned the project when he learnt that the Classic Maya, the Aztecs, and the Toltecs all rose to prominence after the fall of classical Rome, a fact that was known in Lovecraft's time (cf. Spinden). However, although Lovecraft did not write a story about Romans, he did not abandon the Ostrander-like plot entirely.

"The Mound" explores one of Lovecraft's favorite themes—a lost

race, far superior in many respects to humanity as we know it, that
survives in an out-of-the-way spot within the earth. It is a theme
which Lovecraft used in his Arabian tale "The Nameless City" (1921).
Of the origin of the inhabitants of "The Nameless City" we know
nothing. The voyage across space of the people of "The Mound" is
that much more reminiscent of Ostrander's Romans' voyage across
the seas. These ideas dovetail and would be explored even more fully
in 1931 in *At the Mountains of Madness*.

The finds of the Antarctic expedition of *At the Mountains of
Madness* parallel both the anomalous artifacts of Arizona and those of
the intrepid explorer of "The Nameless City," and reflect Lovecraft's
knowledge and love of the ancient world. Exploring Antarctica's ruins, the Miskatonic team discovers the history of the Old Ones not on
leaden crosses, but in murals:

> The prime decorative feature was the almost universal system of mu-
> ral sculpture, which tended to run in continuous horizontal bands
> three feet wide and arranged from floor to ceiling in alternation with
> bands of equal width given over to geometrical arabesques. There
> were exceptions to this rule of arrangement, but its preponderance
> was overwhelming. Often, however, a series of smooth cartouches
> containing oddly patterned groups of dots would be sunk along one
> of the arabesque bands. [. . .] The subject matter of the sculptures
> obviously came from the life of the vanished epoch of their creation,
> and contained a large proportion of evident history. (*MM* 52–53)

These murals are very similar to those of "The Nameless City," in
which a deathless culture portrays its past, but the details have
evolved, and Lovecraft's description seems to spawn from a union of
antiquity's art. Reading history on the walls reminds one of Lovecraft's beloved *Aeneid*. Examining the walls of the temple of Juno in
Dido's Carthage:

> [Aeneas] saw, in order painted on the wall,
> Whatever did unhappy Troy befall:
> The wars that fame around the world had blown,
> All to the life, and ev'ry leader known.
> (Virgil, 1.638–40; Dryden's translation[4])

---

4. Dryden's translation of the *Aeneid* was in HPL's library. See *LL* #906.

But Aeneas saw these things in a new city, a living city. If the men from Miskatonic seem to draw an impossible amount of information from the Antarctic reliefs, it is probably because Lovecraft modeled his encounter on that of Aeneas. Aeneas knew the story of the fall of Troy because he had lived it; it was no great feat to read the history of the Trojan War in the sculptures on the walls of the temple at Carthage. Lovecraft wanted a similar effect—a scene of the sad destruction of a great city written on the wall—but his men could not have honestly read the pictorial history of a race they did not know in the same way Aeneas read the story of his own past. The dot patterns and scenes interspersed with arabesques are reminiscent of the Assyrian panels discovered in the nineteenth century in the dead cities of Nineveh and Nimrud, where images of gods and men are interspersed with designs such as the tree of life. Cuneiform inscriptions, like the dot-writing of the Old Ones, commemorated battles long past to an audience now long dead (Layard). The cartouches of course hearken to Egyptian reliefs. Lovecraft draws on the combined glories of antiquity to create alien glory.

The history depicted on the walls, however, parallels what Ostrander claimed was recorded on the leaden crosses. Lovecraft's explorers discover that the Old Ones, in their decadence, were overthrown by the slave-race of shoggoths whom they themselves created. According to Ostrander's account, the Roman Jews managed to subjugate and enslave the local Toltecs. We are told nothing of the period of their slavery, of how the Toltecs were administered, or what was expected of them, though this seems to have been the golden age of the slave-masters. What we learn is that the Toltecs were liberated by King Israel III, who was banished for this crime, which marked the beginning of the end for the colony. "The earth trembled. Fear overwhelmed the hearts of mortals in the third year after he fled" (*New York Times*, December 13, p. 27), and thus began a war of extermination against the Romans by the Toltecs. The leaden records purport to extend almost to the bitter end of the Romans' society. In the last inscriptions, the historian declares woefully, "It is uncertain how long life will continue" (*New York Times*, December 13, p. 27). Both *At the Mountains of Madness* and Ostrander's narrative of the Arizona Romans describe the destruction of a great people at the hands of what was understood to be an inferior slave race.

Despite their many similarities, the fates of the elder race of *At the*

Mountains of Madness and of Ostrander's Arizona Romans differ substantially from the fate of the entities of "The Mound" or the humanoid reptiles of "The Nameless City." In the former cases, it is a slave race that destroys society. The reptilian humanoids of "The Nameless City" are forced to flee the surface, led to an inner world by a prophet, while the inhabitants below "The Mound" are the last survivors of the descendants of alien colonizers, the rest of whose brethren were wiped out by the deluge. The shoggoths are clearly successful in mostly wiping out the Old Ones; the survivors the Miskatonic expedition encounters are anachronistic members of a society even more ancient than the rise of the shoggoths. Their own highly evolved society had degraded and then been wiped out, not unlike that described by Ostrander.

Another oddity of both the Calalus texts and *At the Mountains of Madness* is the appearance of dinosaurs, though it is unclear whether Lovecraft was inspired by the artifacts to extend his story back to the days of these megafauna. One of the indications pointing to fraud in the Calalus case was the fact that "one of the swords is inscribed with a correct representation about six inches long of a dinosaur, although this prehistoric animal was not reconstructed and drawn in picture form until well within the last 100 years" (*New York Times*, December 16, p. 4). The sauropod appears as an anomaly among the anomalies; it is not referred to in the texts but simply appears in the etchings. Dinosaurs make much more sense in Lovecraft's tale, given that the history of the Old Ones spans the Mesozoic. As early as 1925 Lovecraft was planning tales based upon Sir Arthur Conan Doyle's *The Lost World* (*Letters from New York* 198), and the amateur scientist was ecstatic over the dinosaur bone fragments gifted him in 1930 by Clark Ashton Smith, "actual parts of an entity twenty feet high that lumber'd thro' the fungoid morasses of California and Lemuria 50,000,000 years ago" (*SL* 3.131; see also *SL* 3.119). However, it seems not impertinent to suggest that the appearance of dinosaurs in connection with a narrative of human activity long before such sauropods were known to science may have provided some impetus for Lovecraft's prehuman records of dinosaur–Old One interactions.

The story of "Roman" Arizona did not die in 1925. Excavations by the University of Arizona in 1926, led by Byron Cummings, proved inconclusive. Occasionally the relics are reappraised by fringe archaeologists, both academic and amateur, though mainstream archaeologists have long accepted the site to be a hoax. With the publication in

1974 of *Calalus: A Roman Jewish Colony in America from the Time of Charlemagne through Alfred the Great*, Wake Forest University history Professor Cyclone Covey produced the first, and so far only, book-length treatment of the site, though his defense of the claims of Roman Jewish settlement was designed for a popular rather than an academic audience. As late as 1990, the Epigraphic Society published a series of papers offering several perspectives both supporting and attacking the claims of Roman settlement in Arizona in volume 19 of their journal, *Epigraphic Society Occasional Papers.* The Society's founder, Barry Fell, though a Harvard professor, was heavily criticized for the many Phoenician inscriptions he believed he found in the United States, and the Society in general lies at the fringes of archaeological academia. However, Lovecraft's knowledge of the find probably did not go beyond what was published in the *New York Times.*

Lovecraft clearly learned about and was interested in the claims of Arizonans to have found Roman inscriptions in 1924. He alludes to the event in "The Mound," and the fact that he misplaces the events to New Mexico in that story merely shows that he continued to turn the idea over in his mind as late as 1929, five years after the event. Lovecraft may have read the full week's worth of *New York Times* articles relating to the claims, but he could have gathered all the particulars he needed from that first front-page news story of December 13. In the plot germ he relates to Elizabeth Toldridge just months after writing "The Mound," and in his 1931 treatment of a decadent race of Old Ones overthrown by their biologically and culturally inferior slaves, we seem to see further processing of Ostrander's "history" of the Roman settlement up to a point where the civilization in question is no longer even human. It would be too much to claim that *At the Mountains of Madness* would never have been written were it not for the Calalus find or hoax, but this novel and "The Mound" suggest that this largely forgotten oddity of American history tugged at Lovecraft's mind and perhaps was one of many influences on two of his most substantial works.

Works Cited

"Arizona University Will Study 'Relics: Authorities There Hold an Open Mind on Authenticity of 'Roman-Jewish' Objects.'" *New York Times* (14 December 1925): 1, 10.

"Asserts 'A.D.' Shows Relics Are Frauds: Investigator Says Inscription on Arizona Finds Was Not Used in 775." *New York Times* (15 December 1925): 4.

Bent, Silas. "Bogus Relics of Past Tempt Collectors: Scientists Puzzled by Archaeological Finds in Arizona—Counterfeits Foisted on Public." *New York Times* (20 December 20 1925): 5.

Covey, Cyclone. *Calalus: A Roman Jewish Colony in America from the Time of Charlemagne through Alfred the Great.* New York: Vantage, 1975.

"Explode One Theory Concerning Relics: Experts Hold Arizona Inscriptions Were Written in Classical Latin." New York Times (16 December 1925): 4.

Joshi, S. T. *H. P. Lovecraft: A Life.* West Warwick, RI: Necronomicon Press, 1996.

———. *Lovecraft's Library: A Catalogue.* Rev. ed. New York: Hippocampus Press, 2002.

Layard, Sir Austen Henry. *Nineveh and Its Remains.* New York: G. P. Putnam, 1850.

Lovecraft, H. P. *Letters from New York.* Ed. S. T. Joshi and David E. Schultz. San Francisco: Night Shade Books, 2005.

———. *H. P. Lovecraft: Uncollected Letters.* Ed. S. T. Joshi. West Warwick, Rhode Island: Necronomicon Press, 1986.

"Puzzling 'Relics' Dug Up in Arizona Stir Scientists: Purport to Chronicle the Arrival of Roman Jews There in 775 A.D." *New York Times* (13 December 1925): 1, 27.

Spinden, Herbert J. *Ancient Civilizations of Mexico and Central America.* New York: American Museum of Natural History, 1917, 1922, or 1928.

Reviews

H. P. LOVECRAFT. O *Fortunate Floridian: H. P. Lovecraft's Letters to R. H. Barlow.* Ed. S. T. Joshi and David E. Schultz. Tampa: University of Tampa Press, 2007. xxxvi, 465 pp. $40.00 hc; $1.00 hc (slipcased and signed by the editors). Reviewed by Martin Andersson.

In the course of his career, H. P. Lovecraft corresponded with a great many people, as testified by the enormous number of letters of his that have been preserved, which still constitute only a small fraction of the number he actually wrote. Many of them were only temporary correspondents, but some of them remained his friends for life, regularly receiving bulky envelopes stuffed with dozens of closely written pages filled with personal information, commentaries on the times, witty humour, and learned discussions of everything between heaven and earth. These various major correspondence cycles stand out as true gems in Lovecraft's multifaceted literary production. Hints of them have been presented in various venues, most notably *Selected Letters*, but now the time is finally ripe for the publication of the complete, uncut Lovecraft letters, displaying the Old Gent of Providence in all his glory, warts and all.

Among the many friends he made, the young Robert Hayward Barlow (1918–1951) may have been one of the most unlikely. At the time of Barlow's first letter to Lovecraft, the former was only thirteen years old; yet he soon developed into one of Lovecraft's most interesting correspondents, and his significance for the posthumous recognition of Lovecraft can be rivalled by few. For the last six years of Lovecraft's life, the two engaged in a lively and voluminous correspondence, which has now been published by the University of Tampa Press, meticulously edited and annotated by S. T. Joshi and David E. Schultz and presented in a volume beautifully designed by Sean Donnelly and Richard Mathews.

In their editorial material, Joshi and Schultz provide a wealth of information on the little-known Barlow hitherto unseen in one place.

The substantial introduction constitutes a detailed miniature biography of Barlow, outlining his childhood, his publishing projects, his work on his friend's behalf after Lovecraft died, his subsequent accomplishments as a poet, and his brilliant career as an anthropologist and authority on Mexican Indian culture. It amused this reviewer to note that there is apparently a connection—albeit extremely tenuous—between one of Lovecraft's foremost champions—Barlow—and one of his most famous detractors—Ursula K. Le Guin: in 1941, Barlow worked in the anthropology department of the University of California at Berkeley under Le Guin's father Alfred L. Kroeber.

Joshi and Schultz also do an excellent job in elucidating the friendship of Lovecraft and Barlow. For one thing, Barlow and Lovecraft shared a deep love of literature in general and weird fiction in particular, as prominently displayed in this book. Through Lovecraft, Barlow came into contact with many contemporary luminaries of weird fiction, but the benefit was mutual, since Barlow also introduced Lovecraft to new correspondents such as C. L. Moore. It is also noted that "Barlow, like, Lovecraft was an amateur in the truest sense of the term," enabling them to "engage in unaffected discussion of the merits of authors and works all apart from the *business* of literature" (p. xxiii). Barlow was an inveterate collector of manuscripts and showed an interest in *all* of Lovecraft's literary production, not just the fiction; this may have been a contributing factor when Lovecraft named him his literary executor. And finally, they had some personality traits in common, such as a love of cats and travel, a certain social awkwardness, and similar political views.

The book contains 158 letters and postcards to Barlow, one letter to Barlow's mother, and—in an appendix—two postcards to Charles Blackburn Johnston (the Barlows' handyman). From Barlow's pen, we have "The Wind That Is in the Grass," his memoir of Lovecraft's visit with him in 1934; "[Memories of Lovecraft (1934)]," his journal of the aforementioned visit; and "Autobiography," apparently an outgrowth of psychoanalytic sessions taken before he left for Mexico in 1944. All texts have been carefully annotated by the editors with the level of detail we have come to expect after books such as *Mysteries of Time and Spirit* and *Letters from New York*. In addition, there is a list of Lovecraft's nicknames for his friends, a glossary of names giving brief information on some of the more important people mentioned in the letters, a bibliography, and an index.

The only thing that could be said to be missing is the extant seven letters from Barlow to Lovecraft (p. xxv). They might have shed some further light on Barlow the person. But then again, they might have added little, since the Barlow material that is included, in conjunction with the editorial material, paints a pretty clear picture. In addition, Lovecraft's letters in themselves hint at Barlow's precociousness, wide range of interests, and intellectual depth.

Predictably, as with any new correspondent, Lovecraft's letters to Barlow start out as brief and somewhat reserved, primarily replying to questions. Being addressed as "Dear Mr. Barlow" by his literary idol must have delighted the thirteen-year-old boy immensely. One wonders what the early letters from Barlow might have been like, in light of several remarks on rabbits made with the greatest patience, courtesy, and apparent interest. From the start, Lovecraft displays his customary generosity in offering to lend Barlow manuscripts and articles; and he soon reveals personal things about himself, such as his well-known hatred of typing. (Barlow presently offered, as is well known, to type his stories for him, in exchange for the autograph manuscript—a prescient move for which Lovecraft scholars everywhere owe him thanks.)

Lovecraft soon moves beyond the question-and-answer stage, adopting the conversational style recognisable from his finest letters. When Barlow goes to Washington in the fall of 1932, Lovecraft recommends several sights he must not miss, both in the city and on the way there. In December, 1932, they discuss the death of Henry S. Whitehead, which affected them both deeply. In late 1932, Lovecraft drops the "Mr.," and from there to "Dear Ar-E'ch-Bei" is but a short step.

Literature is a recurring topic; the letters abound with comments on the latest issue of *Weird Tales* and on the great classics of weird as well as general fiction, not to mention the craft of writing. For example, there is an interesting passage on the importance of prose rhythm on p. 204, where Lovecraft states that "Good prose has to be constructed by ear just as carefully as good verse—& the loss or change of any word is just as disastrous to it"; this passage should be required reading to those finding fault with the elaborate prose of fantasy stylists such as Dunsany, Smith, and Lovecraft himself. When Barlow started showing him his own early ventures into fiction writing in 1933, Lovecraft offered him constructive advice and revised some tales for him, clearly seeing a great potential in his young protégé. In hindsight, with stories such as "A Dim-Remembered Story" and "The Night Ocean" (the latter only very slightly touched up by Lovecraft) on which to base our judgment, we can say that Lovecraft's early reaction was entirely justified.

Another recurring topic is Barlow's various ambitious hobby projects, among which can be mentioned a selection of Henry S. Whitehead's letters, a collection of poetry by Clark Ashton Smith, the complete poetry of Lovecraft, and a collection of C. L. Moore's stories. None of the mentioned came to fruit, but Lovecraft invariably treats them with seriousness and discusses them carefully with Barlow (even the idea of his own complete poetry which must have amused him to no end). It is clear that Barlow spread himself too thin and tried to do too many things at once, and every once in a while there is an admonition along the lines of "in the holy name of Yuggoth, drop any *new* projects & *fill your orders for 'The Goblin Tower'!*" (p. 331). But some other projects *were* completed, such as the binding of a small number of copies of *The Shunned House* (printed by W. Paul Cook) and the publication of *The Cats of Ulthar*. The latter was intended as a surprise to Lovecraft; considering Lovecraft's concern with proofreading it is small wonder that he was worried when he got wind of it ("Bless my soul, Sir, but what's this your Grandpa hears about a Yuletide brochure publish'd without permission or proofreading?" [p. 309]), but he was justifiably delighted with the finished product ("Have seen Belknap's copy of 'Ulthar' & must express my owerflowing appreciation! . . . No misprints that I can see—& the taste in format is ideal. Good stuff!" [p. 313]).

A great number of letters are also concerned with philosophy and political theory. In one instance, Lovecraft rather innocently begins, "Expanding to the rather ambitious question which you bring up— regarding the nature & objects of human existence—I will approach the matter as I approach all things; objectively & impartially" (p. 243), which leads into what for all practical purposes is an essay taking up the following six pages. And a discussion of art sets off another fairly complicated essaylike five-page digression that touches upon politics and economic theory before finally—and almost seamlessly—turning into a treatise on "the aesthetic value of certain things which certain persons cannot 'enjoy'" (p. 211). It is a splendid testimony to the agility of Lovecraft's intellect; but it is also a splendid testimony to the high regard in which he held Barlow, since he obviously expected the latter to keep up with his pace.

This is the main charm of Lovecraft's letters—the way the most innocuous remark from his correspondent can lead to a huge fascinating foray in a completely unexpected direction. Barlow's dislike of his own given name leads to a long list of prominent Roberts in history and literature, over some autobiographical information concerning Lovecraft's own given name, and finally ends up in a sketch of the Rathbone branch of Lovecraft's family tree (through which Barlow and Lovecraft were related).

For all the learned topics discussed by Lovecraft and Barlow, it is when Lovecraft allows his emotions to shine through that the correspondence reaches its peak, and he does that remarkably often. There is no mistaking his anguish at having lost a treasured heirloom from happier days: "**Again** I have lost something at the last moment! This time it is the little porcelain ball on the end of my watch fob—the thing with blue designs & the initials W V P. It is about 60 years old, & was my grandfather's. I *think* I lost it *in St. Augustine*, but in case it was yanked off when I was carrying burdens at 128 yesterday, I wish you'd look around the house. . . . I've searched everywhere I went in St. Aug. before I discovered its loss at 7.30 p.m." (p. 284). And again, two days later: "Haven't found my watch-fob ornament yet. Did it by any chance turn up in Daytona?" (p. 285). It is one of the saddest and most touching moments in the book.

Fortunately, there are also moments of humour and happiness. When reading about the spoof collaboration "The Battle That Ended the Century," with its delightful puns on the names of prominent members of the weird fiction community, one cannot help but chuckle, especially at Lovecraft's mock outrage at Charles D. Hornig's suspicion of the authorship of the spoof: "Damn the perspicacity of that Hornig brat! Well—if he mentions the matter to me I'll bluff it out!" (p. 151). "Glad to learn that little Charlie has withdrawn his monstrous accusation. The idea of suspecting us of such a grotesque hoax!" (p. 152). Another amusing anecdote concerns a man that Lovecraft encountered in St. Augustine, who bragged that he had not washed his feet in forty-five years and could not be made to do so by the Board of Health! Writes Lovecraft: "But the old cuss certainly did appeal to my atrophied & undernourished sense of humour. Ain't washed his feet in 45 years, & the Board o' Health can't make him! And how touching was his solicitude to tell the world about it!" (p. 146f).

Finally, it must be said that in addition to its high-quality contents, O *Fortunate Floridian* is also a very beautiful book, from the covers (bound in green cloth with Lovecraft's signature in gold on the front) and the dust jacket (depicting a gnarled old tree eerily draped in Spanish moss) to the interior design (with frequent reproductions of Lovecraft's drawings and various signatures). Donnelly and Mathews deserve a special mention for creating this worthy vehicle for this important collection of letters.

For the Lovecraft scholar, the book is an indispensable, containing a veritable gold mine of data, not only on Lovecraft's life and personal philosophy, but also on Barlow, who has remained an obscure figure in Lovecraft scholarship for decades. For someone who is unfamiliar with Lovecraft's letters, this book is unquestionably one of the best places to start because of the breadth and depth of its subject matter, because it's fun—and because it shows Lovecraft as he would have wanted to be remembered: a patient teacher, a serious thinker, a good friend, and, above all, a human being.

DAVID E. SCHULTZ and S. T. JOSHI, ed. *Essential Solitude: The Letters of H. P. Lovecraft and August Derleth.* 2 vols. New York: Hippocampus Press, 2008. 880 pp. $100 hc. Reviewed by John D. Haefele.

"From my post in Sac Prairie I fished in the wider stream," August Derleth wrote in *Walden West* (1961), remembering a legendary correspondence with H. P. Lovecraft which he said "strengthened my resolution and gave support to my decision to remain in this western Walden and draw from it my sustenance and strength." Derleth never met Lovecraft in person; but so indelible were Lovecraft's impressions that the repercussions occupied him for forty years. Much has already been written of how different these two writers were in temperament and demeanor and how they epitomize the "essential solitude" of two individuals who share essentially the same world. But there were similarities, too. Both were revitalized by a return to "natal regions" from which they pursued respective literary careers that would make them famous. And in Sauk City, Derleth was no less the "outsider" than he coined of Lovecraft in Providence.

When David E. Schultz and S. T. Joshi (with the help of others) began two decades ago amassing, transcribing, and annotating Lovecraft's unedited letters, slotting them among 13 volumes projected in a shadowy "collected works" project, the enormous number sent (usually) from Providence to Sauk City were among the earliest added to the database. Not only were the letters deemed "not as interesting" as other sequences of letters written by Lovecraft—presumably they were missing the social or political emphasis favored by Turner-era Arkham House and used in Lovecraft's *Selected Letters IV–V*—there was also a practical matter that fostered delay: the letters often lacked full dating, which meant that their sequencing would have to be painstakingly gleaned from context. Consequently, nothing much happened until 2002, when another cycle of Lovecraft's letters out of the project was published by Night Shade Books: *Mysteries of Time and Spirit: The Letters of H. P. Lovecraft and Donald Wandrei.* And since Wandrei is inextricably bound to Derleth and Lovecraft, not least because of his role as the co-founder of Arkham House, a "parallel" compilation of Lovecraft's letters to Derleth seemed now to be called for. However, Night Shade stalled, and Hippocampus Press, stalwart for doing Joshi's projects, has become the white knight, releasing it in a two-volume set. Today we review a crown jewel in the Hippocampus lineup of books that is both scholarly and astonishingly entertaining, a beautiful compilation consisting of over 300,000 words on the subjects of the "weird tale," Lovecraft, high literature, Derleth, and much more. It also has portents of Arkham House publishing: perhaps the timing of this release, only months before Derleth's centenary year begins, is just right.

Essential Solitude: The Letters of H. P. Lovecraft and August Derleth is, however, fundamentally a Lovecraft book because of the preponderant use of Lovecraft's surviving letters, and that is why his name heads the book—not because he is axiomatically the greater of the two (though Derleth's work at this writing is much less in vogue), nor even because of editorial bias. And this particular series from the Derleth-dubbed "American master of the macabre" is a fascinating unit indeed. Derleth (probably with the help of Donald Wandrei) wrote the following passage for the jacket of an earlier collection to generally describe what the reader would find there:

Many gems are imbedded in these pages—essays in full or in miniature, serious or leavened with satiric humor, on such diverse topics as
Salem, cats, liquor, smoking, superstition, sex, heraldry, genealogy,
machine civilization, modern art, intellectuals, the beauty of New
England, and countless more.

And that applies to those found in this company. Of especial interest
are the deliberations by the two writers about the "weird tale," a subject initiated (and thoroughly covered once) when Lovecraft wrote
"Supernatural Horror in Literature," but here continued as Derleth
compiled (with Lovecraft's approval and help) "The Weird Tale in
English Since 1890" for his university thesis. Derleth's essay, both a
supplement and a rejoinder to Lovecraft's, didn't end the conversation; it continues unabated throughout this letter cycle. Derleth provides pithy remarks, but more important are the impressions he
elicits from Lovecraft for posterity. Lovecraft, of course, is at the top
of his form during this exact interval. (About his writing, Derleth
wrote for *Dagon and Other Macabre Tales:* "Undeniably, the period
of his most consistent quality in fiction was the decade from 1925
through 1935, and it is evident that death came to him [. . .] at the
height of his creative power.") These later forays were also the likely
impetus for Derleth's use of the Arkham House publishing imprint
to manifest worldwide appreciation for Lovecraft and the weird tale
subgenre. Of course, there is an abundance of subjects that Lovecraft
expounds upon in this gathering, about writing and publishing, about
his methods, and about the "craft" in general. Lovecraft is often amusing and always engaging, and Schultz and Joshi have achieved a worthy goal by bringing into print another capital collection that will find
its way onto familiar shelves of those who are by and large "Love-
craftians," but who know little about August Derleth. (This reviewer,
therefore, will go a little "off trail" in that direction.)

Derleth was only seventeen when the cycle begins and doesn't
come off nearly so well. He is ebullient, over-confident, and occasionally disrespectful—for example, when he unabashedly asks Lovecraft to prod editors to buy his work: "I knew there was something I
had forgotten to write you in my previous letter of this date, and it
was this: I wanted to ask you to push three of my stories. . . ." These
are some of the traits, many will argue, that characterized him all his
life, though they are here thrust into relief as a result of Lovecraft's

demureness. Further, the editors interpret Derleth as aggressively trolling for compliments and discounting the advice of his better, and it's true the reader can occasionally discern a frustrated Lovecraft:

> As for the arguments of last time—I can't say that your rebuttal causes me to change in any way the position I expressed. However—impetuous youth will have its own way. Go ahead, & let later experience correct such minor carelessnesses & errors as you won't recognise when the old folks tell you about them now. Your work is good enough to float in spite of minor slips on rare unlifelikenesses—& after all, there's really no critic like the author ten years afterward.

But Schultz and Joshi profess that Lovecraft, too, had to pass thirty before he "shed the callowness of youth," and so we should allow for the fact that Derleth was younger—often much younger—when he wrote the dispatches within these four covers. And if early in the interval of their correspondence Derleth came to regard Lovecraft as a peer—that is, he didn't see himself as a protégé—it is simply the result of all he was accomplishing at the same time. A measure of Derleth in 1937 shows that locally he was the star pupil of Sauk County, and nationally a writer to be reckoned with on the basis of a speech given by Sinclair Lewis, and that he was selling routinely to mainstream magazines (in addition to the pulps). Derleth had four novels, two short story collections, and two pamphlets in print and was co-editing a volume of poetry with a fifth novel scheduled with the prestigious house of Scribner. Further, work already underway suggested that Derleth's output beyond 1937 would grow substantially (and it did). In 1942 a biography was underway, and that same year Edgar Lee Masters would write the introduction to Derleth's own *Selected Poems*. Is it any wonder Derleth was confident and ebullient, or independent? Lovecraft's last letter to Derleth meanders between "congratulating" him on various accomplishments and "thanking" him for some small favors.

In this early limelight, Derleth would convey that the individuals who had influenced him most were Thoreau, Emerson, Frost, Hardy, and Edgar Lee Masters. It wasn't until later that he credited Lovecraft (along with Thoreau, Emerson, Mencken, and, "closer to home," Max Otto) for shaping his thought. With the proportion that maturity brings, Derleth began to refer to himself as a "youngster" whenever he referenced the period in which he wrote to Lovecraft.

As a youngster, Derleth was full of advice: "Lordhelpus, I wasn't suggesting that you conform to commercial standards. I should have made myself clearer. What I meant was that with your style, you could bring commercial magazines around without any damage to your weird ideals. And you could." To wit, we owe to Derleth "The Shadow over Innsmouth"—one of Lovecraft's best—even though we criticize the audacity: "As to acquiring cash—write more weird tales. If he had them in a shorter length, 10,000 or under, I know [Farnsworth] Wright would use one of yours in every issue, just as he is doing with [Clark Ashton] Smith."

What comes across to the reader as ill-advised tinkering was then axioms in common sense, and as far as Lovecraft took any of Derleth's advice all turned out well. A self-promoter (though he did no less promoting for Lovecraft, and eventually as much for Smith, and ultimately for a host of others), that was how things got done; a lesson Lovecraft might have benefited from employing. In the vernacular of a later era, Derleth would create and then sustain a marketing "buzz."

Throughout this corpus it becomes evident that Derleth had a glimmer of things to come: "Some day I hope that one of the gang has sufficient prestige to force a collection of your stories on to the market; since you don't do much to get one there. I suspect I shall be the one to do it." In the last letter to Lovecraft, but months before the celebrated exchange with Donald Wandrei, Derleth tells Lovecraft this again: "I have also notified Ben [Abramson] of my intention to sometime see to press a collected and selected edition of your stories." Derleth's efforts to secure Lovecraft's literary reputation after March of 1937 are well documented.

But did he affect the person? Undoubtedly Derleth *did* influence Lovecraft, but the degree to which this happened is difficult to measure. Since merely forty-three of Derleth's letters to Lovecraft survive (Lovecraft is notorious for having not saved letters sent to him), and some are incomplete, there is actually very little reported about Derleth, and much in that regard must be extrapolated from Lovecraft's nearly 400 letters, an intriguing puzzle for scholars and ordinary readers alike. Certainly it will be inferred by the preponderance of literary matters discussed that Derleth served as a catalyst for Lovecraft during this important decade, which might have been much emptier had these exchanges not taken place.

The introduction offers a reasonably balanced characterization of the two writers, and for this they are to be congratulated, because the Lovecraft community has been largely critical of Derleth's impact on Lovecraft's legacy. Nevertheless, there are small judgments that should be rescinded if one is inclined to nitpick. For instance, there is nothing odd that "impulsive and methodical" Derleth failed to contact Lovecraft *immediately* upon having his address. Derleth dallied before he contacted Smith the first time and also (as the letters to Lovecraft show) Robert E. Howard the first time. Nor should it be deemed unusual that one who sets out to make a living (even by writing) should endeavor to keep records of works and earnings, or to measure and have as an objective a year-over-year increase in production. I question, too, the suggestion Derleth was offering a "backhanded" compliment when he dubbed Lovecraft "a major writer in the minor division of the macabre," for it was Lovecraft himself who had drummed this idea into Derleth's head: "The fact remains that weird fiction is indeed a very minor & specialized field." Nor do the editors explain why *they* believe Lovecraft may have thought Robert H. Barlow more "sympathetic" and "sensitive" to his work, and that's why he chose Barlow to be his literary executor, when the more obvious explanation might be Lovecraft opting for someone he actually met (in person at length) over a pen pal. And, too, the suggestion that Derleth's preference for the "middle" tales of Lovecraft (such as "The Rats in the Walls") is somehow questionable but which rather betrays preferences of the editors. And finally, it is a curious omission not to give so much as a tip of the hat to Derleth's the Mother-of-All-Lovecraft-Letters projects, the *Selected Letters*.

But this reviewer does object to the *raison d'être* behind including the long excerpt to Frank Belknap Long intended to show the profundity of a "typical" letter of Lovecraft's to someone *other* than Derleth, and to demonstrate indirectly that the youthful Derleth was not the "intellectual peer" of Lovecraft, and to slip into publication for the umpteenth time Lovecraft making a philosophical point by referring to "little Augie" as a "self-blinded earth-gazer" (the one and only time he ever used that or any similar phrase). There is no evidence this reviewer knows of that suggests Long had either native intelligence or general savvy greater than Derleth's. Making this point is disturbing because it has already been said that the relative brevity of Lovecraft's letters in this cycle was primarily due to the frequency with which the two men wrote each other, and the topics discussed were the result of Lovecraft's inclination to match the specific interests of whomever he was writing to. Thus, this feint only underscores the difference in temperament already conceded, and Derleth's maturity at the time, a given. It's a shame the Derleth of the late 1960s would never meet and converse with the Lovecraft he knew—how different that would be! The editors have reprinted in the Appendix several pieces by Derleth (all but one) written shortly after Lovecraft's death, but the reader would be better served with more from Derleth's maturity:

> [Lovecraft's] rationalizations—his beliefs—his attitudes directly and subtly colored my own and helped me to take long strides toward maturity both as a writer and as a man. Looking back now, from the vantage of fifty years, I know more certainly than ever how fortunate I was as a youth to have as mentor the man who was H. P. Lovecraft. ("Lovecraft as Mentor," 1959)

Derleth was dramatically affected by his correspondence with Lovecraft, and his lifelong assimilation of Lovecraft's work; it set the course of his life's work.

But this and nitpicking aside, *Essential Solitude: H. P. Lovecraft's Letters to August Derleth* belongs on the shelf of every Lovecraft aficionado and every Derleth completist. Further, it should interest bibliophiles of many stripes and colors: Schultz and Joshi's annotations are rich with contextual information as only two steeped in the minutiae of Lovecraft's life and times could provide, and they include an index that dwarfs the one found in the "Wandrei companion" book. Publisher Derrick Hussey has provided a deluxe job with superior craftsmanship, and David Schultz the superior design. Cover illustrations by David C. Verba are apt and complete the package. Indeed, this worthy set may be the *most* attractive of the baker's dozen letter-collections (more, if supplements are counted) fielded so far out of the Lovecraft transcription project. But it is "limited." Hussey won't retire off of this book, but unlike others in his business that have produced similar books, he also won't retire with it.

Briefly Noted

The H. P. Lovecraft Film Festival is scheduled to take place at the Hollywood Theatre in Portland, Oregon, on October 3, 4, and 5. Among the guests are Brian Lumley, the artist Mike Mignola, and the band The Darkest of the Hillside Thickets. As of yet, none of the actual films that will be shown has been announced. It is hoped that Frank Woodward, who has been working on an extensive documentary film of Lovecraft, will present at least a preliminary version of his film. The documentary includes interviews with Ramsey Campbell, Caitlín R. Kiernan, S. T. Joshi, and others. For more information, consult the festival's website (www.hplfilmfestival.com). A more academic gathering, the H. P. Lovecraft Forum, is scheduled to take place at the State University of New Paltz later in October. The date of this event has not been set, but it will probably occur on Thursday, October 23. Among the expected guests are Robert H. Waugh, John Langan, Fred Phillips, and S. T. Joshi. For more information, contact John Langan (langanj@newpaltz.edu).